Curriculum Development i

Curriculum Development in Economics

edited by
David Whitehead

Published on behalf of the Economics Association by
HEINEMANN EDUCATIONAL BOOKS · LONDON

Heinemann Educational Books Ltd
LONDON EDINBURGH MELBOURNE TORONTO
AUCKLAND JOHANNESBURG IBADAN NAIROBI
HONG KONG SINGAPORE KUALA LUMPUR NEW DELHI

ISBN O 435 84900 X
Paperback edition ISBN O 435 84901 8

© The Economics Association 1974
First published 1974

Published by Heinemann Educational Books Ltd
48 Charles Street, London W1X 8AH
Printed in Great Britain by
Butler & Tanner Ltd, Frome and London

Foreword

During the last twenty years there has been a remarkable expansion in economics education within both sixth form and further education curricula in Britain. Similar developments have occurred overseas, notably in North America and Australasia. More recently economics education has been extending within the school curriculum to reach much younger, all-ability range children.

These developments not only raise important issues of objective and method in economics teaching, but also of the rightful place of the social sciences, and economics in particular, in the school curriculum. Surprisingly, these issues have received only limited attention in major British educational studies, with the result that most existing studies on the subject are small-scale, fragmented and largely unpublished.

It was therefore decided to call a two-day Conference which would critically examine a number of pre-distributed papers on recent developments in the economics curriculum and then formulate a comprehensive statement on research needs. This Conference was held at the University of Manchester in January, 1973. It was planned and organized by Keith Drake, Department of Education, University of Manchester, with administrative assistance from the University's School of Education and with financial support from the Economics Association. The twenty-five invited participants included practising economics teachers, lecturers in economics and economics education from universities and colleges of education, and representatives of H.M. Inspectorate.

All of the sixteen papers presented at the Conference are reproduced in this publication. The book also contains a general appraisal and summary of future research needs prepared by Raymond Ryba, and a digest of the discussion on the individual papers written by David Whitehead, who has edited the

Conference proceedings. The papers summarize the latest thinking and research work on the curriculum in economics education in Britain, most of which has not previously appeared in print. They should therefore be of particular interest to teachers and lecturers in economics who wish to keep abreast of the latest developments in economics education. In addition, the book contains the first comprehensive statement of research related to the curriculum in economics education in Britain. This should be of considerable value to those directly concerned with curriculum development and education research. It is also hoped that it may stimulate organizations who support educational research to turn part of their attention to this relatively neglected, though increasingly important, component in the school curriculum.

Norman Lee

Contents

viii *Contents*

Notes on Contributors

Vivian Anthony is Deputy Headmaster of the Kings School, Maccles-field, and Chairman of the External Relations Committee of the Economics Association.

Richard Barker is the Director of the 'A' Level Business Studies Project, and teaches at Marlborough College.

David Christie is Lecturer in Economics at Moray House College of Education.

Keith Drake is Lecturer in Education at Manchester University.

Duncan Hancock is Head of the Department of Economics, Madeley College of Education, and Chairman of the Teacher Training Committee of the Economics Association.

Gordon Hewitt is Course Director/Lecturer in Economics at the Civil Service College, Edinburgh.

Brian Holley is Senior Research Associate at the Teaching Research Unit, School of Education, Birmingham University.

Norman Lee is Senior Lecturer in Economics, University of Manchester, and editor of *Teaching Economics*.

Luis Maciver is Senior Lecturer in Education and Psychology at Dundee College of Education.

Pat Noble was Economics Teacher at Rickmansworth School, and from September 1973 is Lecturer in Educational Technology, Garnett College, London.

John Oliver is Principal Lecturer in Economics at Hatfield Polytechnic, and Chief Examiner, 'A' Level Economics, London Board.

Keith Robinson is Director of the Scottish Centre for Social Subjects, and Chairman of the Research Committee of the Economics Association.

Raymond Ryba is Lecturer in Education, Manchester University, and Chairman of the Publications Committee of the Economics Association.

Alex Scott is Research Associate, the Economics Research Centre, Heriot-Watt University.

Simon Smith is Lecturer in Education at Brunel University, and Chief Examiner for C.S.E. Economics, Middlesex Regional Examination Board.

Hazel Sumner is Senior Research Officer, Schools Council Project: 'History, Geography and Social Science 8–13'.

Roy Wilkinson is Senior Lecturer in Economic Statistics, Sheffield University, and Chairman of 'A' Level Economics Examiners, Joint Matriculation Board.

The Editor:

David Whitehead is Lecturer in Education at the Institute of Education, London University.

Other Participants at the January 1973 Seminar

K. Briggs, Head of Economics, Canon Slade Grammar School, Bolton.

A. Gregory, Lecturer in Education, Monash University, Victoria, Australia.

Mrs B. Gregory, Senior Economics Teacher, Methodist Ladies College, Melbourne, Australia.

Miss V. M. Keating, H.M.I. of Schools.

R. Szreter, Senior Lecturer in Education, University of Birmingham.

G. Thomas, H.M.I. of Schools.

H. R. Thomas, Head of Economics and Social Studies, New Mills School, New Mills.

A. Walmsley, H.M.I. of Schools.

I: EDUCATIONAL OBJECTIVES IN ECONOMICS

1: Towards a Taxonomy of Educational Objectives for Economics?

RAYMOND RYBA and KEITH DRAKE

A. The Question Mark

Our interest in the articulation and use of taxonomies of educational objectives arose from a practical concern with economics teaching, examining and teacher education. The taxonomic approach appeared to offer some hope of a reduction in the degree of confusion and of unrecognized argument-at-cross-purposes which often characterizes the dialogue between economics teachers, examiners and teacher educators.

We offer no expert philosophical or psychological assessment, no rigorous analytical approach, only some interim conclusions based on our experience of trying to construct a cognitive taxonomy for economics on the basis of Bloom's work.[1] In particular, this experience has led us to appreciate certain important limitations to the Bloomian approach, at least in relation to economics, to question the entire behavioural approach, and to think a little about alternatives. Essentially, we are exploring some important uncertainties.

B. Bloom and Behavioural Taxonomies

Although this paper includes an incidental critique of major aspects of Bloom's work we recognize an enormous debt of stimulation and example. In the area of assessment and, possibly to a lesser extent, in curriculum development, it has been a powerful influence. The obvious advantages of such an approach are that it is student-centred, that it proposes clear-cut goals and that these goals are to be reached by way of observable, and frequently measurable, behaviours. Its influence is already widespread in testing, e.g. in examination syllabus construction, examination construction and marking. Its relevance to the curriculum in terms of particular subjects is only now being explored at all widely in the U.K., e.g. in natural sciences, history and geography.[2, 3, 4]

Critical assessment of the relevance of Bloom's work is needed in the light of this tardy but growing interest. Taken at face value, the Bloom taxonomy is obviously useful to examiners, but its use in formulating curriculum objectives is more circumscribed. Even then, however, in so far as it makes behavioural objectives explicit it must be a help to the teacher in structuring whatever content he decides upon. But the question of what behaviours it is intended to elicit is not sufficient alone to characterize the educational process. There is no way of being certain that behaviours do more than mediate between intended outcomes and mental changes. They do not mirror either; or, at least, the view that they do is an unsubstantiated hypothesis, which often appears to be accepted by Bloom's disciples as an article of faith. Nor is the degree of relationship of each to behaviour implicit in the posited fact of relationship. Objectives are not simply behavioural, and stating them behaviourally implies the judgment that particular behaviours bear some kind of relationship to mental qualities which, in turn, are the kind which meet the objectives set. These difficulties are compounded if the Bloomian approach is applied directly to the planning of classroom experiences. At least one extra stage of specification is involved and each stage introduces complications which cannot be ignored. Blind application of teaching units and teaching materials constructed on this basis would be as likely, in our view, to stifle education as to promote it.

However, in much work done on Bloomian lines, behavioural criteria have been given special significance, along with an implied relationship of observed behaviours to mental changes and of behavioural objectives to educational objectives. The assessment of behaviour attainment has achieved a special position, in the belief that assessed behaviour can be a good all-purpose indicator of the achievement of educational objectives. As one dimension in our thinking the Bloomian approach has indubitable advantages. The danger is that it will become a Procrustean bed. The purpose of such taxonomies is to clarify and (despite the denials) to prescribe. The effect, so some of the more philosophical critics would argue, may be to confuse rather than to clarify, though a spurious clarification may be achieved.[5] Our evaluation examines the limitations of the Bloomian approach in terms of what it leaves out of account about educational objectives (an external evaluation), but only after some consideration of difficulties arising within the Bloomian framework (an internal evaluation). To do this we must first say something about specific attempts to cast economics in terms of educational objectives.

C. Educational Objectives and Economics

We are aware of recent developments in curriculum development in economics in Australia, the United States, Scotland, and in some English examining boards like the Joint Matriculation Board, in which the influence of Bloom is apparent. Our own exploration of the relevance of Bloom's framework in terms of economics was not carried out with any particular curricular or assessment purpose in view but as an academic attempt to explore its applicability. It is therefore extremely derivative, including even some of the applications to economics quoted by Bloom himself (see Appendix).

In common with others exploring the same road, we have discovered that, starting from the Bloomian taxonomy, it is usually possible to find items to illustrate each category. That this is so, easily leads one into thinking that the classificatory system is a good one. However, reversing the process and starting from particular knowledge or skill items, makes one aware that at least part of this judgment of the system, which starts from the system, is illusory. Any number of examples might be taken from our own taxonomic illustrations in the Appendix.

Thus, items of behaviour do not always fit neatly into a simple category, sometimes overlapping sub-categories within a particular major category, sometimes overlapping major categories, sometimes overlapping domains. For instance, the knowledge category (see Appendix) includes knowledge of methods of inquiry in economics as distinct from the ability to use them. But it is really rather difficult to see how such knowledge can be divorced from understanding and application. For example, is 'Knowledge of terminology' (1.11) or 'Knowledge of conventions' (1.21) in any way separable from 'Application' (3.00)? No doubt the methodology of economics hinges upon empirical

investigation, the formulation of hypotheses and testing. But if
we dig deeper and think about a specific problem, such as how to
eliminate poverty in the United Kingdom, we begin to ask questions. First, what do we know about the size and nature of this
poverty (i.e. the relevant evidence)? This, and the decision on
how to put the evidence to the question, requires imagination
rather than blind application of correctly recalled knowledge of
set rules and formulae. Do we ask ourselves, for example, what
has prevented the self-regulation of the economic mechanism
which would ensure full employment from functioning? Or do we
ask whether there is any such self-regulating mechanism? The
question-formulating aspect of economics is crucial and somewhat neglected. It also involves behaviours which straddle most
of the major Bloomian categories and tie into the affective domain.[6]

Equally important, perhaps, are particular items which, in
behavioural terms, lend themselves to classification in any one of
a number of categories, depending on the context. It is, for
example, easy to find tests of ability to interpret data where the
slightest variation in context shifts the behaviour through categories like knowledge, comprehension and evaluation (see Appendix, 2.20).

Both kinds of problem are familiar to librarians and computer
programmers in their classificatory tasks. The first arises because
the invitation to fill boxes in a given structure seems hard to
resist. The second derives from the multiple dimensions of connectivity between phenomena which is not matched by the number of dimensions in the conceptual structure behind the classificatory scheme in question. In terms of our taxonomy, both
these problems tend to be solved by framing statements about the
items in a form that involves the use of phrases like 'recall of'
or 'understanding of'. This clearly helps us to shunt items into
boxes, but does it solve the fundamental problem? Is it not a way
of living with the problem for classificatory purposes—a pseudo-
clarification which may actually promote confusion?

Thus, where an item seems to overlap categories, is placing it
arbitrarily into one category rather than another any different
from arbitrarily deciding on a call mark for a book in a library?
Or is the alternative tactic of placing it into each of the boxes
any more satisfactory, from the point of view of the user, than
tearing a library book into parts to be placed under different call

numbers? Is it any more satisfactory than placing multiple copies of a book under several call numbers? The classificatory problem is solved at one level, but not the underlying problem which gives rise to it. In the context of a taxonomy for economics these problems are posed particularly forcefully under 'Evaluation' (6.00), where many examples of behaviour might just as properly be placed in the affective domain. This is particularly so where evaluation takes the rapid quasi-instinctive form which Bloom designates as 'opinion'.

The essential points here are two. First, usefulness for one purpose, e.g. classification, is not necessarily going to offer usefulness for all purposes. Second, use of a classificatory system based on a single basic criterion—in this case behaviour—does not offer a complete answer to all the needs of those using it.

Every attempt at systematization involves simplification. Categorization within a particular classification measures only those aspects of the connectivity of things which are implied in the underlying criteria. Other aspects of connectivity—some of which may be important to the user—are hidden or disrupted in the process of systematization. Hence the need for thorough critical assessment of any systematization.

These general remarks may be complemented by a particular case which demonstrates what can happen in practice when taxonomies of educational objectives for economics are applied. In G.C.E. examinations in England and Wales, statements about objectives have traditionally been couched in vague words like 'competence' and 'understanding'. But the most recent syllabuses at Advanced Level from major examining boards reveal an acquaintance with Bloom's work. However, the amount of time and money which has been devoted to the development of an operational taxonomy of objectives, i.e. one which can be translated in any concreteness and at all comprehensively into evaluation, appears to be absolutely minute compared with the well-attested expenditure of such bodies on the psychometric testing of whatever it is (who knows?) that is being tested.

On the scanty evidence which is made public about examining procedures, it seems entirely possible that the weight which is accorded to certain behaviours and certain aspects of economic knowledge is grossly disproportionate to their significance in economic thinking. We refer particularly to the enormous emphasis which is placed on mere recall of obsolete knowledge about institutions and trends in the British economy.

Two points need to be made. First, the use of taxonomies seems to have had little influence on a notorious habit of examining bodies. Years ago Hilda Taba[7] remarked that because of inadequate description of either behaviour or content in expected outcomes 'evaluation tends to be concentrated on the most obvious but not always the most important outcomes, such as remembering information rather than thinking with it'. However, this tendency will not necessarily be counteracted merely by more detailed description, for it reflects an understandable preference by evaluators for relatively simple types of knowledge and low-level skills as against the more complex skills, like evaluation and synthesis, which subsume so much and are so much more difficult to test with any degree of confidence as to reliability. That this tendency remains is an indication of the weakness of current methods of specifying objectives as a means of reflecting the structure of economic knowledge. Whatever this structure may be, it would seem unlikely to practising economists that recall* of information is a skill of such immense importance relative to other skills of the economist.

This leads to a second point, which concerns the critical ability to detect in a mass of information, both relevant and irrelevant, the faint pattern of a familiar problem, or the possibility of such a pattern, given some re-ordering of the data. To think and to behave like an economist, however crudely, requires this ability as a precursor to the application of some mode of analysis. The relevant behaviour is difficult to classify in Bloomian terms. The recent reforms of G.C.E. 'A' level economics scarcely seem to recognize its significance, so that it does not appear to be officially encouraged as a feature of economics teaching. Indeed, the marked absence of project work—the G.C.E. 'A' level Business Studies Project being a welcome exception—strongly suggests that this ability is not adequately recognized as the important objective it should be—or is so vaguely described as to be non-operational.†
Possibly this ability is assumed to develop *pari passu*.

---

* We recognize that almost all recall actually implies aspects of behaviour classified in higher categories, e.g. *choosing* to recall specific items of knowledge must mean more than an almost mechanical behavioural response.

† Some of the most important educational objectives are very difficult indeed to

D. Some Difficulties arising within the Bloomian Framework

Some internal problems of the Bloomian framework have already been noted, in the previous section. Acute critiques of such difficulties have been published already.[8,9] These are not specific to economics but deal with vital general issues such as the validity of Bloom's knowledge/intellectual abilities dichotomy. Pring, for instance, argues that knowledge is a meaningless concept except in terms of comprehension and application, that a false distinction has developed through lack of epistemological analysis of cognitive processes. Indeed, Pring seizes on Bloom's admission that he and his associates failed to discover 'a method of classification which would permit complete and sharp distinctions among behaviours' as admission of a major stumbling block to the whole taxonomic enterprise. On both empirical and epistemological grounds it is not acceptable to treat knowledge and skills in the 'atomistic' way implied by Bloom's framework.

Here is a growing and very important critical literature which we cannot hope to summarize. The two papers by Sockett and by Pring alone, question the 'naïve theory of knowledge' employed in Bloom's work and the 'means–ends' assumption in which behaviours (ends acting as proxies for educational objectives) are distinguished from content (means of achieving ends). This is hardly sufficient to illustrate the radical nature of current criticism of the Bloomian framework, but, since our concern is less with a philosophical critique than with the empirical identification of problems in applying that framework, we shall pass on for the moment to consideration of one example (from several possible areas) of difficulty in terms of economics: the particular difficulty, in our subject, in separating cognitive from affective objectives.

It is increasingly being noticed[10] that the modern emphasis on cognitive behaviours in curriculum development and evaluation has dramatic consequences for teaching styles as well as for

---

examine, i.e. they are difficult to assess to the same psychometric standards as other objectives. This difficulty can also mean that they are very expensive to assess. Is this a reason for neglecting them? Should we examine and teach only what is relatively easy and cheap to examine? Is there a *practical* alternative by loosening the nexus which currently binds teaching so closely to what is examined?

teaching materials and the nature of the curriculum. In the Appendix the emotional dimension is largely ignored; Bloom implies a link between affective and cognitive domains through the 'evaluation' category to which we have already referred. Nevertheless, whatever the attitude of innovators like Bloom and Bruner to the affective domain, the effect of their work has been to encourage a monocular approach to curriculum development and testing; and this is true *a fortiori* in the case of economics. Economics appears almost exclusively as a discrete set of cognitive procedures. Psychic satisfactions (and dissatisfactions) tend to be ignored, and the imaginative skills centred on activities like problem-solving are dealt with most inadequately. What a student feels, expects, and wants to achieve, is surely not without importance even in the cognitive aspects of economics education? However, such considerations are largely outside the remit of Bloom's cognitive framework. Is this treatment a consequence of the Bloomian division? And if so, are the benefits of treating the cognitive and affective domains as if they were logically and psychologically divisible so great as to outweigh the costs of such a division?

A case in point is the synthesis category (see Appendix). This presented us with great and often insurmountable difficulties. There can be little doubt concerning the desirability of specifying effectively synthesis objectives in economics. In current teaching methods there is a common tendency (in turn, largely a function of current examining methods) to overemphasize activities in which, as Bloom puts it, 'the learner functions as a consumer and critic of ideas rather than those in which he functions as a producer'.[11] Moreover, as de Bono points out, 'criticism is one of the easier forms of intellectual effort and one of the more limited. The critical intelligence cannot of itself generate the new ideas that are required for progress and even just to deal with changing circumstances.'[12]

Yet abilities of synthesis remain relatively neglected. One reason is that, under certain definitions, they comprise a form of creative learning which, although a central and exciting educational process, simply will not fit into taxonomic categories and within restricted domains. Bloom discusses the definition of creative learning in terms of a general and a restricted definition.[13] In one sense every experience involves a combination of previous experience in such a way that the learner is permanently changed.

In this sense all learning is creative, involving a novel reorganization of experience (cf. Ernst Mach's definition of science as 'experience, economically arranged', using the word science in a European sense rather than in the narrower Anglo-Saxon meaning). The novelty of the reorganizing experience is what makes the process 'creative'. But some would restrict creative learning to production of something new, unique and original in man's culture—the more traditional meaning.

So we have to choose between (1) 'new to the learner', which is true of almost any experience in some degree since life itself is a Heraclitean flux, or (2) 'new to the culture', which at least has the appearance of being very much more rare. As an educational objective (1) is probably more useful since it defines a synthesizing process ranging from the meanest rearrangement of experience in a new context to a much grander construct which may, or may not, also merit definition (2). Using definition (1) there will therefore be greater variation in the degree of complexity and sophistication of synthesis despite common features. This variation does not square with the simple-to-complex continuum upon which Bloom's taxonomy is based. It suggests that the thinking required in the higher-order, i.e. later, categories is not *necessarily* harder or better thinking. (This higher/lower problem is general to the whole taxonomy, even the knowledge category.)

Since the process of synthesizing involves the use of other skills, abilities and knowledge to construct a product novel to the learner, peculiarly his own personal construct, there are grounds for thinking that synthesizing may have special value in terms of permanence of learning. The motivational advantages of the synthesizing process are obvious, since the task is more clearly creative to the learner than the more routine (and easily assessed) learning tasks: there is a higher degree of personal control of the outcome and the product is more individualized (within the canon). For this reason synthesis can be most absorbing and offer rich personal satisfaction. Project work has long exploited this, and learning by discovery can be structured to do so, although there is no necessary connection. The outcome is by definition more or less unexpected, and the process is concerned with the enrichment and self-development of the individual. The student's attitude to economics (amongst other things) may be considerably altered. None of this is at all easy to describe in Bloomian or even in behavioural terms. It is no easier to assess and measure in any conventional way.

E. Some Inadequacies of the Bloomian Framework

We have said very little about the relationship of Bloom's work to teaching. In our view, it does not help very much in a direct logical way, and the reasons for this indicate some major inadequacies of the Bloomian framework. Thus, for instance, while his taxonomy has a clear sequential pattern of *its own*, it does not offer a satisfactory sequential approach *to teaching*.

The sequential structure of the taxonomy, from lower/knowledge categories to highers/kill categories, might seem to offer a teaching sequence. But many teachers of economics would in most circumstances undoubtedly reject such an approach to the teaching process, preferring to start, let us say, from an application exercise, through which both knowledge and comprehension are likely to be achieved and developed meaningfully. Thus, working with the concepts of credit expansion leads to knowledge and comprehension of the meaning of terms like cash ratio and liquidity. In short, the old adage of learning by doing applies, starting with skill application aimed at developing not only skill but relevant knowledge and comprehension. Anyone who has been subjected to some of the older-fashioned military approaches to learning the parts of a machine gun would know what is meant here. Mechanically efficient they may have been, but they were hardly meaningful!

The taxonomy, after all, is only a classification—a card index, as it were—to the library of behavioural objectives. Consequently, its logic is that of a classification related to use in the assembly and sorting of relevant objectives rather than to the ordering of these objectives for classroom use. For this purpose, the teacher has to look elsewhere, e.g.

(1) in the psychology of learning and in the understanding of the *existing* state of mind of the learners as opposed to the desired one;

(2) in the psychology of the teacher and his understanding of (1), of his subject matter and of his social role;

(3) in a more thorough understanding of the subject matter or content, of its concepts and of their structure.

Many of the problems arising from current use of the Bloomian framework derive from the facts (*a*) that it oversells itself, e.g. as a taxonomy of *educational* objectives, and (*b*) that, because alternative approaches to the specification of educational objectives are so underdeveloped by comparison, it is treated as an all-purpose guide.

Let us examine just two of the taxonomy's major deficiencies, the notion of content-free behaviour and its propositions about educational objectives. Sockett criticizes the concept of content-free behaviours and contends that to consider for example the behaviour of 'remembering' without reference to a content remembered, as implied in Bloom, is 'unintelligible'.[14] 'Explicit reference has to be made to the content . . . for the problem to be coherent.' His view supports the contention that, for example, 'remembering' things of different complexity or kind is hardly classifiable usefully under the same head.[15] This deficiency is amply illustrated, in our view, in the Appendix, in the 'knowledge' category. Moreover, in Sockett's view, 'if the classification of specific objectives is thought to be possible . . . there must be criteria at the simple level and criteria for distinguishing radically different behaviours at the more complex levels'. It becomes clear how very little we do know and how very much we need to know about the psychology of learning economics and about the conceptual structure of the discipline.

But it is the status accorded, in the taxonomy, to behaviour which has attracted some of the heaviest and most effective criticism.[5, 9, 16, 17] Bloom and his associates set out to classify 'the intended behaviour of students—the ways in which individuals are to act, think and feel as a result of participating in some unit of instruction'.[18] It is the concept of identification of achievement of behavioural objectives with the ability to give overt expression to these behaviours which has been questioned by these critics. While the relationship between overt behaviour and the achievement of *a* behavioural objective is self-evident, its identification with *particular* internalized behavioural objectives requires further empirical justification.[9] This is a matter for psychologists and philosophers, but the *identification* of particular *educational* achievements with particular inferred internalized behaviour capabilities is very much the concern of educationists: it is not at all self-evident. Additionally, it is doubtful whether planned behaviour is ever a sufficient criterion of *any* educational achievement. Thus, one would not accept that a parrot which had learned responses to particular 'knowledge' questions was exhibiting an educational achievement, despite its ability to meet the criterion of correct behavioural response to the questions asked. Again, overt behaviours, even when related to educational achievements, are not *identifiable* with *particular* educational achievements without further evidence. Thus, for example, correct responses to quite deep analytical questions in economics can be memorized and recalled. Correct response to such a question cannot, of itself, indicate the achievement of analytical abilities. On the reverse side, such analysis is a complex skill, so failure to give a correct response may not necessarily imply inability to behave analytically—only failure to do so with sufficient accuracy in one instance. May not things be 'known' and 'understood' without the knower being able to *express* this knowledge adequately, or even at all? Or do things only count as 'known' when they can be communicated to others? This seems to be implied by Bloom, but it is surely doubtful. Forms of communication are somewhat arbitrary and conventional, a general problem which is merely more obvious when teaching less-able children.

Overt behaviour is, therefore, a dubious criterion of cognitive processes. But it is accorded an even larger role in Bloom's taxonomy, which was 'especially intended to provide for classification of the goals of our educational system'.[19] Is a behavioural classification sufficiently comprehensive to classify *the* goals of an educational system—*all* of them? Or even all the goals appropriate for the teaching of one subject within that educational system? In the Bloomian taxonomy the cutting edge is achieved by narrowing the description of educational objectives until it is cast purely in terms of the changed behaviour of the individuals undergoing it.[19] Bloom has used a behavioural criterion and, as indicated above, behaviour is only a symptom of psychological development and not the development itself. He and his associates have then adopted a view of education oriented solely in terms of the individual and his (supposed) psychological development. But the goals of education, as generally conceived, must comprise more than the goals of individual development. The well-worn view that education involves mutual interactions between individuals, society and knowledge does not take us very far, as stated, but it does stress that there are 'social' and 'knowledge'* goals in the educational process in addition to the 'behavioural' areas which underpin the Bloomian system.

It is true, of course, that the Bloomian system does not explicitly exclude the other two components of the trilogy 'Individual, Knowledge, Society' nor various aspects of the interrelationships between them which are usually important components of the educational process. Indeed, various categories within Bloom's original taxonomy contain references to knowledge (in the normal, i.e. non-Bloomian sense) and to society. But Bloom and his associates are nevertheless concerned with educational objectives from the *individual's* point of view, from the standpoint of the individual's behavioural patterns. In terms of range of behaviours, and even of cognitive processes, they try to be all-inclusive; but the perspective remains confined to this simple individual-oriented point of view. When they are apprehended at all, society and knowledge-oriented goals are seen only very partially, i.e. in relation to individual-oriented goals.

A classification related solely to individual behaviours would seem to imply a belief that in catering for the individual, through an education designed to modify his behaviour, the preservation and development of existing knowledge and of society will automatically be taken care of. The all-reconciling 'Invisible Hand' is at work again. The basic tenet is not simply the primacy of the individual but also an inevitable coincidence between the needs of society and those of the individual. It is a system-bound view of education not a system-transcendent one: a view entirely consistent with the explicit individual-oriented norms held sacred by most American educationists but challenged by American sociological research, which shows it to be less than the whole basis of even the American education system (see the Coleman Report).[20] In short it is based on an educational philosophy analogous to the economic philosophy 'What's good for General Motors is good for the nation'. This kind of basic tenet is no more self-evident in education that it is in economics, and

---

* 'Knowledge' as employed here, in contradistinction to 'society' and 'behaviour', is essentially different from the behavioural category which Bloom describes with the same word. Knowledge in the sense which is meant outside behavioural taxonomies and in the context of educational objectives is the sum of what is known, the philosopher's multidimensional concept and the subject of epistemological studies.

attempts to justify it logically are just as subject to the fallacy of composition.*

All this is not to say that the Bloomian framework is worthless or that its exploration of educational objectives from the behavioural and individualistic point of view should be ignored. We clearly owe an enormous debt to Bloom and his associates for making it possible to see more clearly and write more meaningfully about what the educational process implies by way of intended behavioural development. But it does suggest that a behavioural taxonomy is not sufficient to delimit discussion of educational goals and their achievement. Our experience indicates that, unless the reasons for this are fully appreciated (hence the foregoing analysis) it may inhibit discussion by acting as a straitjacket. In this respect, it is the initial persuasiveness of Bloom which is itself a problem. As long as societal and knowledge-centred objectives lack an equally powerful medium of expression and articulation, their effective employment as guidelines for the curriculum, and for examining and teaching may be hindered—whatever lip-service is paid to their importance.

It is an open question whether a single comprehensive classification system is really feasible. Any attempts to construct one would certainly have to overcome obstacles even more formidable than those with which we were faced in attempting to apply the Bloomian taxonomy. As the Appendix shows, the thing can be done. But might not a pluralist approach be more promising: one which went beyond a Bloomian approach and attempted additionally to develop separate classifications of educational goals related to economics itself and to its role in the preservation and development of society? One great value of such schemes would be to open out the discussion of economics education beyond the confines of developing particular behaviours in individual pupils.

Of course a great deal of work is going on in this country as well as in America developing non-Bloomian systems of codification, and, in particular, behavioural ones. The state of the art clearly represents a rather high degree of sophistication when it comes to a behavioural approach, with alertness to the dangers of teacher-defined specification of objectives, to the importance of unplanned outcomes, or to the ease with which task perfor-

* See Samuelson's demonstration of the fallacy which so bedevilled pre-Keynesian economics.

mance can be measured compared with the difficulty of knowing what such performance means.[17] When it comes to society-centred codifications, current work seems less impressive, i.e. old-fashioned. As for a knowledge-centred codification, which ought to be the special concern of economists, there is a surprising deficiency in the work already done. Notable work towards a knowledge-centred codification has been done in the U.S.A., following Bruner, by Senesh[21, 22] and many others, concerning the essential structure of the subject and its importance in curriculum development; also, in this country, by Lee, Entwistle and Dunning.[23, 24, 25] However, while stating the 'large ideas' which hypothetically form the heart of a subject's structure is relatively easy, and a favourite academic exercise, it is quite another matter to show that the stated ideas really do so. Like Bruner's famous spiral of increasing conceptual complexity, each notable statement of the essential structure of economics remains a hypothesis. These hypotheses need testing.

Some contemporary economics curricula are probably overweight from birth. Many more certainly become top-heavy very quickly over time. Additions to the syllabus are frequently haphazard: fresh growth points of knowledge inserted here and there, theoretical refinements added in response to the winds of fashion (modernizations!). Many economics curricula are poorly conceived in the first place; others become degraded by a series of unsystematic modifications: death by a thousand additions. What is needed is an explicit subject 'set'. The state of knowledge is not such as to recommend a unique 'set', an orthodoxy. In other words, there is as strong a case for pluralism, for competing taxonomies in terms of the subject, as there is for pluralism in behaviour or society-centred taxonomies.

It might be argued that existing economics syllabuses, cast as they often are in terms of traditional 'topics', are nothing less than (mildly) competing subject- or knowledge-oriented taxonomies. This is true up to a point. Our doubt concerns the validity of the almost universal basic model for a subject-oriented taxonomy, which is grounded on far less empirical and theoretical work than the learner- or behaviour-oriented taxonomies. We are lamentably ignorant of the structure of knowledge and abilities which comprise economics, both as regards the mix and the sequence of thought. We have not even begun the great and necessary task of unravelling this structure in the way that mathematicians and psychologists have been unravelling mathematics for some years.[26, 27]

In lieu of any comparable investigation of the actual structure of economics, there are perfectly plausible basic structures for organizing the concepts which differ radically from the traditional one. The elements of one such structure have, for instance, been outlined by Meno Lovenstein who identified as a major source of confusion—

> the use of the four economic processes (production, exchange, distribution, and consumption) as the skeleton for the presentation of economics. The division is either used explicitly or is the covert design for the presentation. Even with varying emphasis placed on national income analysis, the practised eye can still see the classic pattern at work, especially for the coverage of micro-economics . . . do these four divisions represent the organizing concepts which professional economists are actually using? The ordering concepts of practising economists are scarcity, stability, growth, flow and co-ordination. Sometimes in the texts these categories are imposed on the old divisions. But most often the student must gather that there are two orders of organization—the conventional one which economists use when writing text books and the other which they employ themselves at the professional level. Indeed, graduate work in economics might be defined as the gradual substitution of the new organization for the one in the principles course. It may be the reason why principles courses are clear to the instructor—he is using contemporary insights to teach the old divisions. He sees the light but the student does not.[28]

We know so little about the structure of economics. There are influential opinions, like those of Lord Robbins.[29] From time to time one of the best economists essays the task of defining economics—though it may be that economics, as Skemp argues in the case of mathematics, 'cannot be precisely defined, but only exemplified'.[30] In this country one of the best known recent examples of the genre is the paper by Lumsden and Attiyeh.[31] This is a most valuable essay, the more so because the authors are too experienced as educationists, as well as economists, to claim that they are distilling more than what teachers *believe* to be indispensable economic concepts. They preface their beautifully concise outline of the core with important and revealing caveats. Of the sets of indispensable concepts which are proposed by teachers they say that *'most* of these sets contain a *substantial* common element' (our italics). So even at the level of belief, some do not share the commonest beliefs and those who do only have a substantial element in common. Four concepts enumerated by them merit, in their view, special attention because of their critical importance to economics. But the critical importance of these fundamentals is not demonstrated on the basis of empirical or experimental work. Few economists are in a better position than Lumsden and Attiyeh to assess professional opinion on this matter, but in essence it remains only opinion based, as far as one can tell, on casual empiricism. Indeed, Lumsden himself has drawn attention to the neglect by economists of serious study of their own teaching. He has quoted with approval the view of G. L. Bach:

> We economists like to consider ourselves scientists. Today's Ph.D. theses place great emphasis on carefully specifying models of testable propositions and on rigorously evaluating the evidence to support or reject the models or hypotheses. Armchair speculation is no longer stylish. 'Casual empiricism' —usually an epithet to be hurled at your enemies—is widely scorned. Our journals bulge with econometric tests of elegance and statistical precision. Yet in planning and judging our own major activity—teaching—we are not only unscientific, we are often openly unscientific. [32]

Some of the necessary foundation work has been begun in this country, [25] but the task of tracing the critical path (or paths) by which we learn economics, needs sustained long-term effort by teachers, psychologists, philosophers and economists. If we explored some of the central processes of economics learning with the expertise which is available and is being applied in other fields (e.g. mathematics education) it might be possible to formulate and to structure some rather more certain knowledge objectives and to apply them. In this way the heaps of traditional boxes, hallowed only by time, which serve as subject taxonomies, could be replaced.

F. Conclusion

Beginning with the intention of developing a taxonomy of educational objectives in economics we have found ourselves drawn towards a reconsideration of some of the fundamental tenets of the Bloomian approach and, thence, towards the beginnings of a wider reformulation of the classificatory task.

Bloom's approach has been an invaluable stimulus, drawing attention to the importance of the behavioural dimension and demonstrating the persuasive power of a well-organized framework for the expression and articulation of objectives. But the suggestion by Bloom and some of his disciples that the behavioural approach is not only necessary but sufficient for the purpose of classifying educational objectives seems to us to be both spurious and dangerous, at least when applied to economics education. In our view, progress in this area can best be made by development on a number of related fronts:

First, the continuation of work on behavioural taxonomies for economics education, but as an approach which is complementary rather than alternative to other approaches.

Second, the exploration of ways in which classificatory systems can assist in the teaching of the subject (rather than in curriculum construction or assessment). The formulation of teaching objectives, rather than educational objectives, and their relationship to teaching methods is a subject we have scarcely touched upon. It would no doubt be as difficult an investigation as it is important since means and ends, teaching methods and objectives, may not be separate at all: they may be dialectically joined.

Third, the development of knowledge- and society-centred perspectives, a task which is complementary to and quite as urgent as the further development of the behavioural approach. Not only have knowledge and social objectives frequently been at far too general a level but the rationale underlying their statement has tended to be shallow and unconvincing, a matter of opinion (albeit distinguished opinion) in the case of the structure of economics, and of general goodwill in the case of social objectives.* It is therefore not surprising that it is impossible to tie in convincingly the fairly specific objectives of a behavioural

---

* See, for instance, the increased achievement of so-called 'economic goals' like 'freedom, justice, progress, stability' proposed by Professor Suzanne Wiggins.[33]

taxonomy to statements regarding the need for a well-informed demos, prudent personal budgeting, or clear and logical thinking.

References

1. Bloom, B. S. *et al.* (eds.), *Taxonomy of Educational Objectives, Handbook 1, Cognitive Domain*, Longmans, 1956.
2. Crossland, R. W., 'Defining objectives in lesson preparation', *Teacher Education* (Toronto), Spring 1972.
3. Coltham, J. B. and Fines, J., *Educational Objectives for the Study of History*, Historical Association, 1971.
4. Graves, N. J., 'The problem of hierarchy in the objectives of geography teaching at the pre-university level', in Adams, W. P. and Helleiner, F. M. (eds.), *International Geography*, Vol. 2, Toronto University Press, 1972.
5. Sockett, H., 'Bloom's Taxonomy: A Philosophical Critique (1)', *Cambridge Journal of Education 1*, Lent 1971.
6. Krathwohl, D. R. *et al.* (eds.), *Taxonomy of Educational Objectives, Handbook 2, Affective Domain*, Longmans, 1964.
7. Taba, Hilda, *Curriculum Devlopment, Theory and Practice*, Harcourt Brace, 1962, p. 199.
8. Sockett, H., op. cit.
9. Pring, R., 'Bloom's Taxonomy: A Philosophical Critique (2)', *Cambridge Journal of Education 2*, Easter 1971.
10. Jones, R. M., *Fantasy and Feeling in Education*, New York University Press, 1968.
11. Bloom, B. S., op. cit., pp. 166–7.
12. de Bono, E., 'On the Subject of Thinking', *Times Educational Supplement*, 21.7. 1972, p. 16.
13. Bloom, B. S., op. cit., p. 165.
14. Sockett, H., op. cit., p. 30.
15. Ibid., p. 21.
16. Eisner, E. W., 'Educational objectives: help or hindrance?', *School Review*, 75, 1967.
17. Hogben, D., 'The Behavioural Objectives Approach: Some Problems and Dangers', *Journal of Curriculum Studies*, Vol. 4, No. 1, May 1972.
18. Bloom, B. S., op. cit., p. 12.
19. Ibid., p. 1.
20. Coleman, J. S. *et al.*, *Equality of Educational Opportunity*, United States Office of Education, 1966.
21. Senesh, L., 'The Organic Curriculum—an Experiment in Economic Education', *The Councillor*, 1960.
22. Senesh, L., 'Organising a Curriculum around Social Science Concepts', in Morrissett, I. (ed.), *Concepts and Structure in the New Social Science Curricula*, Social Science Education Consortium Inc., 1966.
23. Lee, N. and Entwistle, H., 'Economics Education and Educational Theory', in Lee, N. (ed.), *Teaching Economics*, 1966.

24. Dunning, K., 'What Economics Should We Teach?', *Economics*, Vol. 8, Part 4, No. 34, Summer 1970.
25. Dunning, K., 'To Know Economics', *Economics*, Vol. 9, Part 4, No. 40, Summer 1972.
26. Piaget, J., *The Child's Conception of Number*, Routledge and Kegan Paul, 1965.
27. Dienes, Z. P. and Jeeves, M. A., *Thinking in Structures*, Hutchinson, 1965.
28. Lovenstein, M., 'Economics, Educational Philosophy, and Psychology', in Knopf, K. A. and Stauss, J. H. (eds.), *The Teaching of Elementary Economics*, Rinehart, Holt and Winston, 1960, pp. 142–3.
29. Robbins, L. C., *An Essay on the Nature and Significance of Economic Science*, 2nd ed., Macmillan, 1949.
30. Skemp, R. R., *The Psychology of Learning Mathematics*, Penguin, 1971, p.27.
31. Lumsden, K. G. and Attiyeh, R., 'The Core of Basic Economics', *Economics*, Vol. 9, Part 1, No. 37, Summer 1971.
32. Lumsden, K. G., 'Technological Change, Efficiency, and Programming in Economic Education', in Lumsden, K. G. (ed.), *New Developments in the Teaching of Economics*, Prentice Hall, 1967, p. 28.
33. Wiggins, S., 'Economics in the Curriculum', in Morrissett, I. and Stevens, W. S. (eds.), *Social Science in the Schools*, Holt, Rinehart and Winston, 1971, p. 102.

Appendix

ILLUSTRATIVE DRAFT OF A BLOOMIAN TAXONOMY OF
EDUCATIONAL OBJECTIVES FOR ECONOMICS:
KNOWLEDGE, INTELLECTUAL SKILLS AND ABILITIES

Introduction

This framework for organizing the objectives of economics teaching is
little more than a crude adaptation of the work of Benjamin Bloom and
others.* It is restricted to the cognitive domain. It draws heavily on
Bloom's structure and, in places, on Bloom's language and examples.
Because it is specific to economics while Bloom's taxonomy is general,
it is a whole degree more speculative than Bloom.

It must be admitted that, though Bloom's taxonomy has greatly
influenced recent thinking about the curriculum, early research and
applications produce a conflicting picture as to its generality and the
validity of its behavioural structure, especially of the simple-to-
complex continuum.† In this country it has received considerable
critical attention and curriculum developers approach it with considerable reservations.‡ Nevertheless, it may be valuable, merely as an
exploratory device, to attempt this application. We would wish to emphasize that this draft taxonomy has been included as an appendix to
our paper for *illustrative* purposes only. The reader needs to be clear that it
is *not, nor is intended in any way to be,* a finished version of a Bloomian
taxonomy. We lay no claim to infallibility in relation to the proper
attribution of items to particular categories. Indeed, as should be clear
from our paper, we hold that such infallibility is unattainable. Nor do
we suggest that our draft offers more than an impressionistic sketch
of a possible full and systematic application of the Bloomian model.

An attempt to construct such a taxonomy would clearly be, in our
view, a valuable enterprise in its own right. However, we have tried
to examine the nature of taxonomy-building itself in relation to

---

* *Taxonomy of Educational Objectives, Handbook 1, Cognitive Domain,* ed. B. S. Bloom
et al., Longmans, 1956. *Handbook 2, Affective Domain,* ed. D. R. Krathwohl *et al.,*
Longmans, 1964. We are grateful to Professor Bloom for allowing us to employ his
work in this way.

† Richard C. Cox and Carol E. Wildman, *Taxonomy of Educational Objectives,
Cognitive Domain: An Annotated Bibliography,* Learning Research and Development
Centre, University of Pittsburgh, 1970.

‡ See, for instance, the *Interim Statement of the Schools Council History, Geography
and Social Science 8-13 Project,* 1972.

C D E—B

economics. We have therefore not taken our construction of a Bloomian taxonomy beyond the stage which seemed useful to us in developing and illustrating our argument. It is essentially for these purposes only that we include it here.

The main categories utilized are as in the *Taxonomy of Educational Objectives, Handbook 1*, viz.,

1. Knowledge
2. Comprehension
3. Application
4. Analysis
5. Synthesis
6. Evaluation

1.00 Knowledge

Refers to behaviour emphasizing memorization of facts or ideas. Learning requires ability to store, and to remember later. Accuracy of recall is only one aspect of remembering. Also very important is development of judgment required to extract from store information which is relevant to situations which may well differ from the original learning context.

Knowledge objectives are classified roughly from specific and relatively concrete kinds of behaviour to more complex and abstract ones. The most specific—primitive—bits of information can be remembered in isolation. The more sophisticated bits, like universals or abstractions, are organized and remembered in patterns or interrelations. This knowledge category is concerned with Ryle's 'knowing that': it extends beyond knowing specifics to 'knowing', in the sense of recalling, that that which is handled is a fact, a term, a skill or a universal.

Later and more complex categories involve use of knowledge, but the knowledge category is the only one in which remembering is the major psychological process. For this reason the remembering process is the prime criterion of classification (simple-to-complex, i.e. isolated bits through to increasingly complex patterns). In later categories remembering is only one of several psychological processes, like relating, judging and organizing.

1.10 *Knowledge of specifics*

Factual hard core, e.g. institutional knowledge of an economy. Applied economics depends upon such knowledge. Low level of abstraction. The wealth of concrete economic information available is such that for educational purposes selection is needed. Students learn those specifics most relevant to a particular field or to a particular level of learning, e.g. *How the City Works* by Oscar Hobson or *Descriptive Economics* by C. D. Harbury. This classification is distinguished from other knowledge classes simply according to the specificity of the information, i.e. it is in isolated bits which have meaning by themselves.

1.10 is capable of division into distinct categories such as those listed below.

1.11 *Knowledge of terminology*

The learner has to know the referents of certain verbal or non-verbal symbols, the shorthand of the discipline. This knowledge is vital to rapid and accurate communication within the discipline. Both symbols and correct referents must be learned.

Bloom (Vol. 1, p. 64) warns of the danger that the specialist 'will attempt to impose upon the learner a larger number of symbols than the learner really needs, can learn, or will retain'.

(*a*) ability to distinguish referents for symbols used in economics, e.g.

M = stock of money
Y = money income
M_t = transactions demand for active money balances
MU_n = marginal utility of money*

(*b*) familiarity with words in general use which have one or more specific uses in economics, e.g.

value	equilibrium	elasticity
scarcity	utility	consumption
wants	welfare	demand
function	deflation	supply
efficiency	accelerator	
factor	incidence	

(*c*) familiarity with words which have one or more specific meanings, more or less peculiar to economics (and related studies, like accountancy), e.g.

monopsony	arbitrage
duopoly	rediscount rate
indifference curve	business cycle

* Referents required will vary according to the level of economics teaching, and some will very probably be needed only for more advanced courses. However, it would be unwise to assume that the relationship between the content of an economics course and the amount of economics a student has done is quite as immutable as it sometimes appears to be: until the introduction of modern maths the idea of teaching set theory to primary school children was not widely entertained.

1.12 *Knowledge of specific facts*

Refers to knowledge of economic phenomena, e.g. the anatomy of an economy, or sources of this information.

Whereas terminology represents agreement within the field (i.e. convention), facts can usually be tested by other means than testing the unanimity of workers. This class mostly comprises findings capable of empirical verification, not conventions designed to ease communication. They are the raw material, the natural phenomena of economics.

(a) recall of basic facts about the national and world economy, including a good deal of economic geography and economic history.

(b) knowledge of basic units of measurement and frameworks used in organizing basic facts, e.g.

   individual—household—firm—industry—economy; economic indicators, indices of wage rates, retail prices, employment, productivity.

(c) knowledge of official and unofficial sources, documentary or statistical, for these facts, e.g.

   Treasury and C.S.O. publications like Blue and Orange Books; specialist journals like Bank Reviews, *The Economist*; reference books like *National Account Statistics: Sources and Methods*.

1.20 *Knowledge of ways of dealing with specifics*

Knowledge of ways of organizing, judging and criticizing phenomena and ideas. This is more difficult for the learner than knowledge of specifics, being at a more abstract level, forms being relatively arbitrary. It includes knowledge of the body of techniques, criteria and classifications used to discover and then to organize facts.

This category does not involve skill in using these ways and means to handle facts, only recall of their existence and possible use. Skills and abilities involved in their use are dealt with later. Knowledge of these ways is akin to knowledge of facts, e.g. knowing that demand and supply graphs can indicate an equilibrium price which is distinct from being able (a skill) to discern the equilibrium price on a graph. Much of this knowledge is the result of agreement and convenience, not of observation and discovery. It reflects the way in which economists think and attack problems.

1.21 *Knowledge of conventions*

(*a*) Knowledge of standard representational devices and symbols used in verbal or mathematical analysis, e.g.

knowledge of conventions used in charting a time series, such as charting time along the horizontal axis and the related variable along the vertical axis; or the difference between logarithmic and arithmetical scales;
knowledge of mathematical symbols and devices used when dealing with problems arising from magnitude of change in one variable in response to changes in another, i.e. the differential calculus;

(*b*) Knowledge of ways of referring to groups of specifics, or of abstracting certain common features among specifics, e.g.

internal, external economies
leads and lags
invisibles
factors of production;

(*c*) Knowledge of accounting conventions, e.g. in national income, company, public or balance of payments accounting, e.g. imputation, profit and loss, double-entry book-keeping principles.

1.22 *Knowledge of trends and sequences*

Knowledge of processes, direction and movement of phenomena over time.

Includes knowledge of trends as attempts to clarify relationships between events which may be separated in time or simultaneous. For example, considering the distribution of income between factors, an increase in the proportion of national income taken by labour must result in a net fall in the proportion taken by other factors. The adjustment is almost simultaneous, but there is a clear temporal connection between the changes in the rewards of different factors.

Economists have selected and then related specific events. They attribute special significance to these relationships. Knowledge of specific facts and terminology is needed for the learner to grasp these relationships. Their full significance, in an operational sense, depends upon more advanced skills which enable the learner to understand the relevant theory—for it is the theory which indicates the significance of the relationships.

(*a*) Knowledge of trends in resource allocation and in the factors of production individually, at varying levels, e.g. world economy, national economy, industry, firm, household, individual. The sort of trends usually considered to be important are those in income levels (or growth rates) throughout the world, in distribution of income within a country or of national income between factors, in patterns of resource use within an economy or industry, in size of productive units, in occupational distribution of working population, in patterns of household expenditure.

(b) Knowledge of different kinds of sequential connection, e.g. monocausal or multi-causal, teleological (beware Marx!), and simple relationships (causality not established), i.e, correlation.

(c) Knowledge of different patterns of change, e.g. dialectical, evolutionary, revolutionary, necessary (determined), voluntary.

1.23 *Knowledge of classifications and categories*

Knowledge of classifications and categories regarded currently as useful in economics for purpose of analysis (though much of it may follow Bullionism, Social Credit, etc. into limbo).

These classifications are used to structure and systematize phenomena. They are useful but arbitrary, and the learner needs not only to know them as isolated bits of knowledge but also where they are appropriate. However, only knowledge is categorized here—application comes later.

(a) Knowledge of categories describing specific types of economic activity and their sub-classes, e.g.

(i) for organizing the field into meaningful areas, e.g.
production—types of input (land, labour, capital, enterprise, with apologies to Hicks) and their combination to produce goods and services.
national income—aggregation of factor incomes, expenditures, value of output.
distribution—determination of factor incomes.
market/mixed/planned economies—continuum of politico-economic systems calibrated according to who makes decisions and who owns the means of production, distribution and exchange.

(ii) for organizing behaviour of units, whether individuals, groups or some other entity, e.g.
monopolistic competition
perfect competition
monopoly

1.24 *Knowledge of criteria*

Knowledge by which facts and hypotheses can be tested: systematic criteria actually found useful for this purpose. Students have to use as well as to know these criteria, but use in problem situations is handled under category 5.00.

(*a*) Knowledge of criteria for judging deductive hypotheses, i.e.

(1) correctness of the process of reasoning, the rules of valid inference

(2) soundness of the basic hypothesis or acceptability of premises (cf. Friedman: does one need 'realistic' assumptions, or is it sufficient to work effectively as a predictor?). How to assess the fruitfulness of an hypothesis? It is the implications of an hypothesis which are usually important, e.g. the implications of the hypothesis that the more of a commodity (or service) which a person consumes the less satisfaction he receives from each additional unit

(3) the extent to which a man acts logically in a relevant contex (and the significance of the law of large numbers)—irrational consumers in particular instances may seriously damage the usefulness of a sound deductive hypothesis whose implications are worked out with rigorous logic.

(*b*) Knowledge of criteria for judging empirical or inductive work, especially of criteria for judging the importance of techniques, statistical or otherwise, for collection and assessment of data to discover significant trends and relationships, e.g. sampling methods, regression analysis, tests of significance. Knowledge of ways of producing soundly based empirical generalizations, e.g. indicating relationships between income and spending habits or income and education.

(*c*) Knowledge of the way in which empirical analysis can be soundly combined with and used to check deductive method, e.g. the way in which the whole apparatus of national income accounting was developed in order to manage the economy and employ the Keynesian model (built from the basic national income identities and translated into fiscal policy prescriptions).

Another example would be the empirical work of Schwartz and Friedman on American monetary history being used to test, qualify and develop a theory about the relationship between money supply and economic growth.

Why is the principle of falsifiability preferable to that of verifiability?

1.25 *Knowledge of methodology*

Emphasis on individual's knowledge of methods rather than ability to use them: methods of inquiry and procedures for investigating particular phenomena, e.g. elasticity.

This knowledge, passive and encyclopaedic rather than operational, is an important precondition to its use.

Problems to be overcome in economics are essentially concerned with scarcity of resources and how to maximize returns from these resources. Methods of attack on such problems include:

(1) investigation of economic evidence to discover present use and distribution of resources and economic trends;

(2) effort to formulate hypotheses to explain economic phenomena discovered by empirical investigation, testing against evidence (What is meant by 'explanation'?). Hypotheses may be statistical or deterministic (cf. R. G. Lipsey, *Positive Economics*, 2nd ed., p. 10);

(3) effort to formulate hypotheses on how to change economic trends, increase growth, change distribution of goods and services, etc., and how to monitor these, e.g. cost-benefit analysis.

1.30 *Knowledge of abstractions in economics*

Refers to major ideas, schemes and patterns in which phenomena are organized, large structures and generalizations which dominate the field and represent the highest levels of abstraction and complexity.

These concepts integrate efficiently many facts, describing processes and interrelation between specifics. They summarize and organize other specifics and the difficulty which the learner often has even to remember them may be related either to inadequate learning of the specifics they organize (the building blocks) or to difficulties with the abstract principle of organization. However, if they can be understood and learned they greatly facilitate handling of economic phenomena and assist retention of specific knowledge.

1.31 *Knowledge of principles and generalizations*

Particular abstractions claim to summarize observations of phenomena. Such abstractions are valuable in explaining, describing or predicting. At this level the student needs only to know the principles or generalizations, i.e. be able to recognize, recall or illustrate correct versions of them. Application of such abstractions to problem situations comes later in the major category of intellectual skills and abilities.

Examples:

> quantity theory of money
> marginal utility theory of household behaviour
> revealed preference theory of household behaviour
> cobweb theory of price change.

1.32 *Knowledge of theories and structures*

These are the most abstract formulations, organizing a great range of specifics (e.g. the theory of price under conditions of perfect competition), by which a body of generalizations is related in a systematic view of a complex phenomenon. 1.32 differs from 1.31 in that the emphasis is on a body of principles or generalizations which have been interrelated to form a theory or structure, whereas the principles or generalizations in 1.31 are treated as particulars which need not be related to each other.

Examples:

> price mechanism
> Marshallian as opposed to Keynesian analysis
> Marxist economics as opposed to capitalist economics.

2.00 Comprehension

Defined as the intellectual ability in a learner, when faced with a communication in some form, whether verbal or symbolic, to know what is being communicated and to make some use of the ideas communicated. This is synonymous with complete understanding of the message. It is simply a behaviour which represents understanding by the student of the literal message contained in the communication.

Evidence of comprehension behaviour is identified by Bloom in three main forms:

> translation
> interpretation
> extrapolation.

2.10 *Translation*

The learner's ability to put a communication into another language, mathematical to verbal or vice versa, into different terms, e.g. another context, or into another form of communication.

Translation involves behaviour which is transitional between the knowledge category (1.00) and the application category (3.00). Ability to translate will depend on possession of relevant knowledge. Clearly the learner must know the parts in order to understand the whole (though the former is usually a necessary condition of that understanding, it is far from being a sufficient condition).

Examples:

(1) ability to transform an abstract idea into concrete or everyday terms to make it useful in further thinking about a particular problem presented by a communication;

(2) an extensive part of a communication may need to be translated into briefer, possibly into more abstract, terms to facilitate the development of an argument, e.g. an algebraic formulation. The form of translation may be made absolutely explicit so that the exercise is largely a matter of recall. Alternatively, the translation may require decisions about appropriate language, degrees of abstraction, precision, etc., so that the behaviour required carries over into analysis, synthesis and application, e.g. a multiple-choice item beginning:

'Which of the following is an exemplification of the law of diminishing marginal utility? . . .'

These translation skills involve:

Translation from one level of abstraction to another:

(1) ability to translate into concrete or less abstract phraseology technical terminology such as the accelerator theory, the foreign trade multiplier or monopolistic competition;

(2) ability to translate a longer into a shorter and therefore probably more abstract communication, e.g. to move from a verbal statement of the quantity theory of money to $MV = PT$;

(3) ability to translate an abstraction like a general principle by giving an illustration or sample, e.g. realization that $MV = PT$ suggests that if money supply is x and velocity of circulation is y then $PT = xy$.

Translation from symbolic to another form or vice versa:

(1) ability to translate relationships expressed in symbolic form, e.g. illustrations, matrices, maps, tables, diagrams, graphs, formulae to a verbal form and vice versa.

Examples:

translate a scatter diagram relating household incomes and food expenditures;

translate standard graphical presentation of equilibrium of a monopolist;
translate supply and demand schedules for a commodity.

(2) given geometric concepts in verbal terms, ability to translate into visual or spatial representation:

e.g. ability to demonstrate that any straight-line supply curve through the origin has unitary elasticity;

(3) ability to prepare graphical representations of physical phenomena or of observed and recorded data:

e.g. ability to draw scatter diagrams;

(4) ability to read and translate data in a specialized presentation:

e.g. read an input/output table;
e.g. understand a company balance sheet;
e.g. understand a balance of payments account.

2.20 *Interpretation*

Facility in translation is actually a prerequisite for interpretation. Interpretation goes beyond translation by involving comprehension of relationships between parts and ability to re-order to get a total view and then relate to the learner's own ideas and experience. Following Bloom, interpretation includes ability to recognize essentials and differentiate these from irrelevant parts of a communication. In turn this involves facility in abstracting generalizations from a set of particulars and assessing the relative emphasis to give to different evidence—abilities similar to those required for analysis and evaluation.

The essential behaviour in interpretation is that, given a communication, a student can identify and comprehend the major ideas which are included, as well as understand their interrelationships.

Testing ability to interpret means offering a communication and requiring the learner to supply and recognize certain inferences to be drawn from it—a behaviour which merges into that required for analysis. Students may be presented with a number of time series relating to one economy, for comment, either with specific questions or a more open-ended essay. Alternatively, the argument for a particular course of action like entry into the European Economic Community or adoption of a crawling peg for the British exchange rate might be put and the student is required to summarize the gist of the argument.

Another way of testing interpretation is to present data and ask whether it is sufficient to establish the truth or falsity of a statement.

The student may be required to judge whether data, related to a statement, can be described as

(*a*) definitely true
(*b*) probably true
(*c*) insufficient evidence
(*d*) probably false
(*e*) definitely false,

Example: a retail price index 1900–73, 1900 = 100 is given.
Answer (*a*), (*b*), (*c*), (*d*), (*e*), as above, on the basis of the information given.*

(1) People were better off in ....*
(2) Between .... and ...., the £ was most valuable in ....
(3) Between .... and ...., more prices went up than went down
(4) Men in the 50–60 age group made most income gains in ....
(5) In .... some loss in real income was probably incurred by people living on interest from gilt-edged securities.
(6) Anyone living on a fixed income was much worse off in .... than in ....

Similar questions might be developed using a table of occupational distribution or of long-period changes in factor rewards. In the example above some of the questions (e.g. question 3) require only interpretation, while other questions require, in addition, skill in translation. So interpretation means

(*a*) ability to grasp the thought of a work as a whole at any desired level of generality, e.g. to grasp marginal productivity theory as a link between theory of production and theory of distribution
(*b*) ability to interpret and comprehend with increasing depth various forms of communication—algebraic, graphic, tabular, etc.
(*c*) ability to distinguish between warranted and unwarranted or contradictory conclusions from a body of data, not on grounds of logic or probability (an evaluative skill), but merely because of an understanding of the interrelationships between data
(*d*) ability to make appropriate qualifications when interpreting data.

2.30 *Extrapolation*

Extrapolation, according to Bloom, involves ability to draw from a communication unstated but valid implications, consequences and ramifications. Extrapolation must be accurate and valid.

The most obvious example of this drawing out of implications is

* Appropriate years would be given.

extension of trends from given data. It involves understanding of the *limits* within which a communication can be extended. For the most part this judgment of the limits of extrapolation depends on recognition that extrapolation is only inference with some degree of probability. Certainty in extrapolation is likely to be limited to cases of entirely logical development.

Extrapolation is distinguished from application because it involves only extension and not application. Rules of procedure which are needed for application are unnecessary for extrapolation, which is a matter of valid inference (statistical as well as logical).

Extrapolation will differ from originals in some of the following respects:

(*a*) time dimension: data on trends and tendencies may be extended beyond and within the time period of the data (interpolation involves the same behavioural skills as extrapolation)

(*b*) topic or domain: extension of ideas from a given topic or situation into another

(*c*) sample or universe: if the data deal with a sample, extrapolation may pertain to the universe from which the sample is drawn (and vice versa: if the data pertain to the universe, the extrapolation may pertain to the sample, e.g. data may relate to motor-car production over a period of years and extrapolation to production of cars by Ford)

Most of these types of extrapolation can be tested with the same sort of five-option answer favoured by Bloom and used in the test in 2.20, e.g. a graph showing public expenditure 1945–73, on defence, education, health, debt, etc. (e.g. from A. T. Peacock and T. Wisemans' *The Growth of Public Expenditure in the United Kingdom*, 1961, and official sources) and a series of extrapolating questions:

(*a*) Less money was spent in ....* than before .... on education and health.

(*b*) The increasing amount of money spent by government for all purposes 1945–73 must have come from sources other than borrowing.

(*c*) Less money was spent in .... than in .... largely because of retrenchment in .... expenditure.

(*d*) Debt charges increased less between .... and .... than expenditure on .....

(*e*) The per capita expenditure of local authorities for education parallels central government expenditure for this purpose.

Of these questions (*a*) and (*e*) are here examples of extrapolation, (*e*)

*Appropriate dates or data would be given.

being an extrapolation from universe to sample; (*b*), (*c*), (*d*) are examples of interpretation and translation.

Illustrative educational objectives of extrapolation:

(1) ability to draw immediate inferences from explicit statements, to form conclusions, including ability to recognize limitations of both data and conclusions;

(2) skill in predicting continuation of trends—heavily dependent on specific knowledge

(3) skill in interpolation where there are gaps in the data

(4) ability to estimate consequences of courses of action described in a communication and therefore to forecast a situation. Includes awareness of limitations of such predictions, i.e. of factors which may render predictions inaccurate. Again knowledge, experience and imagination are assumed

(5) ability to estimate probability of various consequences

(6) ability to differentiate value judgments from predictions of consequences.

3.00 Application

Hierarchical ordering of the taxonomy means that each major classification demands skills and abilities which rank lower in the classification system. Such low-order skills and abilities are subsumed in the higher-ranking classification.

Thus, to apply requires comprehension of the theory to be applied. If a student properly understands a theory he may well be able to apply it correctly, if not—not. The exception is that in some simple cases the student may be able to manage a rather uncomprehending rote-application. So application, though it involves more than comprehension, is one way of testing whether comprehension has been thorough.

The educational objective here is simply experience of applying economic theory to actual economic problems in an attempt to discover how the consequences of scarcity can be mitigated. This involves more precise objectives, e.g. ability to predict the probable effect of a change in an independent variable in a situation previously in equilibrium or in some other defined condition.

In order to test the learning of this skill it is necessary to devise new situations, or at least ones with critical elements which are new to the student, i.e. a strange context, an unfamiliar juxtaposition of familiar features, a new slant on a common situation.

Adequate testing therefore requires minor variations in the kind of problem situation posed and in the extent and nature of the behaviour required to solve it. For example, here is a fictional situation, and a typically Bloomian test item, where the problem is posed in an abstract form—an economic situation so simplified that only one variable at a time is changed. The student has to judge the effect of applying a particular policy on the distribution of income. The policy situation is therefore given, only implication is asked for, and the principles selected by the student to solve the problem and the way they are applied can only be inferred from the solution proposed.

Problem: For each item, judge the effects of the prescribed policy on income distribution, assuming no other policy changes to counteract the effect of that policy. Each item to be marked

A—if the prescribed policy is likely to *reduce* the existing degree of inequality in income distribution
B—if .... to *increase* ....
C—if .... to have *no effect* or an indeterminate effect on ....

Items:
1. Increasingly progressive income taxes
2. Confiscation of rent on unimproved urban land
3. Introduction of a national value-added tax
4. Increasing personal exemption from income taxes
5. Replacing subsidies to farmers, whether producer subsidies or differential payments on prices, by import duties
6. Reduction in degree of monopoly.

4.00 Analysis

To analyse is to break down material into constituent parts, and also to detect relationships between parts and relationships of parts to the whole, in fact the way in which parts are organized.

Analytical skill clearly aids comprehension and is a prelude to complete evaluation. It is therefore difficult to justify exactly its position at this point in the hierarchy.

The analytical skills of economics are varied. They include ability to distinguish fact from hypothesis, positive from normative, relevant from extraneous material, to identify conclusions and supporting evidence, to distinguish between the necessary and the probable, to relate an idea to another, to develop an applicability theorem from a model, to recognize unstated assumptions in an argument.

Although analysis is intimately connected with comprehension and evaluation it can fruitfully be distinguished from them because a student may be able to understand the import of a statement without being able to analyse it effectively. Effective analysis is needed for effective evaluation (although skilled analysis is only a necessary, not a sufficient condition for good evaluation). Analysis is explained by Bloom in three categories of analytical skill:

4.10 Analysis of elements. Ability to classify the elements of a communication.

4.20 Analysis of relationships. Ability to make explicit relationship between elements and to determine the interactions, how they work on each other.

4.30 Analysis of organizational principles. Ability to recognize the organizational principles, the structure which holds all the elements together.

4.10 *Analysis of elements*

Most communications have many elements and frequently some of these are made explicit and identified by the writer, e.g. the hypothesis being investigated and the conclusions. Such elements are easily recognized and classified. But important elements may be left implicit and will be harder to identify, e.g. important unstated assumptions which can only be recognized by careful analysis. The status of statements may also be obscure, and it is necessary to identify and classify them as statements of fact or value, or prediction. So this analytical skill typically requires ability to distinguish between fact and hypothesis, positive and normative, and detection of unstated assumptions.

4.20 *Analysis of relationships*

One of the most obvious relationships to be determined by a student in many communications is that between hypothesis, evidence and conclusions. But other relationships also need to be determined, e.g. between different kinds of evidence being presented. Much analysis of relationships will deal with consistency of element to element or relevance of elements to central thesis.

Typical skills here are ability to distinguish which elements are relevant to what hypothesis, whether elements are related in an inductive or a deductive pattern, ability to distinguish different types of sequential relationships, e.g. causal from teleological, and ability to spot logical fallacies.

For example (following Bloom), it is possible to test 'ability to recognize which facts or assumptions are essential to a main thesis or to an argument in support of that thesis', e.g.

Facts are stated in a table which represents relationships between yearly income of certain families and the medical attention they receive:

Family income	% of family members who receive no medical attention during year
under $1,200	47
$1,200–$3,000	40
$3,000–$5,000	33
$5,000–$10,000	24
over $10,000	14

Conclusion: members of families with small incomes are healthier than members of families with large incomes.

Which one of the following assumptions would be necessary to justify the conclusion?

1. Wealthy families had more money to spend for medical care.
2. All members of families who needed medical attention received it.
3. Many members of families with low incomes were not able to pay their doctor's bills.
4. Members of families with low incomes often did not receive medical attention.

4.30 *Analysis of organizational principles*

The organizational principle or general conception upon which a communication is based is rarely stated in the communication. The analysis of these fundamental organizational qualities is a difficult but often a necessary prelude to evaluation. Often it involves ability to infer (and discount) the normative predispositions of authors and to recognize the general pattern of thinking, e.g. classical, neo-classical, Keynesian, Marxist.

5.00 Synthesis

The gist of Bloom's account is that synthesis means putting together of elements and parts to form a whole, a pattern or a structure not clearly seen before. The process calls for creative behaviour in the student, but within the canon, i.e. controlled by the methodological framework of economics.

Comprehension, application and analysis also involve putting together of elements into meanings. Synthesis differs partly in scale— the process is less partial—and partly in greater emphasis on originality. The product of synthesis should clearly be more than the materials with which the student began work and more than the mere sum of the parts. Several varieties of synthesis may, with difficulty, be distinguished.

Abilities involved in producing a simple and technically unoriginal investigation (e.g. a student project in economics) include ability to propose ways of testing a hypothesis, and ability to integrate results of an investigation into an effective solution of a problem. The product is a synthesis. The personal touch is possible here, since the way in which the student decides to test even the simplest hypothesis can be uniquely his own. In addition, the choice of hypothesis to test and the purposes to be served by the outcome often reflect the personal values of the student.

A rather different kind of synthesis may occur when economists try to communicate certain ideas and produce an excellent and unique organization of ideas and statements, e.g. Marshall's new synthesis of knowledge in the 1890s or Keynes' in the 1930s. The methodology and scope of economics is then a constraint, and the synthesis will be personal in both its structure and its subject.

A closely related type of synthesis produces a set of abstract relations, concerned with either the form or the substance of economics. In the first case, there is a new theoretical synthesis, e.g. Joan Robinson's *Economics of Imperfect Competition*, Samuelson's *Foundations of Economic Analysis* or Leontieff's input–output analysis. This derives from a fresh analysis of deductive propositions and relations. A new framework of abstract relations is produced. The relations are not explicit from the start. Originality in the syntheses lies in their discovery or deduction. Or a set of relations may be derived from empirical work, newly tested hypotheses, which are put together in a new framework. Apart from projects, testing for synthesis is very difficult. On a sample basis, using course work, the problem is that of deciding whether one sample is a fair sample of the student's ability. Written tests can be devised, e.g. a topic is specified upon which the student is likely to have many ideas, such as the working of prices and incomes policy in a specific micro-context. He is required to produce a consistent point of view and specific stipulations are laid down, e.g. aspects of the topic which have to be treated. For instance discussion must consider the moral basis and social effects as well as material consequences and engineering of different policies and the paper must be in the form of an argument in which pros and cons are considered and the argument is clear and logical and supported where possible by empirical evidence. This means that the student cannot produce from memory a coherent argument which meets the requirement. Making a good synthesis requires particularly good powers of comprehension and analysis to ensure that the synthesis fits the requirements of the problem well. For synthesis virtually all other skills and abilities are used to marshal knowledge.

600 Evaluation

In the Bloom type hierarchy it could easily be argued that evaluation should at least precede synthesis and Bloom (I, 185) is well aware of the objections to placing evaluation at this particular point. He seems to have been greatly influenced by a desire to link the cognitive and affective domains by a category which obviously straddles the two.

Value judgments concerning materials, use of criteria of evaluation, are an important cognitive behaviour and clearly linked with affective behaviours where values, liking and enjoying (or their absence and contraries) are central to the processes involved.

Much human appraisal is extremely egocentric and rapid. Bloom calls rapid, almost reflexive evaluations *opinions* and more considered and conscious ones *judgments*, where distinct criteria are applied. The first sort are more common, the second more desirable educationally (?) and it is with these considered evaluations that Bloom is concerned. A major purpose of education is clearly to broaden and deepen the foundation upon which judgments are made, to provide criteria and experience of applying them.

Bloom distinguishes two types of evaluation:

6.10 *Judgments in terms of internal standards of criticism*

A piece of work can be judged from internal evidence as to its accuracy: judgment is by consistency, logical accuracy and other appropriate internal criteria. For example, is the work consistent in use of terms, do ideas flow from one another, do conclusions follow logically from argument? A work might also be judged by the accuracy with which data is reported.

6.20 *Judgments in terms of external criteria*

A work may be highly accurate factually and logically correct without necessarily being highly valued unless it satisfies certain external standards as well. These are derived from consideration of the ends to be served and the appropriateness of the means to achieve these ends, i.e. the economy or utility of means for ends.

There are appropriate criteria by which to judge a piece of work in economics. For instance, Bronfenbrenner has pointed out that some economists (e.g. Friedmanites) would prefer the mathematically simplest of any different sets of assumptions which forecast economic phenomena equally well, i.e. those assumptions involving the smallest loss of degrees of freedom. They therefore prefer linear to non-linear functions and simplifications like 'atomistic markets in which individuals maximize profits and/or utility but where no individual has power to affect prices of anything he buys or sells'.* This is essentially a mathematical criterion. On the other hand, the criterion of a good model is clearly not its internal articulation. Given reasonable logical and mathematical competence the model will follow from its premises and in that sense be perfectly true, and good by the first evaluative criterion, internal standards. But to be a good economic model, i.e. to satisfy external criteria, it must be fruitful. It must, to use Bronfenbrenner's example, be a source for applicability theorems which facilitate useful analysis in the same way as the theorem that prices will approach minimum average costs of production was derived from the perfectly competitive model. So the work is judged by its purpose, the end it happens to achieve. A model is judged by its fruitfulness, an applicability theorem by its applicability, an empirical investigation by its success in testing a given hypothesis. Testing for evaluative ability is by no means easy since it is difficult to establish that the responses given by those being tested are genuine examples of original evaluation or simply regurgitation of stock phrases couched in evaluative form. Clearly the ability to give reasons for a given judgment is necessary. In terms of economics, excerpts from writings on economic matters, e.g. newspaper articles, may form a basis for the exercise of judgment and the statement of reasons for that judgment. Both open (essay type) and closed (objective test type) questions might be asked. Alternatively the setting of essay topics, either under examination conditions or in the form of projects, can be framed to elicit evaluative skills.

* M. Bronfenbrenner, 'A "Middlebrow" Introduction to Economic Methodology', in *The Structure of Economic Science*, ed. S. R. Krupp, 1966, p. 15.

2: Theory of Objectives Applied to the Teaching of Economics

LUIS MACIVER

Background

My interest in objectives derives from participating in courses on objectives and assessment with student teachers representing a variety of specialist disciplines, including economics and business studies, and from increasing involvement in curriculum development. I am *not* a specialist in economics.

The Scottish Working Party in Economics, constituted some two years ago, has to date produced Units on Production, Consumption, and Distribution for use with first year classes in Scottish secondary schools, i.e. with 12-year-olds. Further units, for use with second year classes, are now being prepared. My involvement in the deliberations of the Working Party in Economics has gone somewhat beyond the basic remit of validating course material. I have participated in discussion at all stages of planning and revision of course units and materials. In particular, I have advised on the use of objectives in the preparation of course units, and may claim in a small way to have influenced the Working Party towards increased use of objectives.

Rationale of this Paper

Some illustration is given of the types of objectives listed by the Working Party, both in the final course materials, and in the process of devising course units.

The paper also includes discussion of contrasting and conflicting types and definitions of objectives. It is suggested that various types of statement are appropriate for particular stages or phases of curriculum development, i.e. that no single stipulative definition of an objective is valid.

The concluding paragraphs tentatively advance suggestions for a systematic, rational and reasonably phased approach to preparation and statement of a curriculum. Some final prerequisites and cautions relating to 'an objectives approach' are offered.

Functions of Objectives

It is still relevant to ask 'Why prepare and list objectives?' Both Tyler[1] and Gronlund,[2] the former reputedly the provider of the framework within which most U.S.A. curriculum development over the past 20 years has been formulated,[3] agree that statement of objectives occurs meaningfully within the following framework:

Course Content and Aims→Objectives→Educational Processes
or Learning Procedures→Evaluation.

Tyler and Gronlund, and of course Bloom,[4, 5, 6] all agree that such a framework is cyclical and continuous in process, with evaluation furnishing evidence of relative success and/or failure in attaining educational goals, and leading inevitably to some subsequent revision both of aims and of objectives, and of future learning procedures. While various objections have been raised to such a framework, I consider it a reasonable approach for curriculum planning or lesson preparation, while remaining aware of wider factors, such as home influences or social processes within school and classroom, which admittedly impinge on the learning situation.

One bemoans, however, certain actual imbalances in theory of objectives, especially evidenced in certain text-books. Two such imbalances may be indicated, each involving a relative over-stressing of single elements in Tyler's framework, viz. evaluation or assessment, and objectives. Such imbalances also involve a serious under-stressing or relative ignoring of educational processes or teaching procedures, a topic to which Tyler has appropriately devoted half of his text.[1]

The very titles, *Measurement and Evaluation in Teaching* by Gronlund, and *Handbook on Formative and Summative Evaluation of Student Learning* by Bloom, Hastings and Madaus, indicate a relative over-emphasis on assessment. Each of these texts proceeds almost directly from statement of objectives to methods of assessment, giving relatively scant attention to detail of educational processes or teaching materials.

It is more difficult to fault Mager's[7] definition and examples of instructional objectives, because they are very clearly stated, and have obvious use in generating and assessing suitable educational experiences for pupils:

(a) *Definition of an Instructional Objective*

'3. To describe terminal behaviour (what the learner will be DOING):

    a) Identify and name the overall behaviour act.

    b) Define the important conditions under which the behaviour is to occur (givens or restrictions, or both).

    c) Define the criterion of acceptable performance.

4. Write a separate statement for each objective: the more statements you have, the better chance you have of making clear your intent.

5. If you give each learner a copy of your objectives, you may not have to do much else.' (Mager, *Preparing Instructional Objectives*, p. 53.)

(b) *Examples of Acceptable Objectives, as given by Mager*

'(i) Student is able to write three examples of the logical fallacy of the undistributed middle.

(ii) The student is able to name and give an example of each of six programming techniques useful for eliciting a correct response. To be considered correct, items listed by the student must appear on the handout entitled "Programming techniques" issued by the instructor during the course.'

While, regrettably, the quoted examples from Mager do not relate to economics, they are clearly stated and specific concerning both the learning process, and criteria for immediate assessment of whether specific goals are being attained. [E.g. if the pupil has given only five examples of programming techniques, according to Mager not only the student but the objective has failed!] Nevertheless, Mager's precise complex definition of an instructional objective illustrates the fallacy of emphasizing objectives, however specific, to the exclusion of broader considerations of curriculum content and aims, a variety of possible methods of instruction, and even a flexible variety of assessments of educational success or failure by teacher or pupil!

It must now be emphasized that the use, or statement, of

educational or instructional objectives has no theoretical justi-fication *in its own right*. The statement of objectives is valuable only to the extent that this method improves lesson or curriculum preparation, and ultimately the educational experiences of children.

It must also be stated however that recent analyses of curricu-lum, in terms not only of pupil behaviour, but also in terms of some categorization or taxonomy of areas or levels of human intellectual performance *or* subject expertise, and of learning pro-cedures for pupils, have yielded more meaningful and precise statements than more traditional statements of syllabus content and aims. In short, statements of behavioural objectives seem to have a firm place only within a broader framework of aims and objectives, related learning processes and evaluation, as sug-gested by Tyler in 1949.[1]

Different Types of Objectives with Examples

It seems meaningful to illustrate the different uses of so-called objectives commonly used by curriculum developers. The pro-cess of stating objectives is, however, complex, involving a *variety* of types of statement, a fact disguised by the blanket-term 'objective'.

Curriculum Aims and Objectives

As distinct from many prescriptive writers on educational object-ives, one seeks to stress the synonymity of the terms 'aims' and 'objectives', in the sense of 'things to aim at, goals, or targets'. Whatever the defects of educational aims, educators continue to have intents for pupils, in relation to subject matter, and to express these in terms of aims, as the following examples show:[8]

Aims

(a) to enable pupils to see economics as a dynamic social science of concern to everybody

(b) to provide pupils with an understanding of the basic economic problems which will increasingly face them

(c) to develop in pupils a capacity for economic reasoning and for logical expression of economic ideas based on a study of relevant data.

General Objectives

It is fashionable nowadays to proceed to express the general aims of a course or curriculum in terms of General Objectives. The important element of such a statement seems to be, however, *not* objectives firmly stated in terms of pupil behaviour at this stage, but subject elements, and proposed pupil learning listed under such headings as knowledge, comprehension, application, etc. Such categories are useful both in reflecting a complex balance of 'knowledge' and 'know-how'[9] of a discipline such as economics, and in serving to diversify pupil learning beyond verbal knowledge and understanding of facts, principles, etc., towards finer thought-processes, and especially towards applications of learning and skills.

Examples of General Objectives

1. *Knowledge* of:
   (a) basic terminology and concepts, e.g. labour, scarcity, income, opportunity cost.
   (b) institutions and organizations, e.g. trade unions, industries, banks, etc.
   (c) policies, e.g. full employment, stable exchange rates, etc.

2. *Comprehension* of:
   (a) the existence of economic variables, e.g. supply, investment, costs, revenue, etc.
   (b) the essential nature of personal, local, national and international economic problems, i.e. competing claims on scarce resources, etc.

3. *Application:*
   Application of knowledge previously gained to particular situations and problems; e.g. effects of rapid inflation on levels of employment; effects of investment on the national income, etc.

4. *Analysis:*
   (a) identification of components, e.g. distinction between total and marginal cost; distinction between current account and balance of payments, etc.
   (b) identification of relationships, e.g. between supply and

demand, between price and quantity, between taxation and government expenditure, etc.

5. *Synthesis:*
   Construction of economic models: e.g. circular flow of income; regional specialization, etc.

6. *Evaluation:*
   Identification of positive and normative statements used in economic arguments, etc.

7. *Study and Communication Skills:*
   (*a*) to collect and communicate economic data, e.g. personal and national budgets, population census data.
   (*b*) to explain economic data and principles orally, and in a written statement.
   (*c*) to process economic data in a variety of forms, e.g. charts, equations, concrete models, graphs.

More Detailed Course Objectives

Curriculum objectives cover a wide range, ultimately from general objectives potentially covering an entire school subject, as in the previous paragraph, down to and including specific statements relating to a single purposeful pupil activity within the classroom. From the illustrations which follow it can be seen that more meaningful detail is possible for lessons or units of a course than is possible in a list of objectives for an entire subject. Such detail is possible because of prior focussing on a single subject-topic, e.g. production, and because of the use of dimensions from the taxonomy (Bloom's). Note that for functional simplicity many curriculum developers reduce the categories considerably. For example, knowledge, understanding and application, the last category in effect also embracing a fair number of skills, often suffice in practice. Note also the form of stated course objectives in the following examples:

(i) The pupil firmly figures in each statement.
(ii) The verbs employed still reflect the categories of the taxonomy, e.g. 'knows' and 'understands', rather than the actual behaviour of the pupil.
(iii) However, under the heading of 'Applications', the verbs begin to reflect pupil activity in the classroom, e.g. 'simu-

lates areas of economic activity', 'completes worksheets', etc.

Some Course Objectives on Consumption

A. *Knowledge*
1. Pupil knows the meaning of the terms consumption, production, scarcity, satisfaction.
2. Pupil knows that consumption brings immediate satisfaction of wants.
3. Pupil knows that consumption is a major component of aggregate demand.

B. *Understanding*
1. Pupil understands the relationship between consumption and other areas of economic activity.
2. Pupil understands that advertising can have varying effects on individuals' tastes and therefore on a firm's (or industry's) output.

C. *Application*
1. Pupil identifies different areas of economic activity from various data given.
2. Pupil can represent economic ideas in diagrammatic form.
3. Pupil applies his knowledge of his potential purchasing power to a market situation—e.g. withholds purchase to improve quality of production.

Specific Objectives and Procedures

The next stage of detailing objectives involves stating a short list of objectives for each unit or lesson of a course. In practice, such statements often seem to combine statement of actual procedures with subject-related objectives related to comprehension or application, as the illustrations below show. It must be stressed that full details of procedures and pupil activities are furnished in course notes for teachers, and pupil notes, instructions and worksheets. Such lists have a vital function in directing teachers' and pupils' efforts.

Example of Statement of Specific Objectives and Procedures from a Unit on Consumption

1. Pupil sketches symbols representing the members of his household, and identifies the producers and consumers.
2. Pupil shows that he realizes that all producers consume, although not all consumers produce.

Learning Procedures in Economics for S1 and S2*

An interesting linking of specific objectives and procedures is evidenced above. Pioneering work has been done by the economists on the Working Party in translating firm subject matter into structured, purposeful, and enjoyable pupil activity, always with subject-objectives (i.e. goals) in mind. The teachers' notes and pupils' worksheets quoted below may illustrate this approach.

Teachers' Notes for a Work Unit on Consumption

1. Indicate various items within classroom and ask pupil to state if they are 'Free' goods, 'Economic' goods, and further, if they are Investment or Consumption goods.

   Suggested items: desks, books, pupil's tie, floor-boards, teacher while teaching, sweets, watch, air in classroom.

2. Ask pupils to itemize their spending over past two income periods. What proportion spent on consumption? Why? Does this vary from pupil to pupil?
3. Produce advertisements from press for various goods (luxuries and necessities; capital and consumer durables). Pupil attempts to assess impact on him. Is he convinced? Could he do better?

Possible Pupils' Worksheet on an Aspect of Consumption

1. In the next five minutes you will consume many resources. List these in the space below:
2. With an asterisk mark those items on your list which you think are necessities.

* These are the names given to the first and second years of secondary education in Scotland.

3. Set up the kit to illustrate the circular flow of income between 4 households and 2 firms—one producing luxuries, the other necessities. There is no saving in this model of the economy.
How long can production continue?
Do production and consumption cease at the same moment?
How can production be stimulated if there is no saving by either householder or firms?

Learning Procedures, the Educational Process and Objectives

Any framework for planned teaching or curriculum development must include the Educational Process or Learning Procedures as a core feature. This is indeed *the* core feature not only of curriculum but of a 'pupil behavioural' approach.

The Working Party in Economics for instance has achieved a translation of firm structured subject matter into a very detailed specified structure of pupil behaviours in the classroom. Any single statement of stipulated pupil behaviour may lack the form even of a specific objective, as defined by Mager. This is because the pupil behaviours are defined in much more detail, which is in effect only summarized in any list of lesson or unit objectives.

Theory of Objectives related to the Task of Translating Subject Matter into Structured Learning Procedures

(i) Without doubt, the practice of using objectives, i.e. of stating a syllabus in pupil-behavioural terms, is an aid towards formulating learning procedures.

(ii) The categories of Bloom's taxonomy are helpful for restating a syllabus in a balanced way. A range of cognitive categories and some categories of skills are useful if not indeed essential for translating a content-based curriculum into terms of developing pupil know-how. In short, some list of categories, i.e. a taxonomy, is useful *in its own right*, whether or not the statements are in the form of objectives at this stage of subdividing the syllabus.

(iii) There are other modern psychological models which also seem very relevant, viz. Piaget's[10] developmental theory, Bruner's[11] enactive, iconic and symbolic modes of thinking, and Gagné's[12] hierarchy of learning.

(iv) The members of the Working Party demonstrated an analytical awareness of the subject matter, a sensitive awareness of how the children, for whom the course units were intended, functioned educationally, and the requisite creative imagination to translate abstract subject matter into meaningful and interesting pupil-tasks. Perhaps such awareness is more vital to curriculum development than any theoretical model.

Theory of Objectives must at any rate be placed in perspective as only one of several aids to curriculum planning.

Detailed Objectives, Procedures and Criterion Objectives

During preparation of course units, the Working Party drew up sheets listing Formative and Summative Objectives, in Bloom's language. It now appears clear that simpler terms suffice and clarify, and accordingly the example presented below appears in somewhat amended form.

Example of Sequence of Objectives

Specific Objective	Procedures	Criterion Objectives
1. Pupil knows that if all incomes are consumed, then investment by householders and firms will be affected.	1. Pupil uses kit to help completion of Item 3 in Worksheet 1.	1. Pupils correctly construct model of 'non-saving' economy in Worksheet 1.
2. Pupil knows that non-consumption of present income can lead to a higher level of future consumption.	2. Pupil studies budgets of selected households and firms and identifies saving and investment, etc.	2. Pupil budgets his own present saving to prepare for future spending with accuracy.

Course Worksheets, Criterion Objectives and Assessment

At one stage of course preparation, certain Working Party members opined that no assessment beyond successful completion of worksheets, and the prescribed activities, was necessary. Without doubt, such successful completion is a meaningful assessment of the course materials, and of pupil competence during the learning process. Accordingly, the notion of criterion objectives is useful. (Note however that while Mager includes criterion as an essential feature of any objective, the Working

Various Categories of Statement in Curriculum Planning

Stage	Type of Statement	Examples
1. Syllabus Content	Factual statement or Items or Topics	Production Banking Function of Cheques
2. Syllabus Aims	Teacher intentions for pupils combined with syllabus content	To develop in pupils an awareness of advantages and disadvantages of specialization
3. General Objectives	Syllabus content categorized by cognitive and skills dimensions of taxonomy. Statements tend to *pupil* behaviour, especially in areas of 'Application' and 'Skills'	*Knowledge* Terms: Manufacturer, Warehouse, Factory, etc. *Understanding* The role of insurance in distribution, etc. *Application* Pupils construct models of the 'channel of distribution'
4. Intermediate and Specific Objectives	Intentions of pupil knowledge, understanding and competence stated with increased detail and specificity	Pupil understands that storage problems can be overcome by warehousing
5. Specific Objectives in 'Applications' and 'Skills' Areas	These usually state pupil behaviour in more overt behavioural terms than objectives of knowledge and understanding	Pupil lists main risks against which manufacturers usually insure
6. Learning procedures	Fairly precise detail of structured pupil experiences	See Teachers' Notes and Pupils' Worksheets above
7. Criterion Objectives	Expression of what pupil will be DOING, and criterion of success or failure, when attaining a specific objective	(a) Pupil meaningfully completes experiment (b) Pupil correctly tabulates results (c) Pupil lists at least 3 risks against which manufacturers usually insure
8. Assessment Item	(a) A criterion objective, for assessment in classroom (b) Any form of examination item reasonably related to a general or specific objective	(a) See above (b) A man increases his earnings by overtime from £20 to £30. He will now be in a position to satisfy: A All of his wants B Fewer of his wants C More wants D Exactly the same wants as before

Party—logically, it is contended—expressed criteria in statements quite distinct from specific objectives or procedures.) It is questionable, however, whether absolute criteria for success, as distinct from failure, can ever legitimately be 'written into' the actual material of a course, in view of range of pupil performance, which means 50% accuracy from some is in practice as acceptable as 100% accuracy from others!

In fact, in connection with the use of units in pilot schools, the Working Party has devised and used pre-tests and post-tests, incorporating alternative-choice items, multiple-choice items, and short-answer items, as well as a brief assessment of the pupil's personal reaction to the course unit, in terms of easiness or difficulty, boredom or interest, and the pupil's opinion on whether the course should be done by all, some, or no pupils at his stage. Beyond the usual fairly rigorous assessment of new course materials at the piloting stage, there is always a case for some assessment, independent of the actual course materials and worksheets. This assessment should not be too contaminated with the actual learning procedures of the course, which are bound to represent only one of several possible combinations of methods.

Objectives, or Various Categories of Statement in Lesson or Curriculum Planning?

Various single definitions of objectives have been criticized as being too prescriptive, and too wide-ranging. In fact, any meaningful development of classroom procedures involves several different exercises, with different types of statement at each stage. All of these statements are perfectly respectable in their own place, while only some of them can be called objectives, in any sense. Some distinctive stages of curriculum development might be as stated in the table on page 51.

Objectives within a Wider Framework

The following statement may serve to illustrate a general sequence of topics requiring consideration and decisions by any group of curriculum planners and thus to place theory of objectives further in perspective:

A Wider Framework for Curriculum Development

Topics and Vital Questions	*Answers relevant to Economics for S1 Pupils*

(i) *The Pupils*
   (a) Age and school stage?
   (b) Range of abilities?
   (c) Interests, and likely motivations?
	12+; Secondary 1
	Bright to dull: mean ability—average
	Activity: things: variety of things to do

(ii) *Syllabus Content in Economics*
   (a) Basic for beginners?
   (b) Not too complex?
   (c) Translatable into suitable terms for 12-year-olds?
	Chosen Topics
	Production
	Distribution
	Consumption

(iii) *Choice of Suitable Approach and Methods*
   (a) Suitable to analysed components of subject?
   (b) Suitable to abilities and interests of pupils?
	(a) Use of kit
	
	(b) Interesting, purposeful pupil activities
	(c) Worksheets to direct and consolidate activities
	(d) Still important functions for teacher

(iv) *Analysis of Aims and Objectives (from general to specific)*
   (a) Are various categories of taxonomy covered?
   (b) Is pupil increasingly brought to centre of process?
	See examples in earlier paragraphs, and in Course Units

(v) *Learning Procedures*
   (a) Derived from detailed syllabus content?
   (b) Also related to syllabus statement under headings of taxonomy?
   (c) Whole process expressed in what *pupil* and *teacher* will be DOING?
	(a) Examples in Teacher's Notes and in Pupil's Notes and Worksheets
	(b) Specification in detail
	
	(c) Can be usefully summarized in specific objectives, and criterion objectives

(vi) *Criteria of Success*
   (a) Assessment items in work units?
   (b) Criteria of success in completion of work units?
   (c) Any assessment required beyond completion of work units?
	(a) Structure of worksheets often guarantees that completion of latter items is a fair assessment
	(b) Successful completion a useful criterion, but some flexibility required for a wide abilities range
	(c) Objective items and open-ended items used in pre-test and post-test of cognitive and affective pupil reactions

Some Concluding Considerations

(*a*) Theory of objectives can usefully be applied to syllabus development in economics.

(*b*) This application may occur at two distinct levels: that of general awareness of the theory, or that of using 'an objectives approach' for most of the process of syllabus development.

(*c*) This paper has cautioned against certain ambiguities in the definition of objectives, and against the excessive claims made by certain authors for objectives as a total and tightly prescribed model for syllabus and lesson preparation.

(*d*) This paper has also suggested a fuller framework for lesson and curriculum planning, with objectives having an integral but non-predominating place in such a framework.

(*e*) Detailed analysis of the goals and tasks involved in curriculum development is essential. For successful practice, various kinds of theoretical awareness seem essential. They would include an ability to translate syllabus into pupil behaviours, a central theme of theory of objectives. Various other theoretical 'models', and especially those of Piaget, Bruner and Gagné, seem equally relevant to the task of translating subject-content into learning procedures.

References

1. Tyler, Ralph W., *Basic Principles of Curriculum and Instruction*, Chicago U. Press, 1949.
2. Gronlund, Norman E., *Measurement and Evaluation in Teaching*, Macmillan, New York, 1965.
3. Lawton, Denis, 'Curriculum Reform and Teacher Reform in the Secondary School', in *London Educational Review*, Vol. 1, No. 3. Autumn 1972, pp. 76-9
4. Bloom, Benjamin S. *et al.* (eds.), *Taxonomy of Educational Objectives, Handbook 1, Cognitive Domain*, Longmans, 1956.
5. Krathwohl, D. R., Bloom, B. S. and Masia, B. B. (eds.), *Taxonomy of Educational Objectives, Handbook 2, Affective Domain*, Longmans, 1964.
6. Bloom, B. S., Hastings, J. T. and Madaus, G. F., *Handbook on Formative and Summative Evaluation of Student Learning*, McGraw-Hill, 1971.
7. Mager, Robert F., *Preparing Instructional Objectives*, Fearon Publishers, California, 1962.
8. Source: Scottish Certificate of Education Examination Board, Scottish Certificate of Education. New Syllabus and Examination in Economics at the Ordinary Grade.

9. Ryle, Gilbert, *The Concept of Mind*, Penguin, 1963.
10. Piaget, Jean, *The Psychology of Intelligence*, Routledge, 1950.
11. Bruner, J. S., 'Course of Cognitive Growth', in *American Psychologist*, 1964.
12. Gagné, R. M., *The Conditions of Learning*, Holt, Rinehart & Winston, 1965.

II: VALUES IN ECONOMICS EDUCATION

3: Concealed Values in Economics Teaching

NORMAN LEE

The Issue

A few years ago I was approached by a secondary school economics teacher who was concerned at the 'rightward' shift in the
political views of his pupils, apparently in response to the
economics course he was giving. This was puzzling to him
because (*a*) having been reared on Lipsey's *Positive Economics*,
he naturally prided himself in the 'neutrality' of his teaching and
(*b*) his own political views (to the extent that they inadvertently
intruded) were slightly left of centre. Since this incident a number
of other cases of this kind have been reported, which suggests
that, despite protestations to the contrary, much economics
teaching is still considerably more value-loaded than teachers at
all levels are prepared to admit.

Far from withering away, as 'positive' economics becomes more
widely practised, I can see the problem growing in the future and
centring upon the concealed (rather than overt) value judgments
contained in economics teaching. As the economics literacy
movement broadens and extends down the school curriculum to
younger and less-able pupils, I would expect allegations of political indoctrination to grow. As attempts to integrate the educational contributions of the different social sciences in the schools
are promoted, I would also expect conflicts between the concealed
value judgments in certain forms of economics and sociology
teaching to become more apparent. This general problem was
briefly discussed in *Teaching Economics*[1] but I believe it now
requires a fuller airing, leading to the identification of possible
solutions.

Positive/Normative Economics and Sources of Bias

The controversy over the neutrality of economics and the validity
of the distinction between positive and normative economics is

as old as the subject of economics itself.[2] Robbins, for example, made the well-known distinction between means and ends, holding that economics is neutral between ends and is not concerned with ends as such.[3] Positive economics, according to Friedman, is independent of any particular ethical position or normative judgment.[4] Therefore, it is held, the 'scientific economist' should not and cannot pronounce or advise on ends, though he can pronounce on the means that will promote specific ends.

This is the predominant view to which economics teachers (and, through them, their pupils) have been exposed during the last 10–15 years. In at least one respect it has had a favourable effect on economics teaching. Writing in 1961, the U.S. National Task Force on Economics Education stated, 'on economic issues it appears that teachers often insert their own value judgments and "answers" on economic issues as to what the student should believe, all too often without identifying them as such'.[5] Almost certainly this was also true in this country at that time. Since then, through the attempted separation of means and ends, the more blatant use of value judgments in economics education has diminished, though it has not been entirely eliminated.

However, the value judgment problem cannot be fully resolved by this positive/normative distinction since there are important sources of bias in positive economics itself. Further, under the guise of alleged scientific objectivity, their influence can be every bit as great as the more overt forms of bias with which many economics teachers are now fully familiar.

Hutchison[6] has identified four ways in which value judgments may influence the content and presentation of economics as follows:

(*a*) ethical or political value judgments, overtly stated or latently implied, regarding the objectives or 'ends' of societies;

(*b*) value judgments or premises involved in choosing the problems to be studied;

(*c*) value judgments or premises involved in choosing the types of procedure (methods) by which the problems are to be studied;

(*d*) biased subjectivity in positive empirical statements.

Only part of the first of these (latently implied value judgments regarding the ends of society) is alien to positive economics. All of the remainder, unless care is taken, can flourish unchecked in the teaching of positive economics, without conscious appreciation by the teacher that this is taking place. The sources of bias are considerable and, in the present situation, their collective impact is strongly conservative.

The Conservative Bias within Economics Education

One of the many urgently required pieces of research into economics education concerns the importance of concealed value judgments and the short examples which follow should be regarded as no more than a brief introduction to this subject. Five types of bias are identified; the first arises from the blurred distinction between positive and normative economics, the other four relate to positive economics and the manner in which it is taught.

(*a*) Despite considerable progress in propagating the positive normative distinction, a considerable number of teachers still appear to be confused as to what the distinction really is. Whilst some teachers will be very circumspect in informing their pupils that, *if* the policy objective is optimal resource allocation then, *given* certain specified assumptions, this can be achieved through perfectly competitive markets, others still treat perfect competition (or, worse still, 'greater competition') as if it were a welfare ideal enshrined in the body of economic theory itself. The problem here probably lies mainly with the older teacher who will be less familiar with recent developments in welfare economics, though even some present-day university courses are weak in this area.

(*b*) This effect can be heightened where, on grounds of insufficient time or the need to simplify the course content, the syllabus concentrates on the analysis of particular hypothetical markets and their application to practical economic problems. In many courses elementary price theory is synonymous with the perfect competition and single-firm market models. The prevailing view still appears to be that the essentials of oligopoly theory can only be grasped after a thorough treatment of the perfect competition model—though this is questionable. In the absence of sufficient appreciation of other market forms, applied microeconomics becomes the application of supply and demand analysis in markets (e.g. housing markets) which are demonstrably far from perfect. Students are then in danger of inferring welfare consequences from market solutions which they believe to be scientifically based but which, in fact, are derived from the unjustified transposition of perfect market analysis.

(*c*) Even where policy objectives are explicitly stated, and the examination of ends is separated from that of means, bias can arise in the selection of the objectives of an economic system to be incorporated into the analysis. Generally speaking, in current economics education, our main preoccupation is with the objective of optimal resource allocation, followed by the objectives of economic growth and economic stability. In turn, the concepts and analytical techniques that are developed and used in teaching are mainly related to these objectives. We may plead neutrality in our attitude towards ends, but we show little interest or concern for certain of these ends judged by the content of our courses. The optimal distribution of income (sometimes called 'economic justice'), though it is referred to as an objective of an economic system, rarely receives much more than a passing mention. Too often it is regarded as an analytical inconvenience to be circumvented by the qualifying assumption 'that the existing distribution of income is optimal'. Whether such selectivity in ends is consistent with neutrality is seriously open to doubt.

(*d*) One of the consequences of restricting economics courses to the content of positive economics has been to discourage the explicit examination of the ends of economic systems. The normative/positive distinction is important in the training of the professional economist in identifying the limits of his professional competence. Appreciating this distinction may be facilitated by constructing certain courses of instruction which are entirely positive in nature. However, in education for citizenship it is ludicrous to foster an understanding of the means of economic action without, or before, a systematic and critical examination of the possible ends to which those means are to be directed. The exclusion of the discussion of ends *per se*, is likely to result in the uncritical acceptance of those particular ends to which the major part of economic analysis is directed. The reinstatement of ends within economics courses does not involve the abandonment of the positive/normative distinction. It does involve, however, a special challenge for the economics teacher: how to promote a study of ends (the examination of which extends beyond his economics expertise) without imposing his own value judgments upon his students.

(*e*) The mainstream of economics accepts fairly restrictive boundaries to the area of knowledge which it studies. For example, the findings of the other social sciences are treated as data given (frequently in the form of assumptions) and are not objects of interest or of analysis within economics itself. This form of specialization has tended to isolate economic analysis (and its teaching) from developments in the other behavioural sciences. This partially explains why we cling to the extremely simplified behavioural assumptions which underpin much of elementary price theory—notably those assumptions which underlie consumer sovereignty. The response of the consumer to the 'hidden persuaders' and the behaviour of large corporations, though central to real market behaviour, are still treated as awkward appendages, reluctantly recognized, which cannot be easily fitted into simple market analysis.

The net effect of these different forms of selectivity is to concentrate economics education on the relatively uncritical examination of certain unrealistic market forms serving a restricted number of economic ends. These market forms (more especially the perfect market form) carry strong welfare overtones, which the promotion of positive economics has not yet been able to eliminate. This inevitably encourages the tacit acceptance of those ends that are given the greatest attention in the course (and the subordination of those that are neglected) and the search for solutions to economic problems which are competitive-market orientated. Hence the conclusion that economics education contains a concealed conservative bias.

Possible Solutions

Before discussing possible solutions to the conservative bias in economics education, it is important to recognize that, in some instances, there may exist an overt or concealed left-wing bias in economics teaching: for example, arising from preoccupation with Marxist economics or, more subtly, discrediting received theory in a biased manner. Such biases are equally undesirable and it would be counter-productive if 'solutions' to a conservative bias mostly resulted in the substitution of a left-wing one. For this reason, certain of the changes discussed below would need to be developed with considerable care before they were implemented in the classroom.

A. *Economics Teacher Training*

(*a*) Strengthening of the welfare economics component in undergraduate and college economics courses, so that future economics teachers are better skilled in the handling of economic policy issues and have a greater appreciation of where value judgments are implied in the analysis they use.

(*b*) The incorporation of welfare economics topics in refresher courses for practising teachers, together with certain of the topics discussed in B. below.

(*c*) Greater emphasis in teacher-training courses for economics teachers on the detection and correct handling of value judgments in economics education.

B. *Content of Economics Education*

The main proposals in this section mainly relate to a change in emphasis rather than radical changes in course content.

(*a*) Fuller and more critical examination of the ends of economic systems and the development of the pupils' facility to exercise their own thinking in evaluating those ends.

(*b*) Greater attention to the examination of alternative economic systems and comparisons between systems.

(*c*) A more balanced allocation of teaching time between topics related to the different ends of economic systems. In particular greater allocation of time to topics connected with income distribution and economic justice objectives (e.g. problems of poverty, conservation, housing, education, etc.).

(*d*) Greater use of the contributions of other behavioural sciences in studying consumer behaviour and greater attention to more realistic market forms and their possible welfare implications.

C. *Implementation*

(*a*) Review of course syllabuses with a view to the incorporation of items B. (*a*)–(*d*) where this is presently not provided for. The form of incorporation will depend upon the age, ability, previous experience, etc. of the pupil and not *all* items will be incorporated into *every* stage of the economics education pro-gramme. To make room for these items, others will have to be pruned.

(*b*) The development of resource units in each of the areas B. (*a*)–(*d*) for the different points in the curriculum where they are to be introduced. The early stages of this work might be undertaken by small working groups of teachers, educationists and economists and would focus on objectives, resource unit content and teaching methods and aids. Basic teaching materials might be generated at this stage (corresponding to the J.C.E.E. leaflets).

(*c*) Incorporation of these topics in new basic economics text-books, teaching manuals, workbooks, etc. Preparation of satellite booklets, case studies, visual aids, etc. in each of these cases.

(*d*) Critical study (possibly as part of an educational research project), of the extent of overt and concealed value judgments in existing text-books and other publications (e.g. Hobart Papers and bank reviews) used in economics education in schools. The results of this study could then be made available to teachers and would be of assistance to them in selecting the literature they use for teaching purposes and as recommended reading for their students.

References

1. Lee, N. (ed.), *Teaching Economics*, Economics Association, Sutton, 1967, pp. 54–6.
2. Hutchison, T. W., *Positive Economics and Policy Objectives*, Harvard U. Press, Cambridge, Mass., 1964, Ch. 3.
3. Robbins, L. C., *An Essay on the Nature and Significance of Economic Science*, 2nd ed., Macmillan, 1935, p. 151.
4. Friedman, M., *Essays in Positive Economics*, 1953, pp. 3–4.
5. National Task Force on Economic Education, *Economic Education in the Schools* (Joint Council on Economic Education), N.Y., 1961.
6. Hutchison, T. W., op. cit., Ch. 2.

III: SOME RESEARCH PROBLEMS IN ECONOMICS EDUCATION

4: Research into Economic Efficiency in the Teaching of Economics: Some Fundamental Problems

ALEXANDER SCOTT

The economic method as applied at the micro level is concerned with the question of optimum resource allocation and there is a generally recognized set of tools which can be used in principle to examine the functioning of any production process whether it is hairpins or education. In general terms, the procedure to be followed would be to establish a measure or measures of output in education, perhaps according to the amount of learning assimilated by the pupil, and to identify the inputs used up in the production of this output. A production function would be specified according to some *a priori* notions of the production process and the measured inputs and outputs would then be combined together in this production function and the parameters estimated using econometric techniques. Having gained this knowledge on the process of production the attempt would be made to come to conclusions on the possible variations of inputs and outputs which would lead to an optimum allocation. It is clear that the application of these principles to the teaching of economics is desirable from the theoretical point of view in so far as resources are scarce and the teaching profession as a whole is short of formal efficiency criteria. But the application of the economic method in teaching is a business of considerable complexity and care must be taken not to adopt a simplistic approach based upon quantification which has a superficial appeal but is in fact of a dubious nature. In the first instance it is necessary to determine what is meant by the terms 'output' and 'teaching input' before proceeding with any quantification, and this paper is intended to illuminate the issues which must be dealt with before any serious work can be undertaken or meaningful conclusions drawn.

Educational Output in Economics

The determination of output is a problem which can be roughly split into two stages, the first of which is the identification of the concepts and methods which constitute an understanding of the subject at the level at which attention is applied. An attempt in this direction has been made by the Economics Education Project to produce a 'Core of Basic Economics'* which is based upon a consensus view of what economics is about. This 'core' sets out the concepts which the student should have at the basic level and, broadly speaking, the logic which should be appreciated in arriving at these concepts. There is bound to be a measure of dispute over the components of such a list, particularly at this stage, and this is an issue which can only be resolved by further discussion on the nature of the subject. But it is of particular importance to the Economics Education Project because a series of tests have been devised, for the purpose of assessing output, which are based on the 'core'; those teachers who regard the components of the core as being deficient may quite legitimately consider any results arising from their use to be meaningless. From the practical point of view it has been found almost impossible to do justice to all of the elements of the 'core' as it was defined, and hence the tests of the E.E.P. could be regarded as more or less a minimum requirement in terms of knowledge on the part of the pupil. Although this is a problem which can be accepted in the initial stages of research it is something which will have to be resolved before major policy implications can be drawn.

The second-level issue here is how to test the understanding of the concepts which have been decided upon. Broadly speaking there are two possible types of assessment available: the essay-type exam and the so-called objective tests in which the correct answer has to be chosen from a number of alternatives. The choice of which method is used is a matter of fundamental importance

* This paper was prepared by the staff of the Economics Education Project and members of its Advisory Board and is available on application to the project office at the Heriot-Watt University, Edinburgh.

for the research because in principle the two methods measure different things, or at least they can do. In the former case the process which goes on in the student's head is made clear and this can be evaluated so that on the whole credit is not awarded for getting the right answers for the wrong reasons. On the other hand, there is no such safeguard in the latter case and this has serious implications. If one group scores on the average higher than another on the objective test it is concluded that they 'know more about economics'; this allows no weight to be attached to the thinking process, and it does not allow for the possibility that certain of the questions may be more amenable to answers on the basis of 'common sense' than others, and hence the meaning of 'knowing more about economics' on this criterion is not well specified. In the aggregate, the way in which answers to objective questions are arrived at is a mystery, and until more is known about it, it would be premature to be completely confident of the results. But the practical argument in favour of objective testing has particular force: that the degree of standardization which it introduces into assessment compared to essay exams more than compensates for any methodological problems. However, in view of what has been said above on the nature of objective tests this can only be regarded as a naïve answer based on expediency. Certainly the objective test standardizes for getting the answer right, but this is only part of the problem. The real choice is not between the objective or essay-type tests but on how either of these can be developed to be more consistent with whatever it is we wish to test.

An interesting point here is that both methods of testing appear to test the same things to some extent: at the school level correlations of up to ·5, and at university up to ·7 have been obtained between essay exams and the E.E.P. objective tests. But the real significance of this finding is somewhat obscure; it is not surprising to find some correlation between the two because in the essay exams one would expect on the whole that papers with the 'right answer' would tend to gain higher marks than those with 'wrong answers', and these cases would relate to high and low objective test scores respectively. But what is perplexing is that in some institutions there is no correlation whatsoever between the two, and this is in fact more difficult to account for than a moderate degree of correlation.

The implication to be drawn from these points is that the method of assessment may have systematic effects of considerable importance on the output measure and until more is known about this subject it must be regarded as a potentially serious drawback in the evaluation of economic efficiency. But there is a yet deeper problem than this involved in the assessment of the degree of knowledge or understanding, and this is concerned with the definition of output in economic terms: strictly speaking this is the value added to the pupil as a result of the teaching undergone, and to arrive at this requires the evaluation of the amount of knowledge at the beginning of the course as well as at the end. The problems of assessment outlined above apply here, but there are in addition some rather serious implications for the notion of output. If the objective method is used both at the beginning and at the end of the course then it is necessary to make an important assumption in order to arrive at the value added. This assumption is that those who get the right answer at the beginning do so for the right reason, and no value is attributed to the fact that they understand why the answer is correct by the end of the course. Since it is not known to what extent certain types of question are amenable to answer on the basis of 'intuition' or other non-economic types of reasoning, this important aspect of education is given no weight in the final efficiency model. Thus by using the objective method to arrive at the value added it is possible that we are missing out a considerable proportion of what education is about.

The importance of these fundamental problems on the nature and methods of measuring outputs can hardly be overemphasized. For example, in the E.E.P. it has been found almost impossible to attribute the performance of pupils to different syllabuses in any systematic manner, whether it is done on the basis of the total performance or on the basis of individual questions. There are a number of possible explanations for this; that teachers do not proceed strictly in accordance with the syllabuses laid down but tend to teach what they understand by economics; that the 'economic way of thinking' overlaps into different areas of the subject; that some of the questions appear to pupils in aggregate in a different manner compared to the way in which they appear to those who do the testing.

It will be noted that one of the omissions from the preceding discussion has been any reference to the aims of education, the attempt being made to confine the discussion to the methods of measuring the outcome without making any value judgments as to whether or not the various factors are educationally desirable or not. Another factor is the evaluation of education as a consumption good in terms of the value placed on it by the pupil. The introduction of such issues into the analysis will, of course, complicate the problem even more. But the conceptual and practical issues discussed so far are prerequisites to any sensible process of quantification and policy making.

Inputs in the Teaching Process

As in the case of the outputs there is a considerable amount of basic conceptual thinking to be done prior to quantification and estimation of educational inputs. There is a tendency to think that the identification of the teaching inputs is much more straightforward than in the case of the outputs, but as will be seen this is by no means the case.

In the first instance the pupil is usually taken to be one of the inputs into the teaching process in the sense that he constitutes the raw material which is worked on and to which it is hoped to add some value by the end of the day. The problem which arises is that this input is not homogeneous, and this makes the production process rather more difficult to relate to the normal industrial case on the basis of which production functions are usually specified. Even if the extent of knowledge at the beginning of the course has been adequately measured, the problem still remains that some pupils will learn more than others for a given amount of teaching, as a result of some inherent ability, and it is necessary to standardize for this in order to draw any conclusions on the efficiency of teaching, given that the ability factor is unlikely to be randomly distributed across different institutions. The important issue here is to set out the principles on the basis of which standardization is to be carried out. From the value-added approach this amounts to identifying the extent to which different pupils will learn different amounts for a given amount of teaching, and there is little known about this. The problem is not the same as that of intelligence testing which essentially relates the level of performance on one test to that on another; it has been found in the E.E.P. that there is a strong relationship between performance on the A.H.5* and on the T.E.C. (Test of Economics Comprehension). But the fact that a person who does well on one test also does well on another will hardly come as a surprise, and in any case it is not too clear what it tells us; certainly the A.H.5 is of little value in predicting the value added. It is likely that it standardizes for the ability to do the objective types of test to some extent, but the efficiency with which it does this is not known. In the cases where it is not possible to use the value-added approach it can be argued that the use of some intelligence test is preferable to none as it at least removes some of the influences which confuse the picture. But since it is not known which factors it removes, or whether these really are the ones we wish to have removed, this must be regarded as an empirical as well as a conceptual question on which nothing more can be said in the absence of specific research. Thus so far as the general types of intelligence test are concerned, the standardization of pupils must remain an open issue; but there is certainly little to suggest that they are appropriate in the value-added case.

An alternative method of standardization is to consider the previous evidence of performance at the particular subject, and to use this as an indicator of innate comparative ability at the subject. Again, this is an issue which could be resolved on empirical grounds, but at this stage there is no reason to expect that the outcome will be any more satisfactory than in the case of the general intelligence measures. This is because the previous level of performance will be partly a result of the efficiency of teaching at the previous level, and it does not follow that a comparatively high level of performance at school will result in a comparatively high level of learning in the new teaching environment. The general result which emerges from the E.E.P., and other studies, is that the better the performance at school level in economics then the better it tends to be at university, but the relationship is much the same as that for the general intelligence tests and does not tell us anything about learning. In fact the results obtained with respect to value added in the E.E.P. indicate that those who have had school economics have a lower value added in their first year at university than those who have not. This raises the considerable practical difficulty that not all pupils

---

* A. Heim, *Test A.H.5*, National Foundation for Educational Research, 1968. This test was evolved to distinguish levels of intelligence of university students.

or students have had previous experience of the subject, and this is the rule rather than the exception at school.

In the face of all this it would appear that any attempt to standardize pupils is doomed to failure from the start and the best policy is to leave this out altogether, at least for the present, and hope that its effects are random in nature. But given the way in which admission into the various institutions of learning are conducted this is unlikely to be the case. In any case there is the possibility of interaction effects between those pupils who are more able to assimilate the subject and the actual performance of the teacher, and this may be systematic and important; certainly nothing can be learned about it by ignoring the issue. Thus we are in need of research work on the generation of predictive information in specific subjects. At the present time we are in no position to standardize for the 'ability to learn' differential between pupils.

We can now turn to the examination of the actual teaching inputs with which the pupils are provided in the form of the amount and type of teaching. There are a number of possible components here, each of which presents its own problems of identification and measurement.

The formal education and training which the teacher has received is an obvious point from which to start assessing the efficiency of teaching. It is often argued that the amount of training the teacher has had will have a positive effect on his teaching effectiveness and that this is in fact implicitly recognized in the pay scales. If such an empirical relationship could be established then it could lead to very important policy implications and hence there is good reason for proceeding with extreme care on this issue. In the first instance it is likely that the pay scales reflect the demand and supply situation with respect to graduates and other products of higher education and have nothing to do with teaching efficiency. In the light of the difficulties encountered in saying anything sensible about the output of teaching, it is rather difficult to envisage the process by which the relation of pay to teaching efficiency would work. In any case there are a number of very good reasons for doubting that the level of educational attainment of the teacher has anything to do with teaching efficiency. In the first case, the ability to learn, as reflected by the class of degree, is not the ability to teach. There may be an empirical relation between the two, but this is another matter, and in any case it is not clear what should be done with it because of the absence of an *a priori* explanation. It has in fact been found in the E.E.P. that there is no statistical relationship between the teachers' qualification and the performance of the pupils. Secondly, teachers regard what they are doing in different ways and may see themselves as being more than the instrument by which examination performance is maximized; this is related to the problem of determining the output, but it may have a significant effect on the input of the teacher. Thirdly, it is generally accepted that the teacher training schemes are by no means perfect and the extent to which teaching skills can be imparted is still an open question; there is no evidence from the E.E.P. studies that the fact of the teacher having undergone teacher training adds to the performance of pupils in any way. In this type of discussion it is as well to bear in mind the distinction between the ability of the teacher to learn (as expressed by his degree results or whatever) and the training he has undergone which is supposed to relate to the business of teaching; although they are separate issues they have been treated together here.

An alternative approach is to attempt to relate the performance of the teacher to the amount of experience in teaching which he has had on the assumption that the passage of time affects performance in some way. Again this is an empirical question and there is no evidence in the E.E.P. studies to indicate that there is an effect one way or the other. The inevitable conclusion here is that we are attempting to get at the innate ability of the teacher by using very suspect proxies; the deeper problem is that we have no *a priori* guidance in any of this and even if results were obtained their precise meaning would not be clear; for example it may be the case that the more qualified teachers are attracted to the schools which already have a record of scholastic success, and thus any significant statistical results would in fact relate to something else. It is clear that these important problems are not very amenable to a straightforward empirical solution.

Having not progressed very far with the notion of input as implied by the 'paper' qualifications or experience of the teacher we can now turn to what the teacher does rather than what he appears to be. The important differences in teachers are likely to lie in the extent to which lessons are prepared, the way in which the pupils are brought out in discussions and their particular problems identified, the planning of programmes of projects, readings, essays and so on. In other words the teacher's methods must be identified and included in the analysis; but there are two levels of difficulty here. At one level it is not easy to classify properly from a distance the things which teachers do because there will be differences in opinion as to what exactly constitutes tutorials, lectures and so on. But the second-level factor is likely to be of greater importance; it may be possible to say what a teacher does but it is not possible to assess at a distance how he does it. The amount of preparation, the ability to present topics clearly, the understanding of which issues are likely to cause the class difficulty depending on his understanding of the pupils individually, are some of the factors involved and no questionnaire is able to provide information of any depth here. Thus when it comes to the business of assessing the really important details of teaching methods it looks as though the intensive case study method will have to be employed, and even then the research will be faced with severe problems of classification and interpretation.

There are a number of other inputs of interest which are broadly related to the amount of resources which the school devotes to the teaching of the subject. These will include the provision of a separate classroom, an economics library, the number of books in the library and so on. The problem here is that these cannot be regarded as inputs unless they are actually used by pupils, and the extent to which they are used will probably be determined by the methods of the teacher and the enthusiasm which he is able to generate. A further problem here is that the more resources the school makes available then the more likely it is to be able to attract the well-qualified and highly motivated teacher. Thus in the absence of a proper method of standardizing for the teacher (as indicated above) it is not possible to draw any conclusions on the effect of the provision of resources within the school.

Conclusions

The intention of this paper has been merely to set out some of the problems which arise in the economic approach to the evaluation of teaching effectiveness. It may be regarded by some as a rather negative document; but the plain fact of the matter is that these issues are not adequately discussed in the literature and unless some serious work is carried out in the form of sorting out the underlying conceptual problems, as well as those of an empirical nature, there is little likelihood of the economists coming out with any useful results in this important field.

5: Learning Theory and the Audio-Visual Element in Economics

PAT NOBLE

Influences on Curriculum Development

In attempting to anticipate possible changes in education through economics, attention is focussed on changing objectives, on changes in the learning environment and on changes in the age and ability range of students taking courses. Audio-visual techniques will impinge on the subject only in so far as they serve a mediating or criterion test function. However, while the teacher may be manager of the classroom environment, influences external to the subject may well affect the values in terms of which choices are made. Changing status of specialisms in schools alters not only in what is taught, and who teaches it, but also the quantity and quality of resources available.

Curriculum development project and resource centres in schools and teachers' centres are offering a new range of facilities and materials, together with a new set of standards of presentation. R.O.S.L.A. courses and the flexibility of C.S.E. examinations and interdisciplinary courses have created a juxtaposition of materials and teaching techniques that will have what may prove to be an irreversible effect on subject specialists.

Audio-visual technology has developed rapidly in the last ten years though the domestic and industrial markets are the pacemakers. The sheer availability of new techniques has come to constitute a challenge to the teacher, and publicity material from commercial companies may prove a reproach to the traditionalist as much as does the finding of McLeish[1] that only 17% of what is taught by the lecture method can be recalled after one week. Moreover, the student environment outside school now provides in many areas a sophisticated audio-visual experience and acceptance of professional standards of presentation.

However, the point of departure is not the media themselves, although frameworks exist for such an approach in reference books on educational technology.[2] Initially, the audio-visual elements inherent in the subject matter must be identified; it should then be possible to identify how far a-v skills will be a criterion of achievement in the subject. This would help with planning where a-v modes can be harnessed to mediate or assist the learning process. Research on the psychology of perception and reports of classroom-based investigations can be drawn on to guide such an analysis; the classroom work suffers from the number of variables under study and the consequent range of conclusions.

Once the general aims and the more specific objectives have been identified, it is appropriate to turn to the educational technologists and ask how far an optimizing choice can be made in the mode of presenting the material. (It will be borne in mind that few teachers will in fact have a full and free choice of possibilities.) Guidelines are available in Romiszowski,[3] Davies,[2] Allen,[4] and Gagné,[5] with the aids associated with certain teaching objectives such as assisting attitude change or promoting transfer of learning. Surveys of research into audio-visual aids such as that of Helen Coppen,[6] would preclude any firm prescriptions.

How Far is Economics a Visual Subject?

Syllabus elements can be identified that lend themselves to visual presentation. Consideration of the factors land and labour, distinctions between producer and consumer goods, and the nature of social capital, can be illustrated in pictorial form and recognized in real-life contexts. Processes such as trade, income flows and population changes can be illustrated cartographically or by descriptive statistical techniques, though Vernon[7,8] suggests that interpretation of graphs must be taught and that problems arise with both ratios and the difference between relative and absolute changes. Functional relationships such as arise in theories of value, national income determination, and the firm, lend themselves to build-up or animation techniques.

There are, however, some areas of doubtful visual potential. The concept of capital in several of its meanings is not easy to illustrate. The functions of money and the existence of services

can at best be suggested by symbols or elicited by careful inference. The operation of institutions would not appear to be
inherently visual.

The audio element in economics does not arise directly from
the new language that students learn, nor from the natural sounds
of the economic system! It can arise when a commentary is put to
visuals. Sometimes, an interview or case study is captured on tape
or an academic discussion recorded to illustrate the appropriate
modes of response in argument.[9] Material exists on such topics
as issues of monopoly policy, the application of a prices and
incomes policy and the problems of the British economy.[10]

Is there a Role for Visuals in Examinations?

In so far as the audio-visual aspects of the subject are developed,
criterion tests will need to take account of the changes. Hartley
and Fuller[11] stressed the need to test visually those aspects of a
subject selected for visual exposition. Graphical work still seems
to be accepted as an optional garnish to essay answers. Discrimination by multiple-choice questions is almost entirely verbal yet
discrimination can be tested between visuals. At C.S.E., pictorial
stimulus material has been used to enrich short written answers
but inference from pictures and charts should be just as possible
as in geographical studies. Gropper[12] conceded, however, that
'many visuals are used to present information which will be
brought under control of verbal responses, spoken or written.
Only in a few cases do we test the ability to re-create the graph.'

The Learning Environment

The major role for visuals will probably be in a mediating context
both in class and in individualized learning. The teacher needs
the best available information on effectiveness in terms of perception, communication and motivation. Copywriters for Bell
and Howell[13] quoted (in publicity material) that we generally
remember 10% if we read, 20% if we hear, 30% if we see, 50%
if we both see and hear, 70% if we say and 90% if we participate.
Beard[14] claims simply that 10–15% of students tend to favour a
verbal *or* a visual approach and goes on to suggest that 'so many
sources and differences in skills tend to the conclusion that
courses should be flexibly organized, with a diversity of choices,

and teaching methods or evaluative techniques should be varied so that students have some choice of method as well as of content in their studies'. In a study on language learning,[15] a group of teachers concluded that once a student has mastered structures in a target language, visuals will stimulate verbal associations—a point of some significance in a subject that seeks to modify the role of many words.

In abstracting from the reasoning about the contemporary happenings of the real world, economics presents particular visual opportunities. If students see the subject as part of their vocational training, they will respond well to discussion about industry and commerce, but the visuals could suffer by being too detailed, too complex and possibly associated with strongly rooted attitudes. What the economist sees as significant in a picture may itself have to be taught.

Selecting the Media

Few areas of economics would stand as wholly visual and little of the subject can be studied through concrete, observable three-dimensional models. The actuality of a visit is in fact a highly complex activity even when presented selectively by videotape or film. Concepts with observable effects like the balance of payments could be presented by projected aids with or without animation. Recognizing sequences of a process such as compiling a price index involves any mode that permits chaining. Where setting activities or recognition of ideas in different contexts are involved, then sets and sequences of visuals are required. Opportunities for discrimination and for working at the pace of the individual student might be indicated; locational factors might be presented in this way. Films may be used to broaden background, but it is attitudes rather than factual recall that will be affected. Romiszowski[3] offers algorithmic sequences of questions that help a teacher to check out the most promising media in particular cases.

Maximizing the Potential of the Media

The potential of the media depend on their inherent mechanical characteristics, the environment in which they are used and the quality of the software or materials they are used to present.

Non-projected visual aids are the standby of the classroom. As illustrations to text-books, they appear in increasing numbers, despite the cool comment offered by Magdalen Vernon,[7, 8, 16] after a study with children from eleven to fifteen; she concluded that there was 'no decisive evidence that the pictorial illustrations produced anything more than a very limited addition to the information and instruction given by the written texts'. In considering graphical material, it was shown that inconsistencies between the text and the chart went unremarked and that inferences were not readily drawn from charts on family size. What we do not know from these reports is what degree of 'visual literacy' the students had attained and whether the results would prove repeatable today. Perception is a function of physiology, personality and experience, expectations and making the best bet to achieve closure or make sense of images.[17] The connection between text and illustration may be in the mind of the compiler but not conveyed to the student reader. People depicted in situations of commercial activity are often stereotyped, yet the work of Warr and Knapper[18] indicated that students not only read personality into pictures of people but also edit what they recall of the associated incident to fit with the attributed character. These findings would suggest a careful and considered use of illustrations.

Charts are widely available on topics of economics and styles of design are changing. As people are shown to scan from the top of a layout, this should probably guide selection to those where the caption is above the picture or diagram. Most charts are still too dense in ideas, and static wall displays need deliberate integration into teaching. The chalkboard is a continuing but time-consuming aid; if used for elaborate, diagrammatic work it can be seen to represent a poor use of student–teacher contact time. Other media, especially the overhead projector, allow the build-up and annotation of diagrams accompanied by class discussion —whilst permitting some investment of teacher effort that will survive beyond the first lesson. The magnetic board, like the plastigraph and flannelgraph, allow for building up of elements and for discrimination and choice by class discussion. The Coca-Cola game 'Man in his Environment'[19] suggests the way this could be used even with improvised materials backed with magnetic strip. Similar activity is possible on an O.H.P.

Projected aids include, of course, the overhead projector which has considerable potential in economics provided teachers are trained in its use. It is indeed possible to make 1 : 1 copies of material from print originals but this results in transparencies that are too congested. Moreover in the normal classroom the O.H.P. is so close to the screen that magnification is limited. Simplified, purpose-drawn transparencies with overlays to permit build-up of a topic, or discrimination between points, will make better use of the aid, which should be housed flush with the table-top to enable the teacher to sit and maintain face-to-face contact with the class. Stencilled, lower-case letters in indian ink are an improvement on hand-drawn characters; a height of $\frac{3}{8}$ inch to $\frac{1}{2}$ inch with 2–3 foot projected image will be successful in the normal classroom but a larger image and a greater distance between projector and screen are optimal. Full specifications and many suggestions can be found in Vincent,[20], Kemp,[21] and the Technifax booklet[22] on Diazo projectuals. Pupils as well as the teacher can make use of the O.H.P. in reporting back project work with prepared transparencies on which they can structure their comments.

Filmstrips are available commercially[23] and can be made quite cheaply by the teacher photographer. By 1946 P. E. Vernon[24] had established that they can improve instructor performance. The Radiovision materials, many of which are available as study kits for teacher training purposes, show how great an impact is possible with a filmstrip and commentary.

Slides are more versatile than filmstrips in that they can be sequenced to suit the specific learning needed. Using write-on slides, captions, guidelines and diagrams can be added to a set. They are well suited to individual or small group study accompanied by a worksheet. Simple rear projection screens are now available, although the matt-white interior of a box lid is adequate with many small projectors.[25] A simple handviewer perhaps with a modest cassette player would enable a student to study the slide-tape material already available.[26] The work of Hartley and Fuller[11] suggests several provisos to be borne in mind when teaching with slides. Just as much time is needed for note-taking or sketching as would be given by blackboard presentation: it is too tempting to chat on around the slide and fail to consolidate the point that is being made. Some idea of scale and size may be important, especially with panoramic shots of industrial complexes such as oil refineries. Hawkins[27] sets out a scheme to increase the effective use of pictures in social studies, laying stress on identifying location and the function of any people or objects shown, and making inferences that can then be checked with reference material. This approach fits with the geographical aspects of economics, but for some concepts, location is irrelevant.

Cine materials are widely available and catalogued—if not fully evaluated in terms of subject objectives. An interesting study by Craig[28] indicated that a silent version of a film with a teacher commentary geared to student needs resulted in better recall than the commercial commentary. The sheer length and generality of most films creates difficulties of integration into courses and the 8 mm cassettes of up to four minutes promise a useful extension to media with colour and movement. There are, however, limited areas of economics that would seem to demand movement. Where schools have videotaping equipment, multi-media programmes can be recorded off air, previewed, and integrated into teaching as only excerpts need be shown—this does presuppose administratively simple access to the tape and player.

Audio aids probably have a subsidiary role in economics. Popham[29] records that college students liked the relaxed atmosphere of a taped lecture and the freedom to stop the tape for thought or discussion. Open-reel tapes are a cumbersome item in the classroom, but for class use cassette players with less than 'two watt' of sound output may prove inadequate. For individualized study the smaller models are appropriate.

Cost Effectiveness

The aids that can be used involve capital costs, software costs and opportunity costs in terms of teacher time and student time. Effectiveness can only be judged in the light of the objective or intentions of those concerned; modes may be selected for rote learning, for enrichment, for discrimination or for student-paced learning. Boddy[30] indicates that one may select to bring all students to a minimum standard or to maximize the number of high-flyers. It is possible to integrate audio-visual methods into class teaching without multi-media gymnastics on the part of the teacher. A projector that shows both slides and filmstrips, an O.H.P., access to a small episcope,[31] 16 mm projector and videotape should enable the teacher to take full advantage of most of the developments in resources that will accompany curriculum development.

References

1. McLeish, J., *The Lecture Method*, Cambridge Institute of Education, 1968.
2. Davies, I. K., *The Management of Learning*, McGraw-Hill, N.Y., 1971.
3. Romiszowski, A. J., *The Selection and Use of Teaching Aids*, Kogan Page, London, 1968.
4. Allen, W. H., 'Media stimulus and types of learning', *Audio Visual Instruction*, January 1967, pp. 27–31.
5. Gagné, R. M., *The Conditions of Learning*, Holt, Rinehart & Winston, 1965.
6. Coppen, H., *A Survey of British Research in Audio-Visual Aids 1945–1971*, National Committee for Audio-Visual Aids in Education, 1972.
7. Vernon, M. D., 'The use and value of graphical material with written text', *Occ. Psy.*, 26, 1952, pp. 96–100.
8. Vernon, M. D., 'The value of pictorial illustration', *Brit. J. Educ. Psy.*, 23, 1953, pp. 180–7.
9. Larmour, P., 'Sussex Tapes and the organisation of Knowledge', *Visual Education*, December 1972, pp. 19–21.
10. Audio Learning Ltd, 24 Manor Court, Aylmer Road, London N2.
11. Hartley, J. and Fuller, H. C., 'Using slides in lectures: an exploratory study', *Visual Education*, August 1971, pp. 39–41.
12. Gropper, G. L., 'Why *is* a picture worth a thousand words?', *Audio-Visual Communications Review*, 11, 1963, pp. 75–95.
13. Bell and Howell, 'How to use your overhead projector', 1968.
14. Beard, R., *Teaching and Learning in Higher Education*, Penguin, 1970.
15. Audio-Visual Language Association, *The Visual Element and the Problem of Meaning*, 1966, abstracted by E.R.I.C., 1969.
16. Vernon, M. D., 'The instruction of children by pictorial illustration', *Brit. J. Educ. Psy.*, 24, 1954, pp. 171–9.
17. Gregory, R. L., *Eye and Brain*, Weidenfeld & Nicolson, 1966.
18. Warr, P. B. and Knapper, C., *The Perception of People and Events*, Wiley, 1968.
19. Public Relations Officer, The Coca-Cola Export Corporation, Atlantic House, 7 Rockley Road, London W14 oDH.
20. Vincent, A., *The Overhead Projector*, National Committee for Audio-Visual Aids in Education, 1970.
21. Kemp, J. E., *Planning and Producing Audio-Visual Material*, Chandler Publishing Co., U.S.A., 1968.
22. *Diazochrome Projectuals for Visual Communication*, Technifax Educational Division, August 1969.

23. E.F.V.A. catalogues, 33 Queen Anne Street, London W1M 0AL—the full set is part of the V.E.N.I.S.S. subscription.
24. Vernon, P. E., 'An experiment on the value of film and filmstrip in the instruction of adults', *Brit. J. Educ. Psy.*, 16, 1946, pp. 149–62.
25. Consider the small Elmo model CS and the small rear projection screen supplied by Boots.
26. e.g. from C.I.A.V., Durham Road, Boreham Wood, Herts WD6 1LL.
27. Hawkins, M. L., 'A model for the effective use of pictures in teaching Social Studies', *Audio-Visual Instruction*, 16, 1971, pp. 46–8.
28. Craig, G. Q., 'A comparison between sound and silent films in teaching', *Brit. J. Educ. Psy.*, 26, 1956, pp. 202–6.
29. Popham, W. J., 'Tape recorded lectures in the College Classroom', *Audio-Visual Communication Review*, 9, 1961, pp. 109–18.
30. Boddy, F. A., 'Cost effectiveness and cost benefit analysis in the use of audio-visual resources', *Scot. Med. J.*, 16, 1971, pp. 117–19.
31. E.g. Elitescope from Elite Optics Ltd, 354 Caerphilly Road, Cardiff.

IV: ECONOMICS AND SOCIAL STUDIES

6: The Place of Economics in the Secondary School Curriculum

BRIAN HOLLEY

Introduction

Economics has by now assured itself an important place in the sixth form curriculum. For the foreseeable future at least there is no reason to doubt but that economics will continue to gain ground and that the number of 'A' level students will continue to increase, albeit at a somewhat slower rate than has been the case during the past decade.

If, in a majority of schools, economics is now accepted as an important part of the sixth form curriculum, its place in the main part of the secondary school is less certain. The J.M.B. report for 1971–2[1] shows that in 1972 whereas Economics accounted for 11·6% of all subject entries at 'A' level, Economics, and Economics and Public Affairs between them only accounted for 3·5% of all subject entries at 'O' level. At 'A' level the number of candidates in Economics was almost as high as that for Biology (15·5% of all entries) and French (14·2%); whereas at 'O' level Economics and Economics and Public Affairs had only half the number of candidates in German (6·8%) and less than one third of that for Religious Knowledge (9·5%).

It would seem, then, as though economics were poised for a rapid expansion in the lower school. Certainly there is no shortage of advocates for the teaching of economics at lower levels.[2] However, it seems to me that any attempt to bring about a substantial increase in the number of pupils studying economics is unlikely to succeed and, as I shall argue, is in any case undesirable. It is unlikely to succeed for simple political reasons. Whereas the sixth form expansion in economics could take place in a context of a rapidly increasing number of 'A' level candidates which disguised the relative redistribution of effort in the sixth form;

whereas, too, the expansion of sixth-form economics could be interpreted as a choice of specialism by students, in the lower part of the secondary school no such number increase is occurring, and only in the fourth and fifth years can economics become an option, more or less freely chosen. Furthermore, times are changing and beliefs about curricula for our secondary schools are also changing in such a way that any vigorous proselytizing on behalf of economics is likely to meet with resistance from both conservative and progressive forces.

However, I am more concerned with desirability than practicability, since it seems to me that if something is desirable, then practical obstacles are there to be overcome by imagination and political and intellectual skill. Here I will contend that the teaching of economics, *qua* economics, is inappropriate, increasingly inappropriate, in the first five years of secondary schooling. On the other hand concepts, knowledge and theories broadly categorized as economic have a place, an important one, and one worthy of vigorous advocacy, within a social science area of the secondary school curriculum. At sixth form level, too, while a specialist economics course may be appropriate for many students, there are many others who would derive more benefit from a more general social science course which includes salient aspects of economics.

Before developing a justification for my thesis I must point out that it is not my intention to argue that the subject matter of economics is too difficult for the lower-school pupil. On the contrary I think that the 'teachability' of important economic concepts to quite young pupils has been adequately demonstrated in the U.S.A.[3] In outline, what I propose to do is to justify the notion of *general* education as the basis for curriculum planning in the secondary school, to consider the distinctive contribution that economics might make and to conclude that such a contribution is best made through an integrated social science course.

Secondary Schooling and General Education

That we live in a changing world has been said so often that it is in danger of becoming devoid of meaning. However, in discussing matters relating to the planning of school curricula it is important to bear in mind the nature and scope of ongoing changes. For on the one hand our pupils are not unaware of these changes and, on the other, education is at least in part concerned to prepare them for adult life. If the world of the adult is indeed changing and likely to continue changing, we must ensure that our pupils are as well prepared as possible for that life of change.

Because we live in a society that is changing, changing its values, its beliefs, its technology, and even its knowledge and understanding, school can no longer be regarded as providing all that the future adult needs by way of preparation for life and livelihood. Hence the current talk of 'l'éducation permanente'. Moreover what school does provide must be such that it contributes to a flexibility of mind and outlook so that the inevitable changes which future adults will experience do not become traumatic shocks. In other words schools must become less concerned with imparting sanctified knowledge and more concerned with helping their pupils to develop abilities and skills which are appropriate in a changing world. This is not to say that knowledge is unimportant; it is rather to emphasize knowledge as a means to a more important end. If that end can be achieved without knowledge, if abilities and skills can be developed, as it were, in the abstract, then knowledge does become unimportant. This is, however, not what I envisage since knowledge, understanding and the skills and abilities which we may want to develop are I believe logically rather than contingently related to one another.

In the context of social sciences, including economics, this means that less emphasis must be placed on, for example, knowing the details of legislation regarding monopolies and restrictive practices and more emphasis must be given to, for example, developing the ability to disentangle political, legal, social, economic, moral . . . etc. aspects involved in particular cases of monopoly or restrictive practices. More emphasis must be given to the range of mathematical and communication skills in a variety of substantive contexts and less to the learning of vacuous theorems such as $MC = MR$.

Two implications for the curriculum follow from the acceptance of the assumption that the rate of change is more likely to increase than decrease as the twenty-first century draws nearer. Firstly, secondary schools can and must provide a less specialized and more general education right to the end of the secondary school course. Only in this way can we ensure that pupils do not choose a specialism too early, too far from an appreciation of job-opportunities. Only in this way can that degree of flexibility and adaptability, which is necessary for survival, and, preferably, satisfaction in a changing world, be adequately developed. Secondly, a deliberate decision to concentrate on general skills, abilities, techniques and the like rather than on substantive findings of several subject areas tends to make justifiable a much greater degree of interdisciplinary or integrated work in the secondary school than has been the practice to date.

Distinguishing Characteristics of Economics

Granted that the need for more extensive and intensive general education is accepted, what implications are there for our subject, economics? What contribution can economics make to general education? Before attempting to answer the question it is necessary to characterize our discipline, to make explicit what is unique to economics and what it shares to a greater or lesser extent with other subjects. It seems to me that economics is unique, set apart from other disciplines, in only two ways. In the first place it can be regarded as a sort of society, a sub-culture within our larger society, capturing the allegiance of some individuals, repelling others, developing its own values, beliefs and assumptions. Potential economists join this 'society', i.e. become economists by a long process of initiation culminating in graduate status and acceptance both by the economist himself and by professionals in other fields of the title 'economist' as appropriate for him. Economics is unique here in the same way that other subjects are unique; each one has its own set of individuals who profess, and are accepted as professing, allegiance to the discipline and who, by and large, accept those values, beliefs and assumptions which are shared by other members of the 'society'. There are, of course, some who are members both of the 'society' of economists and of other similar 'societies'; these are in sociological terms 'role-hybrids'. There are others who are, as it were, only associate members of the 'society' of economists, practitioners in other subject areas who engage in work of relevance to economists, and who are accepted as 'part economists' though they are not, as we would say, 'real' economists.[4]

The second distinguishing characteristic of economics is the area of man's experience which it is its particular concern to study, i.e. the economic aspects of social life. By definition, no other discipline is directly and mainly concerned to investigate economic phenomena in the way that economists do. Many other subject areas, though, do have a less direct, more peripheral, interest in the area studied particularly by economists. Thus mathematicians, historians, geographers, engineers, praxiologists and numerous others either use the findings of economists or else contribute directly or indirectly to the work of economists. If the world of social phenomena can be regarded as an area, then we can regard economics as a beam of light focussed on a small part of the total area, but shedding some rays on surrounding areas; other disciplines focus on one or other of the surrounding areas but shed light on the area which is of central concern to the economists. Following this metaphor suggests that economics is a *focus of interest*, rather than a discipline, completely separate from other disciplines.

From a consideration of the uniqueness of economics, I now turn to a consideration of ways in which it is affiliated to, and overlapping with, other disciplines. Unique in respect of personal allegiances and in respect of subject matter, economics is not unique in respect of techniques, skills or abilities. The economist develops no special skill; rather he makes use of general skills in coming to grips with problems, both intellectual and practical, which fall within his focus of interest. Just as a paint brush can be used to good effect on different parts of a canvas, so too can the skills and abilities of the economist be used in other subject areas, simply because they are not skills of the economist alone. Thus marginal analysis is but applied mathematics, the ability to analyse an economic problem is no different from the ability to analyse a physical or historical problem. The physicist can analyse a physical problem because he *knows* some physics; *mutatis mutandis* this applies to the economist and to the historian. The difference lies not in the process, ability or skill, but in the conceptual and cognitive background which the specialist brings to bear.

Thus it is my contention that economics is not unique in the skills, abilities, or techniques which the economist uses, for it shares these with a wide variety of other disciplines. In particular economics shares a great deal with those other disciplines which are concerned to foster understanding of social phenomena. Thus sociology, history, political science, to name but three related disciplines, impinge upon and are directly relevant to an understanding of economic phenomena, as is an understanding of economic phenomena for these disciplines.

Economics and the Secondary School Curriculum

If a changing society requires an emphasis on skills and abilities rather than on knowledge, and if economics has no unique skills and abilities, economics has no contribution, over and above that provided by other subjects, to general education. Indeed, given in addition the fact that pupils very often fail to transfer what is learnt in one subject to other subject areas, it could be argued that we need to organize a school curriculum directly around skills and abilities rather than around subject areas. This is one justification for the development of integrated social science courses.

However, while economics is not unique in these respects, a reasonable case can be made out for saying that the social science area is. Social science differs from physical or biological science in being concerned with the *social*, while it differs from history and literature in being concerned with *generalization*. Social phenomena differ from physical phenomena in that we have, as it were, a direct insight into the former but not into the latter. More important from an epistemological point of view is the fact that human beings can *act* for good and adequate *reasons* (and sometimes for the other sort of reason), whereas physical objects simply react to *causes*.[5] As a result any social science, if it is to be adequate, must find a central place for *action*, *decision* and the beliefs and evidence which form the basis for reasoning. In this respect social sciences are logically different from physical and biological sciences; as a result the social sciences require techniques, skills and abilities which are very different from those of the physical or biological scientist.

Correspondingly, the humanities are much more concerned with particular phenomena, situations and creations, and much less, if at all, with developing generalizations, testing hypotheses, and other techniques associated with science generally, including social science. Again, different techniques, skills and abilities are required in this area from those of the natural and social scientists.

Thus I would suggest that a secondary school curriculum should be developed around these three areas, together with a fourth covering communication skills, both mathematical and verbal. Integrated courses in sciences, social sciences and the humanities would help to bring about a degree of order in the life of secondary school pupils who, at present, can be whisked through as many as eight different subjects in the course of one day.

If the arguments for, and the move towards, broader courses of the type outlined are accepted, economics has an important role to play, not as a discrete 'subject' on the timetable, not necessarily using 'specialist' economics teachers, but as part of an overall study of social problems and issues using the perspectives of the several social sciences. A move in this direction is, I suggest, under way; the new J.M.B. 'O' level syllabus in Government and Commerce is a beginning as, at a different level, is the Open University's Social Science Foundation Course.

The development of integrated social science courses is by no means easy, but an attempt in this direction is worth while,[6] both as a contribution to general education and as a means of ensuring a greater social science content in secondary education.[7] While it may be desirable, even essential, for the economist to abstract the economic aspect from social life generally, such abstraction can both mislead and confuse pupils whose main interests may lie elsewhere or who, for some other reason, can only spend a limited time studying social sciences. Hankering after fully fledged economics courses in the lower part of secondary education seems to me to be doing a disservice both to economics and to education.

References

1. Joint Matriculation Board, *Sixty-ninth Annual Report*, 1972.
2. For example, see Robinson, T. K., 'Extending the contribution of Economics to the Curriculum', *Economics*, Vol. IX, No. 2, 1971, pp. 107–11.
3. Senesh, L., 'Teaching Economic Concepts in the Primary Grades', in Lee, N. (ed.) *Teaching Economics*, Economics Association, 1967.
4. King, A. R. and Brownell, J. A., *The Curriculum and Disciplines of Knowledge*, Wiley, 1966.
5. Winch, P., *The Idea of a Social Science*, Routledge & Kegan Paul, 1958.
6. Examples of work which constitutes a beginning are to be found in Lawton, D., Campbell, J. and Burkitt, V., *Social Studies 8–13*, Schools Council Working Paper 39, Evans/Methuen Educational, 1971.
   Also see the work of the Project entitled *History, Geography and Social Science 8–13*.

Relevant U.S. experience includes that outlined in: Senesh, L., 'Organising a Curriculum around Social Science Concepts', in Morrissett, I. (ed.), *Concepts and Structure in the New Social Science Curricula*, Social Science Education Consortium Inc., 1966.

In addition, Bruner's *Man—a Course of Study* is of some interest though it contains relatively little of an economic nature.

7. Social science as such is at present much under-represented in school curricula. For an interesting case study of a school which is establishing a social science course, see Mitchell, P., 'Social Science in the Secondary School Curriculum', *Journal of Curriculum Studies*, Vol. IV, No. 2, 1972.

7: Integration and Sequence in Economics for 8–13-Year-Olds

HAZEL SUMNER

Introduction

This paper addresses itself to two basic questions relating to education in economics for pupils in the middle-school age band. These are:

A. Should economics be tackled separately, or in some kind of relationship with other school subjects? This involves a brief consideration of the nature of economics as a discipline, the question as to which other subjects might be involved, and discussion on the nature of the relationship.
B. In what order should the ideas of economics be tackled? This involves a review of alternatives in the light of conclusions arrived at in respect of question A.

Finally, the implications of the preferred ways of proceeding will be teased out. However, before plunging into these issues there will be a brief review of the educational principles which inform the viewpoints expressed in the main discussion.

Basic Considerations

Strauss has warned of the danger of trying to relate a *general* theory of children's intellectual development to curriculum structuring. 'Generalizations gleaned from different theories produce theoretical ambiguities when the assumptions underlying the theories are examined.'[1] The curriculum developer's tasks differ according to these assumptions so that to work on the basis of conflicting assumptions can only lead to confusion and uncertainty at the level of devising learning experiences for the pupils. In particular, learning theories differ in respect of their philosophical view of man and the way in which he relates to his environment. The epistemological 'How does man know?' question is answered at least implicitly in the type of learning task which is chosen by the curriculum developer.

The recommendations in this article are conventional in that they are based on the epistemological views and related learning theory of Piaget.[2] The central assumption is that the pupil is an active agent in the development of his intellectual structures. The child interacts with his environment and the teacher's role is that of producer of a facilitating environment. He will take into account the changing modes by which the developing child gains an effective grip on his environment. This paper is, of course, concerned with the ways in which middle-school pupils might be helped towards an understanding of the economic aspects of their experience. It is important to stress at this point that the assumptions espoused here are not compatible with a curriculum strategy which progressively initiates passive pupils into reified public thought forms, not surprisingly called 'disciplines'. Compatible with this approach, as Esland has shown,[3] is a view of each pupil being endowed with a given capacity for intellectual mastery of pre-existing theoretical forms. Such a view tends to be found together with a didactic teacher/pupil relationship, with late initiation into the 'mysteries' of the subject (particularly its fundamental uncertainties), and what Bernstein has called 'strong framing',[4] that is, strong control over what kinds of knowledge it is permissible to treat in the pedagogical relationship. It can be readily seen that the two views contrasted above have significant consequences for the authority of the teacher, for the framing of objectives[5] and for the evaluation of the success or otherwise of the pupils. On the second view the 'good' pupil is one who gives right answers. On the activist view the 'good' pupil is the one who asks searching questions and who actively integrates his classroom and out-of-school experiences.

The above reference to timing of introduction to the 'mysteries' of a subject will, of course, have cued readers to the fact that the recommendations of this paper are strongly influenced by the theory of instruction developed by Bruner.[6] The theories of Piaget and Bruner are compatible in that they are both based on an activist epistemology. At first sight, Bruner's insistence on the employment of discipline experts in the construction of learning experiences may seem to be at variance with the preferences expressed above. Bruner aims to help the pupils towards 'disciplined' thinking. That there are differing disciplines, supported by different academic social systems, existing prior to the pupils' educational life, is an undisputed social fact. That these disciplined ways of thinking differ along the lines suggested by Hirst can also be accepted.[7] What must be realized, however, is that these intellectual structures are social creations and that the boundaries between them,[8] as well as the nature of the structures encompassed by them, are continually changing.[9]

Bruner's views take all this implicitly into account. The pupils are to become activists within the disciplines as they exist now, but they are not to be tied by them. As early as possible they are to be encouraged to be creative historians, economists and so on. This requires that they become acquainted early not only with the pre-existing substantive concepts of the discipline, its generalizations and so on, but also with its methodological concepts and techniques together with the criteria by which these may be judged adequate or otherwise. Subsequentialy these criteria would themselves come under scrutiny, but this is to be carried off into heights of sophistication hardly compatible with the intellectual maturity of the age group under consideration.

The assumption, then, is that the most desirable quality to develop in pupils is the idea that nothing is sacred—that everything is available for thoughtful questioning and responsible discussion. The implications of this for economics for 8–13-year-olds will be evident in what follows.

Question A

Most economists seem to agree that their discipline involves study of those aspects of social behaviour which are aimed at satisfying human wants through the productive utilization of human and natural resources. They also hold that economics is a social science in that it uses logical reasoning linked to empirical inquiry in a search for laws of economic behaviour. Its distinctive nature derives mainly from the unique set of substantive concepts which have been developed for the purpose of classifying this behaviour, and from the theories which have been built up from these concepts. The question now to be considered concerns the way in which economics might be most effectively related to the other subjects which have a claim to be included in the middle-school social studies curriculum.

There are *various bases* upon which subjects may be drawn together for the purposes of a school curriculum as well as *various degrees of integration*. Bernstein uses the term 'classification' to refer to the degree of boundary maintenance between contents, or subjects. He distinguishes between curricula of a 'collection' type, where boundaries are firmly maintained, and those of 'integrated' type, where subjects stand in an open relationship to one another.[10]

Both of these types can involve one or more teachers, but this is a separate organizational question. However, it is likely to have practical significance in relation to the organization of content, particularly at the lower secondary level. As Bernstein's analysis is designed to make clear, there is the added factor of likely resistance to changes in organization of content stemming from the fact that teacher identity is often defined in terms of loyalty to a discipline's social system, so that changes of curriculum organization can give rise to anxieties about professional identity. The fact that economics is only now being considered appropriate for younger pupils gives both an opportunity and a responsibility to curriculum developers to make sure that both the organization of the relevant content and personnel are established appropriately from the start.

The 'collection' and 'integrated' types mentioned are polar cases. Integration of this kind refers to 'the *subordination* of previously insulated subjects or courses to some *relational* idea, which blurs the boundaries between subjects'.[11] Such a relational idea is likely to be an interest-centred topic where the relevant knowledge has little or no logical function in the organization of learning. Examples typically found in the social studies section of primary school curricula are 'Water', 'Transport', 'Children from other lands' and so on. Facts about these are collected and illustrated, but there the matter rests, for the pupils are not given help in acquiring the tools for asking and answering socially significant questions about these topics. Clearly this is not compatible with an approach which stresses the value of disciplined thinking.

Economics as one element in a 'collection' type curriculum *would* be compatible with this approach, but there is doubt as to whether it is practicable to try to introduce a single social science into the curriculum of 8–13-year-olds, when the space for a general social science course is proving very difficult to find. There is a more important reason for dismissing this alternative, however, and it relates both to the value premises set out earlier and to the question as to which subjects might usefully be linked with economics, as well as to the nature of the linkage.

Bernstein has a third category in his typology of curricula, that of the *'focussed'* curriculum[12] where the separate identities of the contributing disciplines are respected (as distinct from preserved as immutable). This involves the disciplines contributing to, rather than being subordinate to, a relating topic. Besides giving pupils a chance to develop the techniques of disciplined thinking it affords opportunities for disciplines to throw light on each other. This is essential if they are not to appear as reified and unchanging. Furthermore, the relating topic enables the relevance of disciplines for the study of real life issues to be appreciated from the start, both the methodological techniques and their substantive concepts being brought into play as pupils explore their social experience.

A variant of this approach is to have the disciplines focussed through the means of high-level concepts which embrace concepts derived from the contributing disciplines.[13] Where these concepts are used to locate significant or rewarding content there may be something to be said for them, but where they are used as a teaching objective there is doubt, on the ground that they are too general to be useful to the pupils in helping them to understand their social environment.

The preference expressed here, then, is for a 'focussed' curriculum based on topics. The questions that follow concern the subjects which might usefully be linked with economics.

Lee and Entwistle have given careful consideration to this issue.[14] They point to the links of economics with psychology, sociology and ethics. The value of examining these links has been more obvious as economists have become more aware that scientific inquiry requires empirical as well as deductive procedures and, in turn, as social scientists generally have become aware of the limits to value-freedom in science. Clearly, pupils of 8–13-year-old age group are not going to become sophisticated thinkers about these issues, but it is important that they become at least dimly aware that these disciplines can inform and refine one another as well as having a use in giving a many-faceted perspective on questions of interest to the pupils.

Other likely disciplines which can be used as resources in a focussed social studies curriculum such as this are anthropology, political science, history and geography. Between them they furnish an enormous wealth of substantive concepts from which the teacher can draw. Apart from ethics, they are linked at the level of method, as both history and geography now show increasing tendencies towards social scientific procedures.[15] As Lee and Entwistle say, we are, as yet, nowhere near a unified social science but there are grounds for saying that the differences *within* each particular social science are in many ways greater than the differences between them.

These views have implications for the training of teachers for the middle-school age band and there appears to be a case for a general social science training backed by specialization in one of the contributing disciplines.[16]

Question B

The great difficulty with a topic-based approach is that of ensuring balance and progression. Even when a discipline is learned within a strongly classified system, there are problems of sequence. These become even greater when disciplines are used in conjunction with one another. Lee and Entwistle[17] have reviewed some of the ways in which economics can be approached. Following the influence of Bruner there is a strong trend towards the teaching of economics 'spirally', so that pupils come back again and again to the powerful concepts which they first met in other contexts. These concepts are then available for continual enrichment as experience and sophistication increase. Examples of these syllabuses which are particularly appealing are those which show elegance in the logical sequencing of concepts, together with explicit reference to ways in which a deeper appreciation of the concepts can be developed at a later stage in the educational career. Among particularly good examples in this respect are the ideas of Senesh,[18] Bach[19] and Dunning.[20]

There is much valuable analysis in these schemes of work and this should be used wherever possible to inform the focussed approach suggested in this paper. However, there are shortcomings in these approaches as they stand. They usually contain an implicit suggestion that economic concepts are related on a single unilinear sequence. It may be that the ideas of concept clusters or networks would be a more adequate rendering of the logical relationships involved. If this were so, it follows that curriculum developers would have more scope, for beginnings could be made in any one of a number of places. Also it would mean that clusters could be approached in a variety of orders.

A further disadvantage of the unilinear sequence is that it entails starting at the point which the curriculum developer, with *his* particular theoretical predilection, considers to be central and basic to the discipline. It is probably educationally sounder to start with those economic issues which are central to the experience of the particular *pupils* concerned. This would be very likely to lead back to one or other of the core concepts[21] which are perhaps more perennial to the discipline than is emphasis on any one of them.[22] This sort of approach allows for such criticisms of usual teaching emphases as are made by Joan Robinson.[23]

It should also be noted that the sequences cited are based on the logical relationship of substantive concepts. These are certainly important constituents of any discipline but there is also the possibility of sequencing on the basis of methodological techniques. The difficulty with this is that these cannot usually be meaningfully applied to topics except in combination with one another. For example, the formulation and testing of hypotheses must proceed together with the collection and evaluation of evidence and so on. It would seem therefore that these skills have to be employed from the start, even if in crude form, with the aim of moving towards greater sophistication in their application. Implicit in this argument is a criticism of Bloom's[24] logical hierarchy of cognitive skill objectives as also being psychologically sound or even possible as a basis for the sequencing of learning.

The conclusion to be drawn from these arguments is that adequate sequencing of learning experiences would take into account the need to develop skill in the use of methodological techniques as well as the need to include logical progression of substantive concepts. Where economics is taught in isolation this is a formidable enough requirement. When the logical progression of the substantive concepts of disciplines taught in conjunction with economics also have to be considered, the task seems well-nigh impossible. A possible solution is to emphasize the contributing disciplines *in turn*, meanwhile using such other concepts as are relevant and necessary to the topic under consideration.

This brings up the question of the selection of topics. Where a particular discipline is being emphasized, it will of course be essential to choose topics which ensure its fruitful application. But there is another consideration. At an earlier stage in this paper, passing reference was made to the use of pupils' interests as a possible criterion for the selection of topics. The use of such a criterion is, however, open to the criticisms that these interests do not necessarily arise spontaneously and that in any case, no class of pupils is likely to provide a sufficiently sustained consensus of interests to service the needs of a curriculum shaper. Room must be made for the teacher as facilitator of the pupils' learning, to point out aspects of the taken-for-granted environment which can yield interest for the pupils. In making decisions here the teacher should be guided by the pupils' 'economic' experience. Several writers have shown how to recognize this within the pupils' personal, family and neighbourhood life. Lee and Entwistle[25] also point out the importance of vicarious experience, either using reality as portrayed on film and TV, or through the use of analogy or fable, backed by such teaching methods as role-playing. There is endless scope for portraying to children the interest inherent in the economic aspects of life.

Conclusions

The following interrelated preferences have emerged from the above discussion on integration, sequence and selection issues:

1. That economics should not be taught as a received truth, but that pupils should be encouraged to perceive of it as a kit of tools, conceptual and methodological, which are in process of continuous refinement.

   The idea is that they should develop skill in the use of some of these tools together with an attitude to economics as a study which is at once both potentially critical and creative.

2. This first conclusion leads to a second which is that economics should be taught, at this stage anyway, in the company of other disciplines. In this way psychological, historical and cross-

cultural perspectives become available to the pupil so that he can reflect, for example, on the definition of economic as distinct from other forms of social behaviour, and on the status of the assumptions normally made in the construction of the models used in economic theory.

Furthermore, as Senesh[26] has said, 'No social problem is purely economic in nature. Therefore the economics curriculum has to be related to the fundamental ideas of the other areas of the social sciences.' This is in line with the idea of a 'focussed' curriculum, but as Senesh goes on to say,

> 'It is the responsibility of the curriculum builder in the primary grades to orchestrate the curriculum or to develop units in such a way that some units will emphasise predominantly the use of the analytical tools of the economist, while others will make most use of the analytical tools of the political scientist or of the anthropologist.'

3. That theory and the real world should be linked together from the start. This requires that pupils should be given the opportunity to 'do' economics rather than just to learn it at second hand. It implies that they be encouraged to induce economic concepts and generalizations from social situations selected because they are permeated with economic content. The theory will thus be 'achieved' through reflection on the real world. There should be a continual interplay between this achievement of economic insights and its application to new situations. For one thing, concepts involve a process of generalization. A single concrete instance does not allow a concept to be freed from a specific context. Secondly, the limits of generalizations constructed from conceptual elements are only appreciated through application to a variety of situations. Thirdly, such a procedure would give opportunity for the process of formulating, testing and modifying of hypotheses.

4. That the logical structure of the substantive concepts of economics should be clarified, and that meanwhile we proceed on the assumption that these are linked in clusters. It is suggested that clusters of concepts be selected for their relevance to the needs of pupils in their particular situations. Though there will obviously be much that is common to the needs of pupils generally, to some the world of retailing will be more

immediate than the world of factory production, or of farming and so on. It must be borne in mind that the problem is not just one of links between theory and the real world, but between theory and the world of the pupils concerned.

It is also useful to remember that this approach does not necessarily involve focus on such real world topics as 'The Family' and 'The neighbourhood'. Simulated and imagined situations also have a concrete reality for pupils. For example, children could study 'Our Farm' or 'Our Factory', in which the simulation partakes of the real world through the medium of visits, films, newspapers, radio, etc. but avoids the complexity of the real world. Or pupils could pursue a topic about the economic aspects of life on an imagined island. These approaches are advantageous in that the degree of complexity in the situation is under the teacher's control. In any case, in tackling the economic aspects of total situations such as these, however simplified, care should be given to the development of the understanding of each of the relevant concepts, through the use of simple classroom experiments, drama, stories and so on.

It is assumed that each topic would furnish a new opportunity to apply the conceptual clusters previously met as well as provide a chance to extend the clusters.

There is of course a lot of work remaining concerning the detail of the implementation of these ideas. They are offered in the hope that teachers will be stimulated to experiment with the teaching of economics within the context of a general social science education, to pupils in the middle years of schooling.

References

1. Strauss, S., 'Learning Theories of Gagné and Piaget: Implications for Curriculum Development', *Teachers College Record*, September 1972, Vol. 74, No. 1.
2. Piaget, J., 'Piaget's Theory', in P. H. Mussen (ed.), *Carmichael's Manual of Child Psychology*, John Wiley & Sons, New York, 1970, pp. 703–32.
3. Esland, G. M., 'Teaching and Learning as the Organisation of Knowledge', in M. Young (ed.), *Knowledge and Control*, Collier Macmillan, 1971.
4. Bernstein, B., 'On the Classification and Framing of Educational Knowledge', in *Knowledge and Control*, ibid.
5. Esland, G. M., op. cit., p. 88.

6. Bruner, J. S., *The Process of Education*, Harvard University Press, 1961.
7. Hirst, P. H., 'The Logic of the Curriculum', *Journal of Curriculum Studies*, Vol. 1 (2), May 1969.
8. Schwab, J. J., 'Structure of the Disciplines: Meaning and Significance', in G. W. Ford and L. Pugno (eds.), *The Structure of Knowledge and the Curriculum*, Rand McNally, Chicago, 1964.
9. Kuhn, T. S., *The Structure of Scientific Revolutions*, University of Chicago Press, 1962.
10. Bernstein, op cit.
11. Ibid.
12. Ibid.
13. Taba, H., 'Curriculum Study', in Taba, H., *et al.*, *A Teacher's Handbook to Elementary Social Studies—An Inductive Approach*, 2nd ed., Addison-Wesley, 1971.
14. Lee, N. and Entwistle, H., 'Economics Education and Educational Theory', in N. Lee (ed.), *Teaching Economics*, 1967. Economics Association.
15. Harvey, D., *Explanation in Geography*, Edward Arnold, 1969.
    Holloway, S. W. F., 'History and Sociology—What History is and what it ought to be', in Burston W. H. and Thompson, D., *Studies in the Nature and Teaching of History*, Routledge & Kegan Paul, 1967.
16. The idea of general social science courses is considered by R. Cootes in *Integrated Humanities in the Secondary School Curriculum—A Philosophical Critique*, Longmans, forthcoming.
17. Lee and Entwistle, op. cit.
18. Senesh, L., 'Teaching Economic Concepts in the Primary Grades', in N. Lee (ed.), *Teaching Economics*, Economics Association, 1967.
19. Bach, G. L. 'What Economics should we teach?' in E. Fenton (ed.), *Teaching the New Social Studies in Secondary Schools: An inductive approach*, 1966.
20. Dunning, K., 'What Economics should we teach?' *Economics*, Summer 1970.
21. See Lumsden, K. G. and Attiyeh, R. E., 'The Core of Basic Economics', *Economics*, Summer, 1971, for an example of a set of such ideas.
22. Barber, W. J., *A History of Economic Thought*, Pelican, 1967.
23. Robinson, J., *Collected Economic Papers*, 1965, Ch. 1, 'Teaching Economics'.
24. Bloom, B. S. *et al.* (eds.), *Taxonomy of Educational Objectives, Handbook 1, Cognitive Domain*, Longmans, 1956.
25. Lee and Entwistle, op. cit., pp. 42–6.
26. Senesh, op. cit., p. 78.

V: ECONOMICS BELOW THE SIXTH FORM

8: Economics in the Early Stages of the Secondary School

DAVID CHRISTIE

Introduction

The idea that economics can be included at any stage in a secondary school curriculum is not one that has universal acceptance. Professional and academic economists have been by no means unanimous in their attitude to the subject in schools.[1] Members of the public are often surprised to learn that economics is taught in schools. Yet the numbers being presented for the certificates of the various examination boards have been increasing, in some areas at a very rapid rate.[2]

Concurrent with this increase in numbers studying economics, the curriculum itself has been undergoing changes which seem to result in an increase in the use of economics as a widening influence, e.g. as part of a general studies course. In addition, the mass media have become increasingly concerned with certain aspects of what could be called 'economic affairs'—strikes, floating pounds, inflation, unemployment—and all of this would appear to be increasing the amount (if not always the quality) of awareness of an economic dimension.

For a paper on economics in the early part of secondary school to be convincing it will have to persuade the economist that justice is being done to his discipline; it will also have to persuade the educationist that there is value in including the subject in the curriculum for young secondary pupils. Further, there is a need to consider the final consumer—will the study of economics be of value to the pupil now and later?

Lord Robbins' definition of the subject—'Economics is the science which studies human behaviour as a relationship between ends and scarce means which have alternative uses'[3]—would be as acceptable to economists as any definition ever would be.

Hence, any course studying human behaviour along the lines suggested by Robbins' definition could be described as economics.

Keynes regarded economics as a method of thinking—one implication being that the study of economics could somehow give the student some kind of equipment which would help him to cope with the world as he found it. This would go a long way to convincing educationists that there was value enough in the subject to warrant its inclusion in the curriculum.

The pupil is a highly significant part of the economy, even if considered from the consumption side alone. He may even be, in some small way, a producer, too. Sooner or later, however, he *will* be a producer, and as things stand, he is likely to spend 49 years fulfilling that role. Economics must, therefore, have a lot to say which is valuable to the pupil now and later.

Approaches to Curriculum Design

Before embarking on a detailed description of a possible course in economics for S1 and S2,* a word is necessary about alternative approaches to the designing of new courses.

Basically, there are two kinds of approach. The first is the 'objectives' approach. The curriculum development model would be objectives → content → method and then assessment. This approach is now well known and the majority of curriculum development programmes have adopted this approach. An alternative approach is that followed by the Humanities Curriculum Project which asked: 'What content is worthwhile?', 'What general aim would be appropriate in teaching this content?' and 'What kind of learning experience is most conducive to furthering that aim?' The alternative approach has been developed partly as a result of the realization that it is extremely difficult (if at all possible) to state behavioural objectives which would be sufficiently wide-ranging to cover all the impacts that a curriculum development programme could make.

The project which I have been concerned with has tended to favour the former approach but has not attempted to cover all possible impacts by stating objectives about them. We have remained in the cognitive domain as far as objectives are concerned, but we recognize that impacts will be felt outside this

* First and second years of secondary education in Scotland.

domain. Bloom's taxonomy has been used as a walking stick rather than as a pair of crutches.

Our project used three types of objectives as a basis for the course:

(a) objectives relating to the significant bits of economic knowledge we thought it necessary that pupils should know were called 'target' objectives. (These target objectives relate to the spiral curriculum mentioned later and in the Appendix).

(b) objectives relating to the teaching and learning processes that the pupils had to go through in order to achieve these 'targets' were called working objectives. (Thus, they were also objectives about teaching methods.)

and finally

(c) objectives relating to the expected performance of the pupils after they have been through the course were called 'criterion objectives'.

Readers of the Appendix will find further details on objectives, and on how these three types link up with each other.

What kind of Course for S1 and S2?

The design of the course for S1 and S2 is very important. Questions like 'Who should be taught?', 'Should the course be integrated into a social studies course, or should there be a "combined" or merely "co-operative" course?', 'Should the course be a preparation for later certificate work?' are important questions which have to be asked at a very early stage of course designing.

In answer to the first question—'Who should be taught economics?'—I can think of no convincing reason why everyone normally in receipt of secondary education should not be exposed to teaching and learning situations involving economics.

The question of whether or not economics should be integrated into a social studies course is not really within the scope of this paper. The curriculum project I have been involved in has been developing a course in economics, *per se*. The reasons for choosing this approach are many—the main one being that it was thought easier to assess *if* economics could be taught to young secondary pupils by piloting it (and them) in a 'non-integrated' package.

There are many difficulties facing the integrators—some of these have been outlined by industrial psychologists, and studies in other fields can be revealing, too.[4] The project I have been involved in has taken the view that the course developed should be 'self-contained' in that it assumes that pupils starting it have had no previous formal training in economics and that they will not proceed beyond the course to any further formal study of economics. For the sake of scientific investigation we ignored the many spin-off benefits we fervently hoped would result!

Having decided what kind of course we were to develop the next set of questions related to the content of the course. Economics has been seen as having a spiral nature; it has been seen as having a basic core.[5] It is thus possible to argue for one single syllabus which would be suitable for all courses of economics at all levels. The depth in which any topic is tackled could be a function of the interest, age and ability of the student. Lumsden and Attiyeh identify the fundamental economic concepts in the basic core as being classified under 'Scarcity and Choice', 'Economic Efficiency', 'Income Distribution' and 'Aggregate Output and Income', and, if they are right, any self-contained course should treat of these elements.

Traditionally, scarcity is seen as the central economic problem, and the subject of economics is an attempt to study and codify various approaches to the 'solution' of this problem. Every single bit of economic knowledge, it has been claimed, is somehow connected to the central problem. At the same time as satisfying the needs of a central core, any course which might be the last some pupils follow would have to contain some mention at least of, e.g. the Welfare State and the Trade Unions. There are a variety of possible approaches which could be adopted in an attempt to achieve the objectives of the course. One could work from facts to principles—or from principles to the 'real world' and its facts. An analytical first year could be followed by a descriptive second year; early description could lead to later analysis, using the tools of analysis developed and practised throughout the course.

The Appendix on the spiral curriculum gives an indication of one approach to the problem of combining a basic core with some necessary descriptive elements.

Having settled on a course design and a list of contents for the course, the next major problem area is that of teaching methods. Many studies of the effectiveness of teaching tend to point to one key fact—only a small number of pupils benefit from a formal type of teaching. Since pupils are individuals it would seem logical that different pupils would benefit from different teaching and learning techniques—thus, it can be argued that the greater the variety of techniques used to put over the content of the course the more effective will that course be.

Courses in economics in the first two years of secondary education will require many of the teachers involved to use methods which have not yet been used in schools by economics teachers. Since school economics has usually meant 'S' level, 'A' level, 'H' grade and 'O' level, the methods used have usually been suited to 'academic' streams. Should economics ever become general in the first two years, it is reasonable to suppose that those teaching high-ability young adults in Forms 4, 5 and 6 will at least share in the teaching of economics to all abilities at an earlier stage. The 'academic' approach will not do for the 11-, 12- and 13-year-olds. These pupils have just left primary school where there has been, in recent years, a considerable change (if not revolution) in teaching methods. It is unreasonable to expect pupils to move from group work to rigid rows and from discovering for oneself to 'being told'.

It would be incorrect, however, to imagine that all economics teaching in the secondary schools is of the traditional, formal type. Much valuable work has been done in developing different methods—e.g. case studies, numeracy problems, business games, field studies courses, group discussions, simulation exercises and so on. Great steps forward have been taken in the audio-visual field with, for example, filmstrips, tapes and posters. It goes without saying that the kind of teacher who avails himself of the opportunities provided by these various methods is likely to be an effective teacher, regardless of the age of his pupils. I am convinced that the right approach to economics teaching in S1 and S2 would involve all of the methods mentioned above. But I feel that they do not go far enough. There is a need for kits of tangible objects which the pupils can use to set up real-life situations where they can get 'hands-on' experience of the economy, and which the teacher can use for demonstration purposes.* These

* A kit of tangible objects for S1 and S2 takes note of Piaget's theories on concrete and formal operations and the transition from one to the other. In addition, there seem to be strong pedagogical reasons for an approach which starts with the concrete and moves to the abstract, regardless of the age of the learner.

kits would be 'tool-boxes' for the teacher and pupil alike—a close analogy would be with the equipment found in physics and chemistry laboratories, technical classrooms and so on—where, incidentally, one would also find posters, films, case studies and the like, but as something additional to the direct teaching and learning process.

A kit of objects—like bits of coal, plastic men, models of machines, model cars, lorries, paper money and so on is a most effective means of bringing controllable parts of the real world into the classroom to allow actual models of economic phenomena to be set up by teacher or pupil. Heuristic methods are then very possible, and given a properly structured situation, there is no reason why, for example, a young pupil should not discover for himself the circular flow of income, or the effect of a change in injections or withdrawals, or the effects of an increase in price, or the actual results (measurable by time and quantity) of the division of labour, or the economies of scale, or indeed any part of economic theory. Mathematical models, after all, are a greater abstraction from real life than 'real' models!

The factors of production—labelled 'human', 'natural' and 'man-made' resources—can be included in the kit. Plastic men can cheaply and readily be bought; bits of coal, wood and so on are easily obtainable, 'Lego' can be used to symbolize component parts, bits of wood can be machines, hardboard can be used to symbolize factory floors (or households, or regions, or countries). The fact that the factors are limited can be shown by keeping them in transparent containers—e.g. glass bottles, polythene bags. Thus, the pupil sees at a glance how much labour is available at any given time. Pupils learn that there is a 'recipe of production'— mixes of the factors—and that the amount paid to these factors when used in production is their income, and the total of these is related in some way to the costs of production or the national income. Some suggestions on the use of a kit are given in the Appendix describing the curriculum project in which I have been involved. Readers of the Appendix will also see how a kit can be supplemented by a 'software' package containing teacher's notes, pupil's instructions and pupil's worksheets.

It is worth stressing at this stage that the 'objectives approach' mentioned earlier is very useful in that the stating of instructional objectives in pupil-behaviour terms virtually determines the methods used. The objective becomes the method!

Schools using the pilot course described in the Appendix report encouraging preliminary results—not only about the amount of economics actually learned but also about the amount of interest in the subject and the positive attitudes engendered.

Implications

Now for some crystal-ball gazing. Assuming that economics were to be introduced generally into the common course in the early stages of the secondary school, what are the implications for the various components of the education equation? For the pupil, it means a new subject for him to cope with; it should result in a widening of his horizons and it should lead to his being able to play a more meaningful role in the democratic economic society of which he is a member. It may also mean that he pays a high opportunity cost in terms of, for example, less of another subject or other subjects, since economics cannot be introduced into the fixed school day without something else being excluded.

The question of the crowded curriculum is a very important one, and those economists who are also educators can scarcely fail to be aware of the dangers associated with it. Those taking the decisions about what should be in and what out of the curriculum face great problems in fitting in the demands of 'new' subjects; and these are increasing in numbers—sociology, politics, general studies, guidance periods, outdoor education and so on can all stake reasonable claims for inclusion in the education pattern of the secondary school, and all of this at a time when there is mounting criticism about the amount of the so-called basics which pupils seem not to have grasped at an earlier stage.

The implications for the teacher are many. The economics specialist—instead of spending most of his time with a few of the physical and intellectual giants of the sixth form—will now have the task of dealing with the entire range of 12- and 13-year-old pupils. This will give him a new outlook, whether he likes it or not, on teaching and on pupils. He will get to know a wide range of pupils, many of whom formerly would never have darkened the door of the economics room. He will find himself in a bigger department and he may find that he is no longer required to teach British Constitution, history, mathematics, modern studies or supervise the library! In the early years he will not be so heavily involved in presenting candidates for external examinations, and he may have to re-allocate his non-teaching time so that he spends more of it preparing models for the first year and less on marking turgid essays on the Welfare State. However, the number and ability of pupils taking the subject in later years will probably increase. He will probably enjoy his teaching more (after a period of readjustment to the greater volume of 'busy' noise), and he may go home more tired at the end of the day.

There are serious implications for the 'subject'. It will face exposure to the mass, rather than to the few. Questions will be asked which have never been asked before! And answers will have to be provided. If greater numbers study the subject at school, the universities, too, will be faced with much increased numbers of students who have studied the subject before—and these students may well have seven years of economics behind them when they enter University Departments of Economics in their first year. Let Higher Education be warned!

If education shapes society at all, then society will not be un-scathed by the onset of popular economics education. Attitudes will be changed; management, trade union leaders and politicians will be faced with an educated population trained to consider the facts and policies and able to judge for themselves about such statements as 'the pound in your pocket' or 'price rises will be curbed at a stroke' and so on.

Perhaps too much has been seen in the crystal ball; possibly nothing will happen at all. However, if economics can be taught effectively in the early stages of the secondary school (as it seems it can be), and if it is introduced generally, then many of the possible changes outlined above will become reality.

Appendix

The contents of this appendix follow the curriculum development model used by the project:

(I) *Objectives*— examplars of the objectives
(II) *Content*— a spiral curriculum
(III) *Method*— contents of kit
two suggested uses of a kit
examples of worksheet material
(IV) *Assessment*—pre- and post-test

I OBJECTIVES

A scheme can be drawn up whereby it is possible to see at a glance the links between method, target objectives and the expected performance (or behaviour) of the pupil after he has completed part or all of the course.

Working objectives relate very closely to methods of teaching and learning.

Target 'objectives' are the significant parts of economic knowledge which it is desirable for pupils to know and understand.

Criterion objectives specify, within strict limits, expected performance of pupils.

An example of the scheme is provided on page 115.

II CONTENT

The spiral curriculum (shown overleaf) specifies broad 'topics' for study. More detailed content of these topics can be found by referring to the objectives which have been stated for each of these topics.

Note. At the S2 level, a 'core and module' approach has been adopted. All pupils study the core. The modules allow for private interests, study in depth and the introduction of a more 'descriptive' element into the course.

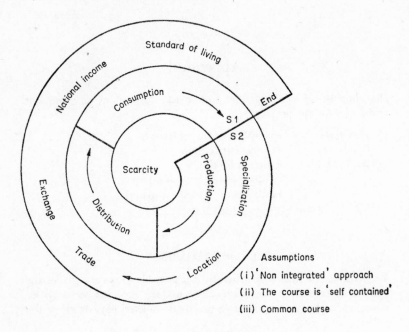

Assumptions
(i) 'Non integrated' approach
(ii) The course is 'self contained'
(iii) Common course

III METHOD

In the early stages, pupils spend a lot of time manipulating a kit of objects. The advantages of this are outlined in the paper.

Contents of Kit

(i) A large number of plastic men ('Human resources').
(ii) Pieces of coal, bits of wood, and Plasticine ('Natural resources').
(iii) Models of machines and tools (or pieces of coloured wood); 'Lego' (for component parts); pieces of hardboard (for factories) ('Man-made resources'). There are advantages in storing these resources in transparent containers, e.g. 'scarcity' can be seen at a glance.
(iv) Model cars, lorries, cookers, TV sets, refrigerators, lamps, chairs, food containers, garages, petrol stations, watches, football, etc. (These can be used as 'finished products' or for other purposes, e.g. transport.)
(v) A quantity of money ('toy' money)—£1 million of different denominations.
(vi) Stopwatch.
(vii) Paper and coloured tape (for indicating flow directions).

Working Objectives	Target Objectives	Criterion Objectives
(1) Pupil lists what he would buy with £10·00.	(1) Pupil writes recipes of production for three finished products.	(1) Pupil completes worksheet 1, within 15 minutes, giving a comprehensive list (80% complete).
(2) Pupil studies list of ingredients in 4 finished products.		
(3) Pupil groups ingredients from 4 recipes into 'sets' (no. of sets determined by pupil).		
(4) Pupil participates in lesson aimed at establishing that all ingredients are able to be classified into the following three groups —human resources, natural resources and man-made resources.	(2) Pupil differentiates between human, natural and man-made resources.	(2) Pupil completes worksheet 2 with 80% accuracy within 10 minutes.
	(3) Pupil understands the symbolism of the kit of materials.	(3) Pupil able to identify, with 100% accuracy, the 3 groups of resources; and, with 80% accuracy, other parts of basic kit.
(5) Pupil sets up production flows for various finished products (after watching demonstration). Pupil uses kit of materials.	(4) Pupil understands that each produced output is the result of several inputs—including at least one input from each of the following list 'human, natural and man-made resources'.	(4) Pupil completes worksheet 3 with 80% accuracy, within 10 minutes.

It should be emphasized that the kit can contain almost anything—and the teacher should be alert to discover new and imaginative ways of using the basic kit. On the question of cost, it is worth pointing out how much equipment is to be found in a physics laboratory. Of course, the use of a kit is not restricted to S1 and S2 pupils.

Two Suggested Uses of a Kit

1. The setting up of production flows involving 'recipes of production'. Different pupils will use different mixes of the factors. Why? The answers can lead to discussions on the price of the factors. The idea of substitution of factors can also be pursued.
2. The exploration of the idea of the circular flow of income is interesting for young pupils and the use of a kit makes understanding much easier.

> E.g. Set up a production flow for any finished product. Isolate one of the 'human resources'. Where has he come from? [Home.] Why? [To earn income.] [Pay him income with a 'marked' note.] What does he spend it on? Food, clothes, etc. [Set up 'shopping centre'] and so on until the 'circular flow' is complete.

There are many variants on this theme.

Worksheet Material

In addition to the kit, pupils are given worksheets to complete. Their successful completion often requires the use of a kit, as can be seen from the worksheet suggested below.

Suggested worksheet for part of course on production:

1. Select any finished product from the kit.
2. Set up the production line required to produce the item you chose in (1).
3. Using kit money, show how much the three groups of ingredients are paid in order to make them join the production recipe. (*You can decide how much they are paid.*)

Answer the following:
1. After the item is produced, what still exists as it was before?

_____

_____

2. What happens to the finished product?

_____

_____

3. What happens to 'Man-made Resources'?

_____

_____

4. What do 'Human Resources' do with the income they receive from having been in the production recipe?

_____

_____

_____

IV ASSESSMENT

The course is assessed by

(*a*) a pre- and post-test which is completed by the pupils. This test includes multiple-choice items, true–false items and some 'short answer' items. Questions are common to both pre- and post-tests— providing a measure of how much has been learned. In addition, the post-test contains a pupil attitude questionnaire;

(*b*) a teacher-comment sheet. This invites teachers to comment on the effectiveness of the material.

References

1. See *Teaching Economics*, Economics Association, 1967, pp. 213–15, for bibliography on this.
2. In Scotland, between 1969 and 1972, the numbers presented for Higher Economics increased by 50%. [In 1972, 3,059 sat Higher Economics. 35,662 sat Higher English.]
3. Lord Robbins, *The Nature and Significance of Economic Science*, Macmillan, 1952.
4. See 'The Integration of Knowledge—Practice and Problems' by D. Hamilton—to be published in the *Journal of Curriculum Studies*, 1973.
5. See Lumsden, K. G. and Attiyeh, R. E., 'The Core of Basic Economics', *Economics*, Summer 1971.

9: Economics for the Less-Able Student

KEITH ROBINSON

The premises on which this paper is based are that the case for the inclusion of economics in the curriculum of more academic pupils at 'O' level and beyond does not need to be restated and that the attention of economists interested in the future development of their subject should be increasingly directed to an assessment of the arguments for its inclusion in the education of all pupils and at every stage of the secondary school. David Christie's paper considers the case for the introduction of economics for pupils of all abilities in the early stages, and accordingly this contribution concentrates on economics courses for the less-academic pupil in the final two years of his school career.

The raising of the school-leaving age has provided one of the most important opportunities in the past generation for a reconsideration of the aims and purposes of secondary education for all pupils. The older definitions of the curriculum which loosely equated it with a syllabus, a course or even a timetable have been succeeded by more wide-ranging explanations such as that of Lawton: 'A selection of those elements of our way of life and of our culture which are so important that their transmission cannot be left to chance.'[1] The curriculum is regarded by Whitfield as 'the tactical centre of the educational enterprise'[2] and its purpose, structure and content have been subjected to a closer examination in the past few years than at any previous time. Traditional academic subjects have been required to justify the place they held in the secondary school course; new subjects such as sociology, psychology and anthropology have been pressing their claims for inclusion and the complex issue of integration and of interdisciplinary courses has received close attention because of the danger of an unmanageable proliferation of individual disciplines.

A major pressure on the curriculum has been the explosion of knowledge and the need to foster modes of study which enable students to grasp the fundamental ideas and concepts of any subject and to apply them to changing phenomena. This is a familiar problem to economists, who are constantly striving to keep abreast of changing events and policies, but fortunately their subject has clear basic concepts and is adaptable to the spiral curriculum where the key ideas can be understood in relation to examples and illustrations chosen to suit the learning capacity of students at different stages of their development. This provides an introductory theoretical argument for suggesting that it should be possible to explain economic concepts in a meaningful manner to less-academic pupils.

An additional pressure on the curriculum arises from the increased demands being made upon it to prepare pupils for life within a complex and changing society, and every subject has to examine its relevance in this context as well as to justify itself as a coherent body of thought. The concern of every individual within a community with economic decisions in his everyday life and the lack of popular understanding of the economic forces which produce changes in the price level, unemployment, the rate of economic growth and the balance of payments combine to produce a powerful case for the inclusion of economics in the education of young adults for whom relevance of their school courses to the world outside is a prime consideration. Dunning[3] has persuasively argued that the most worthwhile contribution of economics education is in the fostering of economic judgments on contemporary issues as a vital part of the education of the individual as a citizen and a member of society, and that the development of the skill of identifying and using economic concepts, even if it is severely limited by the intellectual capacity of the pupil, is preferable to no development at all.

A third potent influence on curriculum is the emphasis on methods of teaching and learning as distinct from the content of what is taught. In this context, the curriculum may be regarded as a series of learning experiences which should provide for the fullest development and growth of the student. At one end of the spectrum there is the 'supermarket approach'[4] which assures that the student can decide to help himself to an array of learning packages, and unless there is careful supervision by the teacher, the 'wants' and 'needs' of the student may become dangerously confused. At the other end, there is the formal instructional lesson situation where the student is the passive recipient of predigested information from the teacher, and his learning pattern is determined for him in an authoritarian manner. Most of present-day curriculum development seeks to find a balance between these two extremes, where the teacher's understanding of the conceptual framework of his subject, and a sufficient knowledge component, are used to guide the student, who still remains an active participant in his own learning. A characteristic of less-academic pupils is that they are unable to absorb lengthy expositions of factual knowledge or to determine their own learning patterns unaided, so that a method of guided individualized learning would seem to be required for them.

This general curricular analysis has highlighted a number of broad and interrelated considerations which should affect the formulation of courses in economics for less-academic pupils:

(*a*) They should be grounded within the discipline of the subject and should 'mediate a grasp of principles'.[5]

(*b*) They should guide the student to learn how to think in economic terms so that he can apply his understanding of the basic concepts of the subject.

(*c*) They should be relevant to the student in the sense that he can appreciate that all the problems he faces and the decisions he is called upon to make as a member of society have an economic dimension.

The term 'less-able' or 'less-academic' is vaguely pejorative and requires to be more closely examined. Its original connotation was probably those students who were not preparing for an external examination at 'O' level or beyond, but with the advent of C.S.E. this approach has already been modified. In Scotland, a recent decision of the S.C.E. Examination Board to rank candidates at the 'O' Grade examination who gain at least 30% of the total marks is likely to mean that a considerably higher proportion of students will take the examination than was previously contemplated, and discussions in England and Wales about a common examination at 16-plus may have the same effect.

It is, therefore, preferable to think in terms of the learning capacity of students who are loosely categorized as 'less-academic', and to suggest that they are not likely to proceed beyond the Piagetian stage of concrete operations to that of formal operations. Accordingly, any attempt to present a subject to them in abstract terms seems likely to prove unsuccessful. The basis of Piaget's argument regarding learning sequence was that a stage of concrete operations is necessary to the understanding of a discipline at whatever age its study begins, and this was reinforced by Bruner's assertion that good teaching consists in the identification of key concepts and principles illustrating these in terms of the experience of the learner whatever his ability may be. The simplicity or complexity of a discipline is thus largely a function of the language and illustrations used to explain it.

Without an understanding of the principles of the subject, a student will be unable to understand economic events or make reliable predictions. Without experience in applying these principles, he will neither understand the relevance of abstract ideas nor retain for long what he has been taught.

In 'The Core of Basic Economics' produced by the Economics Education Project, four key ideas are regarded as essential to an understanding of the economic problems within society:

(*a*) Scarcity and choice
(*b*) Economic efficiency
(*c*) Income distribution
(*d*) Aggregate output and income

If this selection is accepted as a working hypothesis, the problem for the classroom teacher introducing an economics course for students of any ability and of continuing it for those of limited academic attainment, is to translate these concepts into concrete terms related to the experience of his students.

The first concept should present few problems. It is only necessary to discuss with a class the problem each student faces in deciding how to spend his pocket money or how his own family decides to arrange its collective spending, to establish the point that he is experiencing, at both levels, the relative scarcity of resources in relation to the demands made upon them, and that he has to relate the price to be paid for any purchase made to the satisfaction received in relation to the available substitutes. The most likely progression would be to consider in concrete terms the similar problems of allocation of the resources of local and national governments and perhaps to move on to international trade, where although the principles remain the same the outcome of any decision made is so much more far-reaching.

The second key idea of economic efficiency proceeds from the principle of resource allocation to consider the relationship between the input of factors of production and the output of goods and services. It involves discussion of the costs and prices of the producer, the level of employment of factors of production, specialization in production, exchange of the products created and the concept of opportunity cost applied to the satisfaction of wants from one particular factor combination to that achieved by the best alternatives. One way of achieving an introductory understanding of these apparently complex relationships would be to set up a 'production flow' using a kit of facsimiles of land, labour, capital and enterprise. This is the approach taken by the Scottish working party producing an economics course for mixed ability classes in the first two years of the secondary school; and from the limited attempt made so far to apply the same approach to older R.O.S.L.A. students, beginning an economics course at a later stage, it would appear that this very practical approach has greater possibilities of success than more formal methods.

What is the most desirable income distribution within society is a question which involves political and ethical considerations and, as such, it lies outside the strict realm of the economist, but he is able to analyse the effects on income distribution of a particular organization of productive resources and to analyse the economic effects of a given income distribution. It is this type of limitation on economic analysis which poses serious problems for the teacher of less-academic students, for they have considerable difficulty in appreciating such restrictions and they may be naturally more interested in the welfare applications of the subject, where it merges with other social sciences. The responsibility of the teacher in this situation is to enable his students to perceive that each factor is entitled to a return for its part in the productive process and that the balance of factors used in any firm or industry is the main influence on the relative size of wage, interest, rent and profit incomes. It should also be possible to investigate how the National Income 'cake' may be divided in a variety of ways and what are the consequences of slicing the pieces in a particular way. This could prove to be an effective introduction to the idea of the equality of the three methods of measuring the National Income—by output, income and expenditure.

The final concept of aggregate output and income gives the student an insight into the combined activities of all the producers and consumers, including the government, in a national economy, and into the more complex operation of the price system as a means of equating supply and demand at this level. It provides the teacher with an excellent opportunity to remind the class that a community faces the same economic problems as an individual, that the manner in which its resources are used will determine its efficiency and that the exercise of its choices will profoundly affect the present and future well-being of its members. A simple model of the circular flow of income might be constructed to show the consequences for a community of its decisions on the proportion of its resources being consumed, invested and exported. Specific examples of how the government by its fiscal and monetary policies influences the level of output and income could be the culminating contribution to this section of the course.

This is still only a skeleton of a course for less-academic students. It seeks to establish a clear grasp of fundamental principles and recognizes their interdependence, but the flesh on the bones of the course will be the range of realistic examples and illustrations which can be provided in a variety of ways. Some teachers may wish to make use of programmed texts or other structured learning units, but others may prefer to be more flexible in their approach, perhaps using case studies, games and simulation exercises as the basis of their course. The vital factor is that the teacher should decide what precise objectives he wishes to achieve in the course and should devise appropriate methods of assessment as to whether they have been achieved. Since it is unlikely that his students will be able to reach beyond the comprehension stage of the cognitive hierarchy in the Bloom taxonomy, he may decide that his course should concentrate more on such affective objectives as developing in his pupils a concern for the responsible use of economic resources within society, regarding such a concern as a vital element in the education of the citizen of the future.

In relation to these wider-ranging issues, it is legitimate to inquire whether a less-academic student would benefit more from a multi-disciplinary or integrated course in social subjects, rather than from a study of separate disciplines. The supporters of the integrated approach contend that the division of knowledge into subjects is artificial and may lead to unnecessary fragmentation; it reflects a judgment on the relative importance of individual disciplines which may no longer be valid, and it may mean that certain areas of knowledge are largely unexplored in the school curriculum. Hence, some form of integration is essential if the curriculum is to be both more efficient in terms of organization of knowledge and more effective as a medium for preparing students to move into the world outside the school where daily problems are multi-faceted.

This is a significant criticism of the discipline-based curriculum, but it does not necessarily ensure that multi-disciplinary courses would be an adequate replacement. Most of these courses are thematic in approach with the curiosity and free inquiry of the student as the integrating factor. For the R.O.S.L.A. student they usually seek to deal with some of the major problems with which he will be faced when he leaves school—getting a job, setting up home, paying taxes, etc.—and so in terms of relevance and immediate interest they are acceptable, but there must be considerable doubt whether they can provide a basis of understanding of all the disciplines compounded within the course. As a result, students may not be well equipped to deal with situations and problems other than those directly discussed in the course. If it is possible for an economist to make his contribution to such courses in the context of team-teaching, this may overcome some of the major problems of the integrated course from the standpoint of the discipline, but otherwise it is unlikely that economic issues will be analysed satisfactorily, for teachers with only a limited acquaintance of the subject may either under- or over-assess its significance in relation to a particular event or problem.

This paper has inevitably raised more questions than it has answered. Much research is needed into the learning patterns of less-academic students and into the precise objectives of courses planned for them. Experiments should be established to test the relative merits of courses in economics as against multi-disciplinary courses (including economics) but the fundamental criterion must be whether such courses equip the student with the technique of thinking which distinguishes economics from other disciplines and whether he can use this skill in a complex society.

References

1. Lawton, D., Campbell, J. and Burkitt, V., *Social Studies 8–13*, Schools Council Working Paper 39, Evans Methuen, 1971.
2. Whitfield, R. J., *Disciplines of the Curriculum*, McGraw-Hill, 1971.
3. Dunning, K., 'To Know Economics', *Economics*, Summer 1972.
4. Entwistle, H., 'Educational Theory and the Teaching of Economics', *Economics*, Autumn 1966.
5. Branford, W. G., 'Who Wants a Bigger Slice of the Cake?', *Scottish Educational Journal*, 28 November 1969.

Lee, N., 'Economics Education for the Newson Child', *Economics*, Spring/Summer 1969.

Dunning, K., 'A Developmental Course in the Teaching of Economics for the Average Young Citizen', *Economics*, Autumn 1967.

Dunning, K., 'What Economics should we Teach?', *Economics*, Summer 1970.

10: Terminal Economics: The Experience of C.S.E.

SIMON SMITH

The introduction of the Certificate of Secondary Education in 1965 marked a new departure in school examinations in this country. While many external examinations have had the effect of dictating to a considerable extent the content of school curricula, the C.S.E. set out to reflect, measure and enhance the standards in the schools, and encourage their freedom to develop their courses of study in the way they thought best for their pupils.

In order to ensure that the examination was a school-based one, administrative instruments were established whereby teachers in the schools were entrusted with control over the examination. Every school is able to choose from three modes of examination —if a school chose Mode III, for example, the examination would be set and marked internally—and a subject panel of teachers meets regularly throughout the year in order to review syllabuses, and supervise the standard, content and marking of the examinations.

The candidates for the C.S.E. have certain well-defined characteristics. They come from a broad band of pupils extending from those who are of G.C.E. Ordinary level ability to those who are a little below the average in ability; they are estimated to account for about 60% of all secondary school pupils in the country; all but a very few will be leaving school as soon as they have taken the examination. The C.S.E. examination must therefore assess the attainment of a wide ability range, and also provide the sort of information about school leavers which employers and other users of the certificate will wish to have. But what sort of children are these school leavers? Some are no doubt those who had spent much of their career in the lower streams of primary school, and who had neither academic ability nor the motivation to participate strongly in the work of the school. On the other hand, many manifest a 'remarkable degree of independence, seldom needing continual adult approval for their actions. They are ready for responsibilities in class but generally are denied the opportunity. They have a lengthy interest span for that which is familiar to them; unfortunately the majority of what they meet in text-books does not represent the type of life to which they have been exposed, so their attention span is unfairly considered as shorter than that of high achievers.'[1]

It was with problems such as these in mind that the Economics Subject Panel sat down to formulate the aims and syllabus for the Mode I examination in economics for the Middlesex Regional Examining Board. The basic philosophy of both the Board and the Panel is clearly apparent in the statement of aims contained in the handbook of Regulations. These were 'to test the candidate's understanding of the elements of that part of his environment which is concerned with the production and distribution of goods and services. It is believed that the teaching of economic principles isolated from everyday life is of little value to the pupils who are likely to follow this course, and that one justification for including this subject in a general curriculum is the extent to which it adequately prepares pupils for entry into the adult world of earning and living.'

To this end, the detailed syllabus presents economics as an interpretation of the various roles in which the pupils are likely to find themselves. Thus the three main sections of the syllabus are entitled 'Men as Workers', 'Men as Consumers', and 'Men as Citizens'. The syllabus was deliberately set out in detail (i) in order to provide maximum help to teachers, as it was known that candidates in several schools would be prepared for the examination by teachers whose primary qualification was not in economics, and (ii) with the expressed hope that teachers would resist the temptation to prefer depth to complete coverage, for the merit of the syllabus and examination is in the 'comprehensiveness of its treatment of this one aspect of Man's existence'.

Under the title 'Men as Workers', pupils study population size and distributions, factors of production and their earnings, location and organization of firms, and the labour market. The section 'Men as Consumers' comprises an introduction to the determination of prices, retail and wholesale distribution, and money and

banking, while under 'Men as Citizens' comes a study of the
national income, public finance, government intervention, and
international trade. Put in terms of educational objectives, it was
expected that by the end of a two-year course of study a pupil
should

(i) have some knowledge of the elements which go to make up
the British economy;

(ii) have an understanding of the interdependence, the interrelation of the different parts of the economy;

(iii) appreciate the functions of the more important economic
organizations such as the banks and the Stock Exchange;

(iv) have acquired skills enabling him to find economic information, evaluate evidence, and suggest solutions to economic
problems;

(v) be able to read with understanding and interest newspaper
articles, or listen to news and other broadcasts which have
an economic content.

Having considered what it is that is to be tested, the next
problem was to look for the best possible means of testing. The
use of a single type of test, such as an objective test or a written
essay, has obvious shortcomings: consequently the decision was
made to employ several types of tests in a single examination.
Accordingly a written examination paper was devised, divided
into four sections, with a quarter of the total marks allocated to
each section (see Appendix I). Section A contains questions on
the whole syllabus, requiring one-word, one-sentence or short-
paragraph answers. The advantages of this kind of test are well
known. It enables the examiner to map out the field to be tested
quite accurately, and then to test the knowledge, skills and
understandings systematically; it reduces the possibility of question spotting and rote learning; it gives candidates the opportunity
to supply a variety of evidence about themselves; and, particularly important for the kind of pupils characterized above, it
enables the less-articulate candidates to have an opportunity for
scoring marks in the early part of the paper. Section B was
designed to achieve among other things the testing of objective (v)
mentioned above. It consists of a short elementary passage (possibly one adapted from a news item) upon which candidates answer
questions framed to discover the level of comprehension of its

concepts and ideas, and to test the application of their knowledge to real economic problems. The types of test represented by Sections A and B are reasonably easy to set, and are probably more reliable to mark than the essay-type question. They are particularly valuable to use where for some reason it is desired to avoid the multiple-choice test, but when the essay may be placing a greater burden on the examinee than he is able to bear.

Sections C and D of the paper contain short essay-type questions designed, among other things, to test the candidates' ability to understand the interrelatedness of the economy, and to assess their ability to develop an argument, and the quality of their judgment. This style of testing is easily set, though time-consuming to mark, and usually has a lower reliability than the objective style.

As an alternative to Section D of the written paper, candidates may submit a 'Project', and since about 25% of pupils select to do this, it may be instructive to consider the aims and possible outcomes of this kind of activity. The project is usually presented in a loose-leaf folder, and often is the result of work extending over several months. The quantity of work produced varies from 5 or 6 pages at one end of the scale, to 'dissertations' of 10,000 words or more at the other. The quality of work is assessed by the school and also by an external oral examination when questions put to candidates are framed in such a way as to evaluate the level of economic understanding that has been achieved in the selected topic. There is much to commend the project method in economic learning. It can create and reinforce a genuine interest in the subject; it is useful for assessing boys and girls who find difficulty in arranging their thoughts on paper under pressure of an examination, and, since the Regional Board stipulates that the work should consist of a study of current local, national or international affairs, it enables pupils to apply their knowledge of economic principles to the world outside the classroom. Thus, for example, a project may consist of the study of prices in a local retail market carried out over a period of weeks, with an explanation of daily, weekly and monthly fluctuations, involving some of the skills of economic analysis in transforming raw data into a reasoned presentation of causal relationships. It is hoped that in this way pupils will be encouraged to take some responsibility and initiative for their own learning and progress in economics.

We must now attempt to assess the effect that the introduction of the C.S.E. Syllabus and Examination has had on the teaching and learning of economics in the schools. There has certainly been a growth in the number of schools submitting candidates and in the total number of candidates, the latter having increased from under 100 to over 400—a total still quite small when compared with those entered for some of the main subjects (see Appendix II). The Mode I examination is still the only one of its kind in economics in England (though the East Anglia Board has an examination in social economics), and recently candidates from outside the Middlesex region have been entered by their schools for the examination. This was done with the consent of the regional board concerned. One can only form a subjective judgment as to the quality of economic literacy. It is noticeable, however, that the quality of the project work submitted has improved tremendously over the years, and also that in 1972, for instance, the entry of schools new to the subject slightly depressed the overall level of attainment. What can be said about the syllabus and the style of the examination? A few minor modifications have been made to the syllabus by the teachers' Subject Panel as part of a general tidying-up process. There have been no criticisms made about the general format of the examination, and few adverse comments made concerning individual questions on the papers. At a Regional Conference of Economic Teachers held in 1970, and attended by about 36 teachers, there was general satisfaction with the examination. Teachers from two schools expressed some concern that in their view the syllabus was 'not analytical enough', and should in part at least, be of a comparative nature. On the other hand there has been, perhaps disappointingly, no growth in the submission of candidates under Mode III of the C.S.E. scheme, there having been only one school entering candidates for the subject in this way.

In spite of advances made in the theory of educational measurement and the application of improved assessment techniques, the professional examiner in economics is still faced with one fundamental problem. The National Foundation for Educational Research in its *Educational Research News*, September 1969, characterized a good examination as having a 'clearly-defined purpose and [being] composed of questions or items which are tailor-made for that purpose. The teacher or examiner should be clear about his aims and that the items in the examination should have been compiled in strict accordance with those aims.' It goes on to say that more and more teachers are becoming aware of the need to prepare a blueprint of examination objectives, and to provide the test items which match the blueprint. In practice, the situation facing teachers and examiners at present is rather different from this. The field of achievement testing in economics still awaits an analysis of objectives related to those concepts, intellectual processes and skills that are *uniquely* the contribution made through the study of economics. Until the time that such objectives can be defined and measured, some might ask whether it makes sense to call available instruments 'economic examining'.

Reference

1. Strom, R. M., *School and Society*, 1964.

Appendix I

MIDDLESEX REGIONAL EXAMINING BOARD

ELEMENTS OF ECONOMICS (160/1)1972

Certificate of Secondary Education

Section A

Answer all questions. You are advised to spend about 40 minutes on this section.

1. Indicate, by writing 'Yes' or 'No' in the spaces provided, which of the following are legal tender money:

   Cheques ....   Bills of exchange ....
   Pound Notes ......   20p of bronze coin ......

2. Complete the following statements by writing 'current' or 'deposit' in the space provided:

   The owner should give the bank notice if he wishes to withdraw money from his............ account.

   A................account enables its owner to draw cheques.
   The owner of a .... account receives interest on the amount of money held in it.

   A .... account is mainly intended for those who wish to save their money.
   A .... account may enable its owner to obtain an overdraft.

   Complete the following statements:

3. *Two* ways in which the Government can influence the location of industry are:

   (*a*) ....
   (*b*) ....

4. Firms which are run in such a way that their profits go to the community as a whole belong to .... enterprise, while firms whose profits go to the individuals who own them are part of .... enterprise.

5. *Two* factors which cause National Income to change are:

   (*a*) ....
   (*b*) ....

6. The lower the price of a good, the .... of it will be demanded, and the .... of it will be supplied.

7. *Two* reasons why some areas of Britain are more densely populated than others are:

   (*a*) ....
   (*b*) ....

8. When Bank Rate is raised, other rates of interest tend to ....

9. *Two* arguments *against* the nationalization of an industry are:

   (*a*) ....
   (*b*) ....

10. *Two* arguments *in favour* of the nationalization of an industry are:

    (*a*) ....
    (*b*) ....

11. *Two* disadvantages of the division of labour are:

    (*a*) ....
    (*b*) ....

12. Two reasons why the Census of Population is carried out are:

    (*a*) ....
    (*b*) ....

13. Members of the London Stock Exchange who buy and sell shares on behalf of the public are known as ....; members who are prepared to buy and sell securities on their behalf are called ....

14. List the main functions of a trade union.

15. What organizations exist for the protection of the consumer?

16. What is meant by the term *tariff* in international trade?

17. List five items of central government expenditure.

Section B

Read the passage below. Then use it and your knowledge of economics to answer the questions which follow. You are advised to spend about 50 minutes on this section.

The working population of the U.K. is just over 25 millions. Of these just over one-third work in manufacturing industries, while another third are engaged in industries providing various services, such as the distributive trade. The remainder of the working population is employed in primary industries, such as farming. The total money value of all goods and services produced by these industries in the U.K. in one year is called the National Output or National Income.

Many different forms of organization can be found in the various industries and trades, from one-man businesses to the public joint-stock companies and nationalized industries. The one-man firm is still the most numerous form of organization. A special type of firm which occurs in retailing is the co-operative retail society; both co-operative societies and public joint-stock companies distribute dividends.

18. What is meant by the term 'working population'?
19. Name *two* classes of people not included in the working population.
20. (*a*) Give *two* examples of service industries (other than the distributive trade) in the U.K.
    (*b*) Give *three* examples of manufacturing industries in the U.K.
21. (*a*) What is meant by the term 'primary industry'?
    (*b*) Name *one* primary industry other than farming.
22. Explain why National Output must equal National Income.
23. Give *two* differences between a public joint-stock company and a nationalized industry.
24. Give the names of (*a*) *two* well-known public joint-stock companies, and (*b*) *three* nationalized industries.
25. Give *two* reasons why one-man firms are still the most numerous type of business organization in the U.K.
26. Give *two* of the special features of a co-operative retail society.
27. What are the differences between the *dividend* issued by a co-operative retail society, and the *dividend* distributed by a public joint-stock company?

Section C

Choose *two* of the following questions and write a short essay in answer to each, using the blank ruled pages immediately following this section. You are advised to spend about 30 minutes on this section.

28. Give reasons why the people of the underdeveloped countries generally have a low standard of living.
29. Why are workers often reluctant to change their jobs?
30. Describe the main ways in which firms raise money for expansion.
31. What are the possible advantages that monopoly may bring to the community?
32. Why do doctors usually earn more than railway porters?
33. What are the ways in which either the Central Government or Local Authorities raise the money needed for its expenditure?

34. How may the bank help a customer who (*a*) needs a loan and (*b*) is planning to spend a holiday abroad?
35. What are the factors which may alter the size of a country's population?

Section D

This section is to be attempted only by those candidates not submitting a project.

Answer one question from this section, using the blank ruled pages immediately following this section. You are advised to spend about 30 minutes on this section.

36. The Index of Retail Prices showed an increase of more than 10% between July 1970 and July 1971. Describe carefully how changes in prices from one year to the next are measured by the Index.
37. Distinguish between the balance of trade and the balance of payments. How may the balance of trade be affected by changes in the terms of trade?
38. In 1971 the Chancellor of the Exchequer cut purchase tax on certain goods and eased hire purchase restrictions. Why did he do this, and what are the likely effects of these measures on the economy?
39. Motor-car manufacturers generally operate in very large factories, while motor-car repairs are often carried out in relatively small garages. Give reasons why this is so.
40. Describe the work done by retailers. How may they benefit from the functions performed by the wholesalers?

Appendix II

MIDDLESEX REGIONAL EXAMINING BOARD FOR C.S.E.

Summary of Examination Entries

Economics

Year	MODE I		MODE III	
	No. of Cand.	No. of Centres	No. of Cand.	No. of Centres
1966	58	6	16	1
1967	86	10	11	1
1968	143	14	10	1
1969	199	15	12	1
1970	340	20	18	1
1971	310	19	10	1
1972	450	26	—	—

VI: ECONOMICS AT SIXTH FORM LEVEL AND ITS RELATIONSHIP TO UNIVERSITY ECONOMICS

11: The Educational Value of Economics: Some Practical Implications

JOHN OLIVER

I hope in this paper to take one theme and illustrate a number of problems and provisional solutions in economics teaching. The theme is the very nature of economics and how it illuminates any consideration of the teaching of economics, with respect to both what might be done (which thus specifies the *limits* of what might be done) and how it might be done.

Perhaps I can deal with some hostile counter-arguments before I begin. There is an easy, and not undeserved, ironic comment on those who set themselves up on how to teach; that in discussing how to be interesting, they are themselves boring, that in explaining how to be clear, they are themselves confusing. My reply is simply 'do as I say and not as I do'. If any such comments are just, they make my position hypocritical rather than my theme invalid.

There is much to be proud of in modern economics but, I fear, much less in what is known about the teaching of economics. I am, in consequence, unable to pass on a synthesis or overview of mainstream established doctrine on the teaching of economics, and I am unlikely to erect single-handed a comprehensive and reliable model. I am not, therefore, some self-appointed Messiah but I do hope I have come to light the way of the Lord—so I might just be John the Baptist.

My aims are uncharacteristically modest. To specify carefully what I am not doing, to take a necessary but not sufficient theme in the teaching of economics and, in passing, to abuse some of what is currently passed off in the teaching of economics.

First, what I am not doing. I do not propose, save by implication, to discuss syllabus content or relationships with other subjects. Nor do I propose to discuss economics as such. My interest is in discussing different ways of teaching, for instance, the U-shapeness of cost curves and not whether they are, or are not, U-shaped. The illustrations are reasonably non-controversial so that we may concentrate on pedagogic technique rather than economic content. I will illustrate the discussion with examples that seem appropriate to G.C.E. 'A' level. Quite clearly, the principles with which I am concerned would manifest themselves rather differently in different courses and at different levels and no doubt you can modify the principles to particular courses ('O' level, non-examined courses, etc.) as I go along. The main task is to convince you of the theme rather than teach you your job.

The theme is easily stated: no proper consideration of the teaching of economics can ignore a consideration of the nature of economics. I believe this to be important for course content, objectives and pedagogy but will concentrate on the latter. I feel that such a consideration will not lead us to 'ideal' syllabuses or novel methods, but teach us to regard the first as a delusion and the second as not only irrelevant but also a minefield.

I take it that we all have in common some orthodox view of the nature of economics, so I will not offer a blow-by-blow account, but simply draw attention to particular facts relevant to the present context, and refer only briefly to the views of Robbins, Keynes and Popper.

A hurried overview of the nature of economics would be something like this. The problem of economics is the allocation of scarce resources between competing ends, and the classic manifestation is the micro-concept of opportunity costs. But the same problem is apparent in macroeconomics and in economic growth. This is hardly to say enough but it does no great violence to the use of words to embrace within this definition a modish concern with normative decision-making or a system approach. Indeed, if we are to consider the economics paradigm it is rather useful to define one's discipline in none too strict a fashion.

This approach *does* hardly say enough but for quite a different reason. It is quite inadequte to define a discipline by referring to the subject studied: such an approach would fail to distinguish astronomy from astrology. Clearly we must look to method as well as content and there is a prestigious precedent, Keynes: 'The theory of economics is a method rather than a doctrine, an apparatus of the mind, a technique of thinking, which helps its possessor to draw correct conclusions.'[1]

Emphasis on method is as much a distortion as emphasis on content, for merely looking at method would fail to distinguish algebra from geometry since both are deductive in method. In defining a subject we must refer to both content and method.

Keynes talked of *a* technique of thinking. What is/are the technique(s)? There are two answers and they are complements, not substitutes. The first is more widely trumpeted than the second.

Robbins can help us with the first, for the first answer is that the economist's method is deductive. Robbins: 'The nature of economic analysis . . . consists of deductions from a series of postulates, the chief of which are almost universal facts of experience.'[2] Or, again, 'The propositions of economic theory, like all scientific theory, are obviously deductions from a series of postulates. And the chief of these postulates are all assumptions involving in some way simple and indisputable facts of experience, relating to the way in which the scarcity of goods, which is the subject-matter of our science, actually shows itself in the world of reality.'[3]

It is, for instance, a simple and indisputable fact of experience that inputs are not perfect substitutes for one another, that an extra farm worker is not the same as an extra farm field. Because they are not perfect substitutes we have the phenomenon of diminishing returns at the margin and we deduce something about short-run behaviour of both costs and firms. The origins of some quite sophisticated conclusions in the theory of the firm are to be found, at least in part, in that workers are different from fields.

The deductive method is certainly widespread in economics and its pervasiveness has many implications for the teacher—not least that in this side of the trade there is no room for dispute. Once a firm's objective is specified as profit maximization, then it follows as a matter of logic, and not of opinion, that the relevant price–output strategy is that which equates marginal revenues and costs. And that is an end to that.

It is this very deductiveness that can make some economics teaching so difficult. If the topic is non-disputatious then there is practically nothing to do except make sure that the pupils do understand. And that means we are examining/assessing rather than teaching. At least part of the answer to *that* difficulty lies in a problem-solving approach of which more anon.

Two other teaching points emerge when dealing with this deductive part of economics. First, if an answer is necessarily true, if it is entailed by its assumptions, then it is odd that so many teachers use notes for this kind of teaching. Like teachers of mathematics we should be able to work out the conclusions on the board, that for example,

$$MR = P\left(1 - \frac{1}{e}\right)$$

or whatever. Like them we need sheets of problems, not sheets of proofs. Second, the deductive nature of much economics (and in particular G.C.E. economics) means that in teaching we should be self-evidently using the deductive process—of which also more anon.

Popper has reformulated our vision of deductive reasoning in emphasizing, in summary, that a theory can only have empirical content if it has predictive powers and its predictions have laid it open to refutation rather than proof. So the most we can hope for is the status of the *tentative plausibility of not having been disproved*. This is a modest status and it should be reflected in our teaching of so-called Applied Economics of which also more anon. (*Pace* the Phillips Curve.)

This kind of approach, with various modifications and qualifications, is probably reasonably common ground among us. What is unfortunate is that this deductive aspect is greatly overemphasized in many courses and text-books. If we were simply concerned with the necessarily true then there could be no arguments of the current kind on inflation.

For deductive reasoning is not the only form of good reasoning and not the only kind found in economics.

Inductive reasoning is the second aspect of the Keynes technique of thinking. An inductive conclusion is not necessarily true, not entailed by its postulates. The conclusion is tentative and it can have respectable rivals. There might be an apparent relationship between the output of bacon and the price of eggs and the latter might be 'explained' by reference to the former. However 'good' the statistical techniques and results, there could soon be equally convincing 'explanations' that refer to personal income levels or the number of chickens.

The distinction is now clear enough. Deductive reasoning is necessarily true, inductive is merely plausible and reasonable. *And in our teaching the logical status should be quite explicit.*

One set of conclusions are deduced, the other reasonably inferred. These are not the same animals at all: only some of the latter are 'true'. The Cobb–Douglas results that:

$$\text{A.C.} = \frac{TC}{q} = \frac{wq^{1/a-1}}{b^{1/a}} + \frac{F}{q}$$

are non-analogous with Pratten and Dean cost-estimation.

Now what kind of support do we look for in inductive economics? Clearly the answer is statistical support. And the statistical techniques are broadly those of inference and probability.

Three teaching points: first, there seems no analytic reason for stressing the deductive against the inductive although this is exactly what most text-books do. Second, what are we to make of courses that ignore or minimize statistical techniques? Fraudulent might be the first word to come to mind. Third, once this inductive aspect is acknowledged, then a modish 'problem-solving' approach becomes attractive.

Before I return to these issues, I would like to develop the pedagogic implication of the deductive and the inductive nature of economics, but first, there is a question of 'language' and of objectives. In deciding how to teach we must consider not only what is being taught but also *who* is being taught. Cohen and Cyert: 'In the deductive process, a number of different languages can be used. . . . In the past, economists have commonly used three types of language: ordinary prose, pictorial geometry and mathematics. . . . There is no particular honorific ranking of theories on the basis of the language used. The scientist chooses his language primarily as a matter of convenience, both in terms of the requirements of the problem and of his facility in handling the language.'[4]

We might re-phrase to: there is no particular honorific ranking of teaching methods on the basis of the language used; the teacher chooses a language appropriate to the problem and to the students' facility in handling that language. Now deductive models might be taught verbally/mathematically but it is difficult to see inductive economics that is not either statistical or mathematical. Any other approach makes for teaching the economics as received doctrine, and since inductive conclusions are tentative and non-disproved, *such an approach falsifies their nature and is a false method*. (Here lies the great problem of G.C.E. Applied Economics.) The students just do not need conventional answers to contemporary problems. Techniques are much better and have less built-in obsolescence.

Before we return to the nature of economics and classroom practice we might direct ourselves to implications so far for G.C.E. in general and objectives in particular. *We find ourselves led to the conclusion that many contemporary G.C.E. courses undervalue or ignore the inductive techniques and so give a view of economics that is bogus.* The specific question then becomes: either we must introduce some substantial syllabus changes or we must realize that we are teaching a view of economics that is out of focus. It may be that the benefits of even limited economics exceed the costs of teaching no economics and so we may countenance this distortion. (Of course no G.C.E. reaches professionalized standards but this is not the point: a sixth form history student who only studies the nineteenth century has a limited historical view but the explanations he meets may be genuinely historical in nature. Our case is different; the students are not facing genuine economics.)

A consideration of the nature of economics should lead us to some idea of its objectives and values, and realizing the unnatural state of sixth form economics would help us to choose from the list of objectives those which are applicable to the sixth form.

I do not offer a Bloomian taxonomy but a succinct list which I then discuss rather summarily. I think we might claim that our subject is/might be

    (1) vocational
    (2) intellectually rigorous
    (3) that it has a citizenship value.

The vocational aspect is clearly very muted in the sixth form course.

To offer rigour is to say nothing about the problem of curriculum choice as most other likely subjects make the same claim;

to include economics is to incur the opportunity cost of excluding an alternative subject.

Any claim with regard to citizenship is to claim that certain problems are important to everybody—inflation, unemployment, etc. This, however, gets us only a little further forward since I do not know of a subject that claims it deals with trivial problems. Opportunity cost rears its head again.

It might help to think that economics holds a good claim in offering a rational approach to experience that might well be distorted without some social science. Self-evidently, people trained in Natural Sciences do not apply the same standards of rigour and verification to society's problems that they expect, as a matter of course, in their professional lives. They might hold that savings depend on interest rates, that devaluation is a disaster and that capital punishment deters murderers. The point is that people who should know better never think of these propositions as testable. So economics teaching might lead to a more rational, as opposed to superstitious, approach to social experience.

All this simply amounts to saying that economcs is a worthy subject. And to support economics teaching for that reason is a disguised value judgment. Economists of all people should be jumpy about the opportunity cost of their subject and the normative nature of its rationale.

All this may seem a heavy-handed approach to the obvious, but the point is made in this way just because too many people identify some values/objectives for economics and then perpetrate the *non sequitur* that 'therefore' it 'ought' to be taught.

Confidence in our subject is not enough. We must be explicit about our claims for our subject, and careful that we really do meet them, or we may go the way of classics as a school subject.

In summary, our subject offers a rigorous intellectual training, a rational approach to social experience, and it treats of inescapable real world problems of the firm and economy. This is an attractive menu: research is needed on the correspondence between the menu and what goes on in the kitchen.

If these are the sort of objectives suggested by a consideration of the nature of the subject, what is suggested about classroom techniques? Let us start with deductive reasoning. If a student is to learn real economics then to be faithful to the subject the teaching procedure must be deductive. (We would have no time for a biology teacher who only 'taught' his subject by referring to Mother Nature and her wondrous works.)

Thus comparative costs might be taught by a Socratic question-and-answer method that presented pupils with output figures for two countries each producing two goods and then (all usual assumptions) showed the increased world output effect of each country concentrating on the product with the greatest comparative advantage. If the case of a country producing advantageously one kind of goods is followed by the case of one country producing advantageously both goods the pupils can *deduce for themselves* (doubtless with much hinting and prompting) that the case for international trade is an opportunity cost ratio argument and *not* an appeal to Smithian specialization or division of labour (see Appendix I).

These latter benefits are common in the world but not necessary to the argument. Yet most text-books concentrate on the latter, and also often argue by analogy: painful comparisons like 'why do pop-stars pay chauffeurs to wash their cars when they could do it more cheaply themselves?'. The *argument* for international trade is not proved by demonstrating that I pay somebody to paint my flat which I could do more cheaply myself because it is a better resource-use for me to mark G.C.E. scripts. Such a teaching technique may be helpful but *it is certainly not sufficient and probably not necessary.*

Let us look at five ways of teaching profit maximization.

First, we might take the derivative of a profit function to yield the well-known marginal revenue-cost equality conditions

$$\frac{d(PQ)}{dQ} = \frac{dC}{dQ}.$$

Taking a further derivative will determine whether we have a maximum or minimum turning-point. The method has three advantages: it is deductive, it is succinct and it emphasizes necessary and sufficient conditions. Its two problems are its 'language' and the awkwardness of moving from a differentiable model to a world of incremental change and its discontinuities. It is a helpful method for the appropriate sixth form students but it cannot be sufficient.

Second, we might use the parallelism of tangents to total revenue and cost functions (Appendix II). This has the merits that it is clear and visually easy and conveniently distinguishes profit, revenue and sales maximization. The disadvantage is that the marginal revenue and cost equality is indicated by the equal slopes of the tangents/functions. It is hardly apparent to the mathematically maladroit that equal slopes have the same meaning as equal marginal revenues and costs.

Third, and worst, we might resort to an arithmetical table (Appendix III). The advantages are that it is incremental, and so realistic, and easily understood.

The shortcoming is just that it is 'wrong'. Profits are now maximized at two levels of output, 3 and 4 units, and at only one does marginal revenue equal marginal costs. It thus 'proves' the opposite of what is required for it shows that profits can be maximized without equating costs and revenues at the margin. And the explanation—that it is a discontinuous function with the variable making discrete changes—is of little use to the average student.

This example does point up something important about the relationship between models in economics and the real world—but that is a different matter.

Fourth, we might use a diagram like that in Appendix IV. This is easily understood and merely requires a particular syllabus sequence in that it must be preceded by the notion of a negatively sloped marginal revenue curve. But it gets nowhere near necessary and sufficient conditions.

Fifth is a diagram like Appendix V which neatly makes the necessary and sufficient distinction. Of these methods it probably offers the most with the least risk of ambiguity.

Three points emerge. Decisions on teaching methods cannot be taken independently of the curriculum, or vice versa. All methods must acknowledge the deductive nature by deducing rather than by asserting profit-maximizing conditions, comparative advantage or whatever. It is the technique of thinking that helps to identify economics and not a particular set of results. The third point is that this kind of emphasis is likely to make the student more adept at problem-solving. (As I am keen to discuss other classroom methods, I now incur the opportunity cost of not discussing by example the teaching of inductive economics.)

A general class of teaching methods is illumined by reference to the nature of economics. *Case studies* are much in vogue, so it is their disadvantages that need emphasis. Some are simply extended examples and as such are plagued by diminishing returns. Put another way they easily become anecdotal rather than analytic. A more pressing difficulty is that they work the wrong way round, for they may seduce pupils into moving from a particular case to a general law though this may not be in fact general. Economics proceeds in the opposite direction: it is the careful application of general principles to particular problems.

It is, of course, quite possible to devise cases that do manoeuvre students into deductive processes, and what is good about that is that it acknowledges the nature of the discipline and not that it is a case study. Too many zealots believe that case studies are 'good' because they are case studies, but there seems to be no analytic reason for this prejudice. Just like verbal teaching they can be ranked from good to bad, and a relevant criterion is their correspondence to economics as such.

I do believe that they can perform a useful tutorial/assessment role as part of a battery of problems. Appendix VI contains an example to which I shall return in the context of problem-solving.

Diagrams, other than deductive geometry, have no explanatory powers whatever, though they may be good memory aids. Cost curves are certainly not U-shaped because we draw them so, and we do, after all, feel free to draw them L-shaped. Similarly for the Phillips relationship, which is neither false nor true because we can portray it. If they do not involve a technique of thinking then they are not part of economics as such. If they are interesting as memory aids then we must be clear that *that* is their objective and their value.

Appendix VII is an almost classic case of the important line between literally seeing that outputs have increased and conceptually 'seeing'. Much the same can be said of analogies, to reiterate an earlier point. An argument conducted *solely*, or mainly, by analogy is not properly conducted although to read some books and hear some lessons one might well think so.

Let me finish this catalogue of abuse with a look at *visual aids*. I think that the general principles must be clear enough. Devices such as overhead projectors, filmstrips, factory visits, etc. are unlikely to lead to inductive/deductive reasoning although they may reinforce what has gone before or is to come. These techniques are at the best trivial and at the worst bogus, and I might hope I was stating the obvious and paying insufficient attention to such merits as they do have. But I fear that too many publications trumpet the virtues and ignore the limitations. These, and other, techniques may indeed rouse interest and, where true, that *is* in their favour. Since they do not correspond to the nature of the subject we must judge them as ways of arousing interest *and on that criterion alone*. It is difficult to see any analytic distinction between that method of arousing interest and, say, putting a live ferret down your trousers.

Further points—perhaps debating points—are: is interest what we are trying to maximize? And it is a poor subject that gains interest only from its presentation. I see no reason to be ashamed of the intrinsic interest of economics.

Problem-solving seems aimed at two main objectives. Firstly an objective of economics is an ability to solve problems and, secondly, if diligently constructed, they are a teaching/tuition device which may correspond to the nature of the subject and so can reach other objectives.

Multiple-choice problems are, I would suspect, simply a way of checking understanding and they can certainly reveal ambiguities in the understanding that might be masked in the traditional essay form. This is true of other problem-solving techniques like that shown in Appendix VI.

In these cases, the student must put to precise operational use an idea he has already 'learnt'—rather like a dental student might proceed from hearing about extraction to actually taking a tooth out.

Appendices VI and VIII give excellent examples of problems that can be relied on to sort out good essay-writers about 'fixed cost changes do not alter marginal costs', 'bygones are bygones', and so on—from those who really understand these matters.

A greater emphasis on this kind of work rather than traditional essay/discussion methods (they are complements, not substitutes), offers the hope that by manœuvring the student into using the ideas he will reach a better understanding.

Perhaps, in summary, I may defuse some possible opposition. I have advanced a necessary but insufficient theme. Of course, a comprehensive account would cope with other problems and refer to other criteria, but it does seem clear that no proper understanding of either the role of teaching economics, or methods of teaching economics, can ignore some reference to the nature of economics.

I have leaned hard on the present form of some 'A' level economics because we must sometimes ask the fundamental questions. The answer may well be that if all we can do is to teach economics that is somewhat out of focus, then that is what we should do.

I have leaned harder still on visual aids not because they have no value because quite self-evidently they may be more legible than some handwriting, and prepared O.H.P. material may well save classroom time. They have real practical values of this kind rather than as a substitute for conventional methods. Unfortunately, my impression is that, at the moment, it is their limitations that need to be clarified rather than their advantages, for they have too many naïve supporters. And the same goes for case studies, integrated sessions, and so on.

Excessive reliance on these modish techniques is for fools and zealots, and I personally hope to live and die an old-fashioned sock-it-to-them teacher.

References

1. Keynes, J. M., Introduction to the *Cambridge Economic Handbooks*, which is common to all volumes in the series.
2. Robbins, L. C., *The Nature and Significance of Economic Science*, 2nd ed., Macmillan, 1935, p. 99.
3. Ibid., p. 78.
4. Cohen, K. and Cyert, R. M., *Theory of the Firm*, Prentice-Hall, 1965, p. 20.

Appendix I

Production		WITHOUT TRADE			WITH TRADE	
		Good X	Good Y		Good X	Good Y
Country						
	A	10	5		20	–
	B	5	10	→	–	20
	total	15	15		20	20
					1X ↔ 1Y	
		X	Y		X	Y
	A	15	10		30	–
	B	5	5	→	–	10
	total	20	20		30	10
				$1\frac{1}{2}$ – 1X ↔ 1Y		

The new opportunity cost ratios are clearly advantageous.

Appendix II

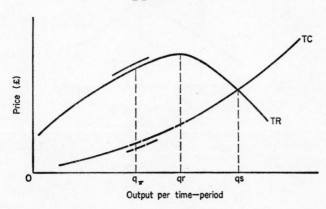

Output per time—period

Appendix III

Q	P	TR	MR	TC	MC	π (Profits)
0	0	0	0	1		−1
1	10	10	10	10	9	0
2	9	18	8	16	6	2
3	8	24	6	20	4	4
4	7	28	4	24	4	4
5	6	30	2	28	2	2

Appendix IV

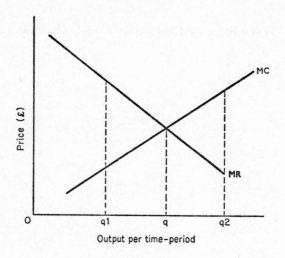

Appendix V

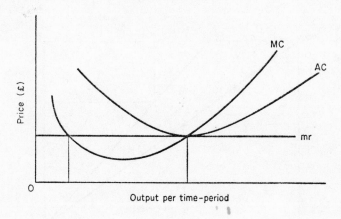

Appendix VI

Q	TC (ooos)	TR (ooos) per week
4	47	76
5	57	90
6	66	102
7	74	112
8	80	120
9	85	120
10	91	130
11	99	132
12	110	132

Find the profit maximizing output.

Find the effect on price and output of a change in local authority rates of £4,000.

Suppose, in the initial situation, the firm is offered £100,000 to produce 5 per week and that any other quantity can then be sold on the open market. Should the firm take the contract? How much would it then sell on the open market at what price?

Appendix VII

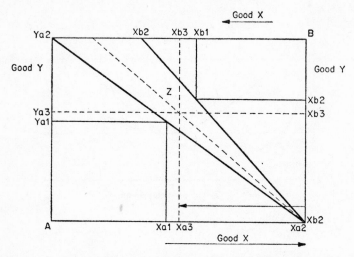

Before trade: A and B both produce X and Y and consume Ya1 + Xa1 and Yb1 and Xb1

After trade: with A only producing X and B only producing Y they exchange to the advantageous positions Xa3 and Ya3 and Xb3 and Yb3

Appendix VIII

A company produces 200,000 suits a year for wholesalers in 9 months each year with January–March 90% idle during which maintenance, etc., is carried out. The company is offered a contract to produce 50,000 suits, to be delivered in the first two weeks of April if the price is less than £30.

The internal decision is to refuse because—

Labour	£14·00
Material	13·50
Depreciation	1·48
Overheads	2·13
Administration	1·15
Repairs, etc.	1·92
Total cost per suit	£34·18
10% mark-up	3·42
	£37·60

A consultant advises	
Direct labour	£11·90
Material	12·90
Spoilage	00·60
Total direct costs	£25·40
Indirect labour	3·00
General factory	2·20
Depreciation	1·80
Repairs, supplies, admin.	2·68
	£35·08

Also overtime would be necessary at 20% of direct labour, extra supplies necessary from a new supplier who refused usual 2% discount. The consultant fee was £2,000.

(*a*) Should the company sue the consultant?
(*b*) Should the company take the contract?
(*c*) In what circumstances would you reverse your decision on (*b*)?

12: The Effect of Recent Developments in Sixth Forms on the Relationship between Economics and Other Subjects

VIVIAN ANTHONY

In the past decade or so there have been developments in the sixth forms of most schools which have had significant effects on the teaching of economics and on the relationship of this subject with other subjects being taught at this level. The forces responsible for these developments are in many cases still with us and the process of evolving relationships is therefore a continuing one. Before examining in detail the relationship between economics and other subjects in the sixth form it would be helpful to analyse some of these forces.

The place of economics in the sixth form curriculum at the outset of the 1960s was generally much more rigidly determined than it is today. In most schools it had grown up as an offshoot of the History or Geography department, and it was unusual to find a candidate offering Economics at 'A' level who did not partner it with one of these subjects. The teachers of the subject were still, all too often, regarding this activity as subsidiary to their main subject. The aspirant to a University Economics Course was commonly advised that it would be better not to do the subject at 'A' level. With the sixth form organized in 'Sides', the scientists were all offering their Physics, Chemistry and Biology or Mathematics Combination, the specialist mathematicians their 'Double Maths' and Physics, the linguists their French, German and English, and Economics was placed firmly on the modern side with History and Geography. In a few enlightened schools it was possible to cross 'the iron curtain' but the ire of the man doing the timetable was a known hazard.

The developments which have revolutionized the situation during the last decade are not easily disentangled. A huge growth in numbers staying on into the sixth form (the numbers of 'A' level candidates more than doubled between 1959 and 1967), making possible a larger number of sets in each subject, coincided with a gradual change in the philosophy underlying the curriculum. The need for a bridge between 'the two cultures' was being preached.[1] A plea for the literate scientist and the numerate arts man appeared in the report of a Royal Commission,[2] while the newer universities were designing courses which combined subjects of different disciplines.[3] Schools responded by first modifying and then scrapping the rigid frame-work of 'Sides'. The 'grid' system, which had been the tool of the enlightened few, became the standard pattern of organization in all but the very small sixth forms. This system enables the student to choose one subject from each of the three or more columns offered. The way was opened for hitherto impossible combinations. This is not the place to debate whether or not the loss of the old-style, coherent, tightly integrated combination, and the danger of ill-chosen largely unrelated subjects outweighs the gain of the sensible new-style combination of subjects from different disciplines. Suffice it to say that the new system has liberated economics from the strait-jacket binding it only with modern arts subjects. Its role as a useful bridge between arts and science subjects came to be widely recognized, and the resulting growth of the subject was phenomenal. In 1959, the number of candidates for 'A' level Economics was less than 4,000, and by 1970 this number had grown to more than 25,000. The growth in the combined areas of Economics, Economic History and British Constitution in this period was such (364% in 1960–70) that their total of 'A' level passes exceeded the totals from History and Geography (growth rates 109% and 187% respectively in the same period).[4] How the position has changed since the fledgling subject was nurtured by teachers from established modern subjects! No wonder some historians and geographers believed they had a cuckoo in the nest.

Pressures for greater flexibility of subject combinations in the sixth form have emanated not only from the universities and the educational theorists but from employers, parents and the students themselves. Many sixth-formers have no clear idea of their career objective when they begin their course, and they wish to keep open as many options as possible. Economics appears to many, falsely perhaps, as the key to a wide range of job opportunities. So in choosing their subject combinations, many students are anxious not to limit their job opportunities, and parents are a powerful reinforcing factor in this.

We have spoken of the growth of numbers staying on into the sixth form, but this is not the only reason for sixth forms becoming larger in the last decade. The spreading of the comprehensive principle in the organization of secondary education has meant that schools have been amalgamated and units of 1,000 plus have become the norm. The grammar school of 500 pupils with 100 or so in the sixth form has been replaced, where reorganization has taken place, by the comprehensive school with 200 or more in the sixth form. It is true that the expansion of further education, and the widespread provision of 'A' level and courses of a similar standard in colleges, has provided the student with an attractive alternative in many localities, but this has not prevented a considerable growth in the size of sixth forms. However, the existence of highly flexible alternative arrangements in colleges has been yet another pressure on schools to reorganize their curriculum.

A good deal of verbiage is being produced on the emergence of the 'new sixth-former', who is less academically orientated than his colleagues returning for the 'A' level course. Even before R.O.S.L.A. there had been a great increase in those voluntarily continuing their education, and comprehensive schools, in particular, are developing courses to meet the needs of these students. These courses will have to be at a lower academic level, more career-orientated and less formally structured than the traditional 'A' level course. Economics will no doubt come to play a valuable part in such courses, and the relationship between subjects in the curriculum for the 'new sixth-former' will be of a different kind from that between traditional 'A' level subjects because of the differences in objectives and academic standards.

We are still being treated to the fiction that examinations are the servants of those who plan the curriculum and that they follow changes in the teaching of subjects in schools rather than producing the changes. There is not much doubt in my mind that they are a powerful influence for change in schools and that this fact is well recognized by the theorists and administrators who wish to bring about the change. Nowhere was this more obvious than in the 'Q & F' level debate. There is a strong body of educational opinion which believes that the present system of three 'A' level subjects is too highly specialized and not productive of a good general education. They want to see the present trend, which allows greater choice of subjects and a mixture of disciplines, taken further and an element of compulsion introduced to achieve a balance of science and arts subjects. They complain that as things stand some students will choose three closely related subjects, and point to the limited nature of such a combination as Economics, Economic History and British Constitution. The proposal was to institute at the end of the first year in the sixth form a 'Q' (Qualifying) level examination in five subjects, the study of which would have occupied about five-sevenths of the week, the remainder being devoted to unexamined subjects. The choice of subjects was to be guided to produce a 'well-rounded person' with a 'wide variety of skills'. To this end a choice from groups of subjects was suggested which, with the minimum of bridging between arts and sciences, would have involved a predominantly arts student (for example) in taking at least one science (or mathematics). The Schools Council Working Party making the proposals[5] wanted no bypassing of the 'Q' levels, which suggests that they saw the examination system as a vital factor in bringing about the reform. The implication of the proposals for Economics teaching was discussed by R. H. Ryba in *Economics*.[6]

It would, however, be wrong to suggest that proposals for 'liberalizing' the sixth form curriculum come only from Schools Council Committees and its working parties, or that, because the Q & F proposals have been shelved, we shall hear no more of the need for a curriculum covering a wider range of disciplines. Nor, as teachers of a subject which has a valuable bridging role, should we necessarily be opposed to such proposals. The International Baccalaureate, for so long canvassed by A. D. C. Peterson, has a similar wide base of subjects including both arts and sciences.[7] The first economics papers for this examination appeared five or so years ago. Furthermore it is hardly likely that our entry into the Common Market will bring about a diminution in the demand for a qualification based on a broad pattern of education and acceptable all over Europe. And is this the only implication which entry into Europe will have for the teaching of economics?

The actual methods of examination in economics and other subjects have been subjected to a rigorous 'grilling' in recent years and as a result significant changes have been made, or are about to be made. It became clear that the process of testing candidates purely by means of essay questions was too limited in its scope. While it provided a good deal of information about certain of the candidates' abilities in the subject, e.g. the ability to write creatively, to develop a line of thought or to present the two sides of an argument, there were other important abilities which were not being suitably tested.[8] Moreover grave doubts have frequently been expressed about the reliability of the marking of the papers. The 'A' level Boards have therefore decided to supplement the essay questions with questions of a more objective nature designed to test a wider range of abilities and knowledge. Some Boards have gone to a great deal of trouble to set out clearly the objectives of their syllabus and examinations and the methods by which they will attempt to achieve them. The J.M.B. Syllabus 1974[9] is worthy of attention for this reason. For most Boards the questions which supplement the essay type will be of the multiple-choice variety. The J.M.B. also intend to set a single question (one-hour paper) designed to test comprehension of economics including the interpretation of quantitative data. These changes in the nature of examination papers are already having their effects on the work in the classrooms. Some emphasis is going from the literary aspects of the subject to a more careful consideration of the analytical and logical aspects. More teachers are turning to a more mathematical treatment in some areas of the subject albeit at a very simple level. It is not every teacher who welcomes these changes and the backlash against the inadequacies of objective testing is already being felt.

The relationship between economics and other subjects in the sixth form is also being affected by the introduction of subjects not previously taught in schools. Still in the early stages of development is the Business Studies 'A' level Project, which Richard Barker has described elsewhere in this volume.[10] Perhaps one factor in the development of this course has been the argument that economics has no direct vocational relevance to business, and the demand from students that such courses should be available. Economists have emphasized the intellectual rigour of their subject in the sixth form and have tended to play down the vocational role. There are a number of ways in which Economics and Business Studies impinge on each other. In the first place they share in part a common syllabus. The parts of economics which relate to business appear in the Business Studies Syllabus, e.g. profit maximization, monopoly and competition, price theory. Secondly, students have to make a choice between the two subjects at 'A' level: the Cambridge Board will not allow both subjects to be offered at the same sitting. In this sense the subjects will be in competition for candidates and the growth of Business Studies in a school could well be accompanied by a fall in the numbers doing Economics. Thirdly, the subjects are likely to be grouped together in one department and will often be taught by the same person. It is to be hoped that economists will be given reasonable training before they are asked to take on the many aspects of Business Studies which lie outside the normal Economics syllabus. If the Business Studies course is to offer a significantly different approach from that of Economics, and particularly if it is to be that of vocational relevance, then this training of its teachers should surely include some experience in business itself.

Sociology is another subject which is new to the sixth form curriculum. No doubt the thousands of graduates emerging from universities with degrees in this subject will be grateful for the opportunities of employment in schools. There has in fact been a rapid growth of the subject at 'A' level, although the total numbers are still relatively small. The implications for economics of the growth of this subject depend partly on whether it is regarded as a competitor or a complement. Although it has considerable differences in the subject areas covered by its syllabus, the methods of approach inculcated by the subject are similar to those of economics. This raises problems of narrowness of specialization, if the three 'A' level subjects provide the student with a narrow range of academic tools. As a firm believer in the value of economics as a sixth form discipline, one can be excused for regretting the introduction of sociology as a competitor for potential economics students. I doubt if one can also be excused for arguing that a good understanding of sociology requires an experience of the world that no sixth-former could possibly have gained, for this sort of comment was being made of economics for sixth-formers not so many years ago.[11]

The relationship between economics and other subjects was one of the themes taken up recently by Keith Robinson in an article in *Economics*.[12] In discussing 'Economics and the Raising of the School Leaving Age', the argument was put forward that 'such students should be prepared for life in society in a broader sense when they are unlikely to take up the subject as an academic study at a later stage'. More significantly perhaps, he went on to say that 'Economics should be related to other social sciences so that meaningful courses of an interdisciplinary kind can be devised in relation to those issues and problems with which potential school leavers will be soon confronted.' This theme is obviously directly related to one of the popular gospels of the Schools Council, namely 'Integration'. We must look forward, we are told, to a time when the defined boundaries of subjects will become increasingly blurred. Students will be asked to tackle a particular question with the tools of the economist, geographer and historian all part of his integrated awareness. It will increase the ability of the students to follow their own learning paths. It will no doubt be a good thing if students are taught to appreciate how all the different aspects of a problem interrelate, with an awareness which would not be possible as long as a particular approach remained the sole property of a particular subject. This will facilitate the study of human issues of great complexity and breadth. However, we would be deluding ourselves if we thought that a course which ranged over the combined areas of Economics, Geography and History would cover the same ground in total that the separate subjects previously achieved. The advocates of the integrated approach would in any case not want this. It must be stressed however that this approach brings with it its own limitations. On the other hand, economists must be aware of the important role the subject can play in integrated studies within the humanities or the narrower field of the Social Sciences. It is disturbing to see what a small part Economics plays in Project Technology,[13] in Environmental Studies Courses (usually dominated by geographers) and in the Integrated Studies so far prepared by David Bolam and his Schools' Council team,[14] though it must be said that this is aimed below the sixth form. The Humanities Curriculum Project,[15] on the other hand, includes material for the 16 + group, and it anticipates 'radical changes in the organization of the school and in the attitudes of teachers to students'. It aims to meet the problems of giving 'every man some access to a complex cultural inheritance, some hold on his personal life and on his relationships with the various communities to which he belongs, some extension of his understanding of, and sensitivity towards, other human beings'. Materials published will cover such topics as war, education, the family, poverty, and people and work. Radical changes will result from the need to develop a teaching strategy which meets the specification outlined above and the need for self-training of teachers. So says Lawrence Stenhouse, Director of the Humanities Project.[16] You may or may not agree with the argument. We must, however, be aware of the changes and developments which are occurring in our sixth forms, and see to it that the position of economics in the changing situation is not an accident but a carefully thought-out role. There are many economics teachers who are not altogether happy that such integrated projects as have been mentioned above stem from the work of the Social Studies Subject Committee of the Schools Council. There is no separate subject committee for economics, which therefore takes its place along with all the other social sciences. The concern of economics teachers is that the Subject Committee seems to be dominated by sociologists and that any project that does not harmonize with the gospel of integration has little chance of survival. Attempts to improve the representation of economics on the Committee have met with very limited success.

While we must be jealous for the role which we believe economics should play in the sixth form, it would be ridiculous to pretend that we have a monopoly of educational virtues. We must remain alert for the improvements which can be introduced into the teaching of our subject from other subject areas. A good deal of use is being made elsewhere of a multi-media approach to teaching. In the Schools Council Projects—Technology, Humanities and Integrated Studies—much emphasis has been placed on the use of visual materials and audio methods to supplement the written word. Much of the work is pupil-controlled with the teacher in a guidance role. Some economists have begun to make use of this approach, but the Manchester Economics Project,[17] which is perhaps the first attempt at a multi-media approach by British economics teachers, is much more limited in its use of media than the projects mentioned. David Christie has written elsewhere in this volume[18] of an economics teaching project in Scotland which makes use of a wider variety of media. American economics teachers have been writing of their efforts at the multimedia approach to teaching for some years past. We have also begun to learn from geographers and biologists the value of field trips, and Brian Robinson, in a series of articles in *Economics*,[19] has been showing how experience from the field study brings economics alive for the student by contact with the real world of the subject and how 'it enables the student himself to make some tests of economic theories and policies'. No one will deny that there is much more to be learned from other disciplines. How long will it be for example before 'A' level economics students are encouraged to offer a major written study or project as part of their final assessment—a practice already well known in other subjects? And could it be that economics has something to offer other subjects in the use we have begun to make of case studies as a means of teaching the principles of the subject? By real-world case studies, not the neatly rounded hypothetical cases, the student is led to 'understand the limitations as well as the power of economic logic and measurement', wrote Keith Drake of the case studies of Sandford, Bradbury and Associates.[20]

There is undoubtedly a new spirit abroad in the world of economics teachers and this spirit is much more self-critical and self-analytical than anything that has been known before. Various studies have been set up to see how teaching can be improved. The Economics Association has been playing its part in this and the Research Committee has begun to compile a register of research. The Economics Education Project is perhaps the largest single venture, set up by Lumsden and Attiyeh from the United States and financed by a grant to Heriot-Watt University from the Esmée Fairbairn Charitable Trust. Lumsden describes the Project[21] as an attempt 'to provide a profile of current teaching, studying and testing practices and to assess in quantitative terms the importance of different factors in the learning process'. Some of the early findings of the Project throw some light on the relationship between economics and other subjects in the sixth form. It was suggested that some subjects studied with economics appear to help the candidates' performance in the Project's 'Test of Economics Comprehension' more than others. Most helpful of all the subjects was 'A' level Economic History, while 'A' level

Mathematics and 'A' level General Studies also had a significant positive effect on performance. An 'A' level in History was said to have little positive effect, while the preliminary findings suggested that an 'A' level in Geography had a significant negative effect. The reader will no doubt think it strange that to do an 'A' level Geography course would actually reduce one's chance of performing well in a test of Economics Comprehension. However, Alexander Scott[22] has warned us that the Economics Education Project is a long way from solving the numerous problems associated with such research and the above findings should be regarded as highly speculative. Even so, several possible explanations can be offered for the apparently poor performance of the 'Geographer-Economists'. This combination is in fact frequently chosen by those who are among the weaker academically in the sixth form. Even where there is common material, differences of approach employed by geography teachers compared with that used by economics teachers may be as much a source of confusion as it is a means of reinforcement, particularly for the weaker pupils. It remains however an important question to ask, i.e. does a student's performance in economics depend to some extent on the other subjects he combines with it? The E.E.P. will be attempting to check out these preliminary findings in the second phase of the Project which is just beginning.

The External Relations Committee of the Economics Association has been discussing this important matter of the relationship between economics and other subjects in the sixth form with other interested subject associations. Two Joint Working Parties sat through most of the academic year 1971–2. The first consisted of the Mathematical Association, the Royal Economics Society and the Economics Association, with the Business Studies Project represented at one of the meetings; and the second consisted of the Economic History Society and the Economics Association.

The relationship between economics and mathematics in the sixth form is probably, at this time, the most important single issue facing economics teachers who aim at laying firm foundations for the more advanced study of their subject in higher education. The problem has recently been given an airing by Scott, Chalmers and Hill, all members of the School of Social Sciences at Sussex University, in an article in the *Times Higher Education Supplement*.[23] They say that nowhere are the difficulties of those inadequately prepared in mathematics more evident than in the case of social science students who are 'launched on courses which have elements sometimes heavily dependent on quantitative expertise. That they fail to get full benefit from these courses is as much the fault of the system which brings them there as it is of the undergraduate himself.' This mathematical inadequacy could of course be regarded as the responsibility of the universities, pure and simple, and indeed many universities have come to offer remedial courses in an attempt to rectify the situation. But this seems a less satisfactory solution than one in which the students are wherever possible well prepared in the sixth form for the courses they will follow at university. For most intending economics specialists a course in 'A' level Mathematics would seem to be highly desirable. The fact that we can all quote examples of our students who have successfully completed an economics degree course without this mathematics qualification does not cause me to modify this statement. Furthermore, we must remember the economists who have chosen the subject for its apparent relevance to the occupation they will take up immediately upon leaving school. Whether it is the civil service, insurance, banking or whatever, likely as not a good grounding in mathematics will be a valuable asset. These students are not however the main concern at this point, which is the mathematical training for potential university economists. There can be little doubt that both the theoretical and analytical elements of economics courses at university involve a mathematical treatment of ideas, while a knowledge and understanding of statistical techniques and theory is often essential for more empirical work. Many of the new developments in the subject are on the mathematical frontiers, which makes it essential for the intending researcher to be mathematically well equipped.

While Scott, Chalmers and Hill have initiated a project, financed by the S.S.R.C., 'to investigate the characteristics of university social science students and to develop retrieval mathematics programmes designed to bring students up to a fitting standard', the Economics/Mathematics Working Party concentrated on the provision of a suitable course at 'A' level. The findings of a conference of university teachers which debated 'the complex issues involved in the teaching of statistics to social science students' will appear in the *International Journal of Mathematical*

Education in Science and Technology,[24] and the report of the Working Party will appear in the *Journal of the Mathematical Association* and in the *Journal of the Economics Association*, early in 1973.

If we accept the thesis that mathematics should be taught in the sixth form to all potential university economists the vital question which must then be asked is: 'what mathematics should be taught?' or perhaps more pertinently, 'are the mathematics courses traditionally provided in schools suitable for students going on to read economics at university?' The *T.H.E.S.* article was concerned primarily with simple 'numeracy', 'such low-level skills as multiplication of decimal fractions, the reading of scales and graphs, and the use of algebra as generalized arithmetic', so it is not so much the 'A' level course which it calls in question but the lack of suitable courses for the non-'A' level Mathematics student doing economics. The Economics/Mathematics Working Party reached a number of conclusions after discussing this question at several meetings, after considering the replies from university social science departments to this question, and after looking at 'A' level syllabuses and examination papers. Traditional 'A' level Mathematics courses have been based on a combination of Pure and Applied topics. There have been double Mathematics courses with Pure and Applied Mathematics counting as two separate subjects, and there have been single Mathematics courses with one paper each of Pure and Applied. The syllabuses for these courses have been developed largely to meet the needs of the natural scientist and, while they provide an opportunity to practise various mathematical techniques and give a good insight into the problems of mechanics, there has been no attempt in these syllabuses to meet the special needs of the social scientist. The 'A' level Mathematics with Statistics syllabus has grown up partly to meet these needs, but here it is the absence of certain of the mathematical techniques used in economics which is the problem. Obviously, the syllabus must not only meet the future needs of the economics student but also satisfy the mathematicians. The Sussex group have described a similar problem in university remedial courses when they talk of 'a compromise package' in which 'the demand for rigour and technical competence made by the statistician or mathematician is balanced against the need to make material relevant to the social sciences at an introductory level'.

Designing any syllabus is, of course, a question of what should be put in and what left out. It would be difficult to design a mathematics paper consisting entirely of assumptions and laws that relate to economics and still containing a satisfactory mathematics content, and if this could be achieved only by gross simplification of concepts, it would be of questionable value. The solution, which seems to have most to commend it, is one in which there is some modification of the traditional syllabus, leaving out some of those concepts which are more useful to the natural scientists and including some which are needed by the social scientists, and a recognition of the interest of the students by the type of question set. Such a solution depends on a clear identification of the mathematical skills required by economists which are not adequately catered for in existing syllabuses. Among the topics identified for this purpose were basic calculus, mathematical statistics, significance tests, difference equations, graph theory and functions of more than one variable, some of which are already included in 'A' level syllabuses. To make way for the inclusion of these topics there could be some paring of the trigonometry and co-ordinate geometry content. Kinematics, mechanics and electricity could also be omitted. Naturally it is much easier to modify the double Mathematics syllabus without leaving out skills which the mathematicians consider important. Various attempts have been made to design a syllabus to meet the needs of the social scientist but the Working Party found that of existing syllabuses M.E.I. (Mathematics for Education and Industry)[25] and S.M.P. (School Mathematics Project)[26] were the most appropriate.

The Joint Economics/Mathematics Working Party has been concerned with the counsel of perfection, i.e. 'In a combination of "A" level subjects which includes both economics and mathematics, what mathematics should be taught which will enable the student to make the most of his university economics course?' The Sussex group are concerned with the more fundamental question of 'how do we ensure that the economics student has the basic minimum numeracy to derive some benefit from his university course?' There are still those who deplore the limitations beginning to be imposed on the teaching of economics in the sixth form by the demand for a good mathematical background. There are many sixth-formers who are convinced that by 'O' level, or even before it, they have reached their mathematics ceiling. This number is likely to increase as more students stay on into the sixth form. The conflicting needs of 'The new sixth-former' described earlier and those of the potential university economist become only too apparent.

The other sixth form subjects with which Economics inevitably has a close relationship are Economic History and British Constitution. The latter is usually grouped with Economics in the same Department, and, as many Economics teachers have done some British Constitution as part of their degree, both subjects are often taught by the same person. F. W. G. Benemy, in his letter to *Economics*,[27] suggested that many economic ideas can be introduced by means of British Constitution, and that the subjects are good running mates for the purpose of giving the 'new sixth-formers' a course of relevance to their life after school days are over. A good understanding of the workings of political institutions is an important prerequisite for an appreciation of the economic policies of the government. We have already raised the question whether or not the combination of Economics and British Constitution, or indeed, Economics and Economic History, in the same 'A' level sitting encourages too narrow a specialization for the sixth form.

The Joint Working Party of the Economic History Society and the Economics Association considered, among other things, how the close relationship between the subjects could be exploited to further common aims. The Report of the Working Party appeared in *Economics* in Autumn, 1973. There is concern among many economics teachers in schools that the growing emphasis being placed on the use of statistical, mathematical and other analytical tools in the teaching of economics, and the increasing use of objective methods in examining the subject, will have a serious and detrimental effect on the knowledge and understanding of the historical background, for clearly there is not time to teach all that we should like to teach. 'Historical', in this context, covers all but the last year or two. There are few topics in applied economics which can be properly understood without a good grounding in the developments since World War II, and for some topics—trade unions, balance of payments, industrial location— one would expect to delve back into the last century. The value of case studies for demonstrating economic principles in action has been alluded to earlier. Economic history is, of course, a rich fund of such case studies and has the added advantage of describing real-life experiences. There are lessons to be learned too by the economic historians from economics. A scrutiny of the syllabuses and examination papers of the various Boards leaves one with the impression that very little use of the techniques of the economist were expected: the questions encouraged a descriptive rather than an analytical answer. The coverage of twentieth-century economic history in most papers has been sadly lacking and where it is offered candidates have been reluctant to attempt the questions. The very period which covers the most relevant developments of present-day economic institutions is being largely ignored. Small wonder then that there has been an actual decline in the number of candidates taking the subject at 'A' level, and the pass rate, among the lowest of all subjects (53%—1970), has shown little improvement.

One can sympathize with their objectives, but in some ways it is a pity that the Scottish and Welsh Boards have discontinued the joint Economics–Economic History 'A' level. The Oxford and Cambridge Board still offer such a combination. There is, of course, a greater limit on the amount of either subject that can be included in such a syllabus but it does maintain the important link between the subjects. We have recently heard of plans by the London Board to introduce an alternative Paper 2 which will cover the twentieth century and require rather more economic analysis and statistical interpretation. It is hoped that the paper would be a useful complement for candidates doing economics at 'A' level. Two subjects which share so much must obviously continue to look for ways in which they can be complementary. The Working Party has suggested the preparation of a bibliography of material suitable for the teaching of very recent economic history, including books, articles, novels, tapes and so on. Where there are obvious gaps such material should be commissioned, perhaps in a series similar to that published by Macmillan with the Economic History Society.[28] Joint Conferences could be held at regional and national levels to discuss topics of common interest, and university Departments of Economics and Economic History could be requested to widen the range of facilities offered to school teachers of both subjects to enable them to keep up to date with developments in the subjects.

In such a wide-ranging paper it has been impossible to deal in detail with all the subjects in the sixth form which are offered in combinations with economics. This attempt to show how external and internal developments in sixth forms have affected the relationship between economics and other subjects aimed to emphasize the importance of being well prepared to meet the changing situation in which we find ourselves. We must be willing to discuss with teachers from other subject areas the impact of these developments on subject relationships and to work out how the developments can best be channelled and directed for the benefit of our students.

References

1. Snow, C. P., *The Two Cultures and the Scientific Revolution*, Rede Lecture 1959.
2. *The Crowther Report. 15–18*, H.M.S.O., 1959.
3. *The Prospectus of the University of Sussex*, 1961, and *University Central Council on Admissions (U.C.C.A.) Handbook*, 1961.
4. *Statistics of Education*, Vol. 2, H.M.S.O., 1972.
5. S.C.U.E. and Schools Council Joint Working Party, *Proposals for the Curriculum and Examination in the 6th Form*, 1969, and Briault, E. W. M., *Q & F and all that*, 'Dialogue' Schools Council Newsletter, No. 5.
6. Ryba, R. H., 'Economics Education and the Q and F Proposals', *Economics*, Vol. VIII, Part 5, No. 35, Autumn 1970.
7. See e.g. Peterson, A. D. C., *Arts and Science Sides in the Sixth Forms*, Report to the Gulbenkian Foundation, Oxford and Cambridge Schools Examination Board, 1960.
8. I have developed this theme at some length in the introduction to *Objective Tests in Advanced Level Economics* by V. S. Anthony and D. P. Barron, Heinemann, 1971.
9. *Joint Matriculation Board Regulations and Syllabuses, 1974*, 1972, pp. 49–53.
10. Barker, R. P., 'Lessons from the "A" Level Business Studies Project', Ch. 14, pp. 179–95 of this volume.
11. Szreter, R., 'Attitudes to Economics for Secondary Schools, 1918–45', *Economics*, Vol. VI, Part 2, No. 22, Autumn 1965.
12. Robinson, T. K., 'Extending the Contribution of Economics to the Curriculum', *Economics*, Vol. IX, Part 2, Autumn 1972.
13. Schools Council, Schools Science and Technology Committee, *Project Technology*. See Report of Working Party 18, *Technology and the Schools*.
14. *Exploration Man*, Schools Council Integrated Studies, O.U.P., 1972.
15. Schools Council and Nuffield Foundation, *Humanities Curriculum Project Material*, Heinemann, 1970.
16. Stenhouse, L., *Pupils into Students*, 'Dialogue' Schools Council Newsletter, No. 5.

17. Manchester Economics Project, *Understanding Economics*, with Satellite texts, Ginn, 1972.
18. Christie, D., 'Economics in the Early Stages of the Secondary School', Ch. 8, pp. 105–17 of this volume.
19. See e.g. Day, M. and Robinson, B. R. G., 'Combined Schools Field Studies in Economics—Organisation and New Techniques', *Economics*, Vol. IX, Part 2, No. 38, Autumn 1971.
20. Drake, K. B., [book review of] *Case Studies in Economics: Principles of Economics*, by C. T. Sandford, M. S. Bradbury and Associates, *Economics*, Vol. IX, Part 2, No. 38, Autumn 1971.
21. Lumsden, K. G., 'Economics Education Project—Report on Preliminary University Study', *Economics*, Vol. VIII, Part 5, No. 35, Autumn 1970.
22. Scott, A. 'Research into Economic Efficiency in the Teaching of Economics: Some Fundamental Problems', Ch. 4, pp. 65–74 of this volume.
23. Scott, J. F., Chalmers, A. D. and Hill, B., 'Remedial Mathematics for Social Scientists', *The Times Higher Education Supplement*, 24 November 1972.
24. Scott, J. F., Chalmers, A. D. and Hill, B., *International Journal of Mathematical Education in Science and Technology*, Vol. V, No. 1, 1973.
25. *Mathematics in Education and Industry Project*, Oxford and Cambridge Schools Examination Board.
26. *The School Mathematics Project*, Westfield College, London.
27. Benemy, F. W. G., *Economics*, Vol. VIII, Part 3, No. 33, Winter 1969–70.
28. Flinn, M. W. (ed.), *Studies in Economic History* (started in 1968), published by Macmillan in association with the Economic History Society.

13: An Approach to the Teaching of Economics in Schools

ROY WILKINSON

Introduction

It is perhaps audacious (or foolhardy) to offer comments on the scope for and purpose of economics teaching in schools without having had any first-hand experience. My qualifications to express a view come from my experience as a university teacher and as an 'A' level examiner. In the latter capacity I have been heavily involved during the last two or three years with the revision of the J.M.B. 'A' level syllabus and examination system and have, therefore, been forced to think about the fundamental objectives of each.

The Problems

There have been noticeable changes in the last decade in the attitude to the teaching of economics in schools, both inside and outside the schools. Apart from the rapid growth of the subject at sixth form level and its increasing acceptance by schools as a normal part of the curriculum, it is true to say that from the point of view of university teaching, the possession of a good 'A' level in economics a few years ago was by no means regarded as an advantage; by some it was regarded as a positive disadvantage. This is much less true today and some first-year courses have been adapted to take account of the fact that many students have a substantial grasp of parts of the subject. Partly as a consequence of these changes, the problems of economics teaching have become more sharply defined.

One of the basic problems which teachers have been aware of at all levels is that in addition to the grasp of sometimes fairly complicated models, an element of judgment is required in applying these models to concrete problems. When I first began examining 'A' level economics, the general level of competence in dealing with the analytical parts of the subject was very low, and I was led to the view, by analogy with other subjects, that whatever the degree of maturity which might be required, there was no reason why some basic principles could not be taught successfully, albeit in a fairly mechanical way. Therefore, in drafting examination papers, I began to set questions parts of which demanded a precise knowledge of quantifiable concepts such as elasticity, the multiplier, comparative cost and definitions of income. At first these questions were avoided or done badly: it was clear that many students could memorize definitions of concepts without understanding how they were to be applied. A learning process has taken place over the years, however, which has resulted in such questions becoming popular with the arithmetic parts especially being done well. This has tended to highlight the inability of many candidates to interpret numerical concepts; the weaker merely manage the calculations and show no real appreciation of the meaning of what they have done. It seems that although fairly sophisticated ideas can be taught to and assimilated by sixth-formers, it is equally clear that understanding remains fairly superficial. The examination papers show evidence of a good deal of 'drilling' in parts of the subject and whilst a certain amount of this may be regarded as inevitable, there is a danger that it will get in the way of understanding and inhibit real education.

Another aspect of weakness in the understanding and application of principles is apparent in the approach of examinees to 'applied' or 'descriptive' questions. In general the technique has been to submerge the examiner with facts in a fairly undisciplined and often stereotyped manner. I regard this as a consequence (and illustration) of a further difficulty of learning and teaching economics, viz. the achievement of a 'fusion' of description and analysis. The application of even the simplest economic theory (particularly static theory) is not easy and it is not made easier by the tendency to teach 'principles' and 'applied economics' more or less in isolation from one another. Good applied or descriptive economics arises out of 'theory' in that factual information is collected, ordered and evaluated not haphazardly but on certain well-founded principles.

Consequently, in order to make 'applied' questions more precise and also to test the ability to sift and appraise evidence and apply concepts, questions have been set in recent years which have been based on numerical data. Whilst these questions are becoming more popular, one is aware (as with conventional essays) that some candidates merely use the data as a convenient peg on which to hang their accumulated knowledge of a subject. They either lack the confidence to bring their minds to bear and to apply their knowledge, or they lack the imagination and flair to deal with the problem, or both. This is disappointing, because not only is it true to say that such problems are what economics is really about, but also it seems to me that the purpose of study is lost if the student does not have the confidence or the insight to apply his knowledge. I think that these attributes can be taught to the average pupil in much the same way that the ability to calculate an elasticity coefficient can be taught. To do so, however, calls for a different emphasis in school teaching, and a more explicit consideration of what the subject is about and what the purpose is in teaching it. My own experience suggests that if students are encouraged to look at real economic problems (however naïvely and superficially) their motivation and interest become enhanced and they tend to develop greater (and more soundly based) confidence in handling ideas and evidence. I am not claiming that we can teach the maturity required to make judgments in economics but that by changing the *emphasis* of the teaching, pupils can be encouraged to think for themselves on real issues and thereby be given the chance to develop a more mature approach to the subject.

A Problem-Oriented Approach

It has frequently been suggested (with a good deal of truth) that public examinations impose heavy constraints on teachers and that they have a stultifying effect on the education process. (It is significant, but not surprising, that the conventional distinctions of advancement in most subjects are made in terms of the short-hand of public examinations.) Examinations tend to be regarded by candidates and teachers as assault courses constructed by malevolent men whose purpose it is to trap the unwary candidate. Armies of candidates are trained and drilled each year in how to overcome the obstacle and outwit the examiner (usually by predicting questions and learning by rote volumes of facts and theories). Not unnaturally a tension exists between the examiners, the examined and their teachers. This is partly a result of the secrecy which surrounds all public examinations, and undoubtedly an improvement of the flow of information to and from the examiners might help to bring about some improvement. It would be salutary for examiners (and teachers) to consider and make explicit the purpose of examinations, and perhaps to be allowed to write more detailed reports indicating how questions are assessed.

Although the system of examining is important, it is not the sole cause of these problems nor the sole means of dealing with them. It seems to me that a change in the attitude of examiners and in the system of examining can only have a beneficial influence if there is simultaneously a change in the approach to the teaching of the subject in schools. The purpose of teaching economics to schoolchildren might usefully concentrate on developing an awareness and way of thinking about current problems at local, national and international levels rather than simply trying to communicate a body of knowledge which may be more or less unrelated to their experience. Thus emphasis would be given to thinking about problems, looking for the evidence of the operation of economic forces and generally developing an appreciation of how an economist goes about his work. Many, perhaps most teachers, for example find the examination syllabus a major constraint on what goes on in the classroom. It is interpreted by some as a definitive statement of the subject which must be followed strictly to the letter rather than as an indication of the scope and analytical level of the examinations.

The main pedagogic argument for starting from a realistic problem is that for many people a concrete problem is easier to think about, that it draws attention to the relevance of the theoretical apparatus and scientific method and simultaneously may illustrate how theories are developed as well as used. In addition, however, problems can be selected which are within the pupils' experience and ability. One of the main difficulties in teaching is that of making the student aware of the problem which individual theories have been developed to deal with. The development of an awareness of problems can in principle begin at any stage and could well be integrated in the general curriculum at the primary school stage. This is not to suggest that any form of specialization is desirable but simply that this aspect of the study of society can in principle be started as soon as social awareness begins to develop and as part of the process of developing social awareness. The purpose would be simply to draw attention to the existence of questions and the body of knowledge about them. This approach would be constrained by the age and experience of the pupil but this applies to any subject area (e.g. the natural sciences) and the approach which is increasingly adopted is first to stimulate the interest and awareness of the pupil. In the socio-economic field children become aware at a relatively early stage of, for example, differences in social backgrounds, their parents' jobs, housing, shops, traffic, and other environmental factors in localities. These are all potential areas of stimulation which could be developed in a methodical way to provide the basis for (further) study. By the middle-school years an enhanced awareness of the problems and the kind of information relevant to their solution would undoubtedly provide a sounder basis on which to build more advanced studies. It is conceivable that in the early years especially, careful integration into the general curriculum might have 'external' benefits (e.g. on the teaching of arithmetic, geography and history) and thus prove to be generally beneficial. It is necessary to emphasize the importance of the approach however; one is aware that 'Social Studies' appears in school curricula, but this is often simply a mixture of traditional history and geography.

The principle of developing an awareness from the pupils' experience would seem to be generally applicable at any stage. For the older student, the study can be widened to encompass the systematic collection and categorization of information, the development of theoretical principles and the construction of hypotheses and simple models. From any given starting point in the pupil's career we can recognize two kinds of progression: (1) a widening of the awareness of the number of questions; and (2) a deepening of the scientific search for answers (which means a greater emphasis on analysis). Thus more advanced courses are characterized by greater breadth and depth. The objective and criterion of success is that the pupil should understand something of the workings of an economy, appreciate what economic questions are and how an economist thinks, and be able to take an intelligent interest in 'the news' or current affairs as reported on television, radio and in the newspapers. This means that pupils should be expected to know something about the social and economic framework of the British economy, that they should be aware of the main problems confronting it and should have developed a way of thinking about and analysing these problems. For those not wishing to take the subject further it is important that they should have acquired knowledge which is relevant to their future activities, and I would claim that this kind of knowledge (which includes the ability to look critically at information and its relevance to certain questions) satisfies this requirement. For those who wish to study further, this kind of approach will not hamper or limit their progress but rather provide a sounder basis for it.

Conclusions

In concrete terms this means that in order to look at the theory of markets it is first necessary to acquire some knowledge of what markets are and how they operate. This knowledge needs to be developed on the basis of the pupil's own experience. Similarly, to understand the theory of consumer behaviour necessitates observing how consumers behave. To understand the theory of competition it is necessary to know something about the firms in the economy. All this information needs to be acquired (cf. passively absorbed) by the pupil, and to do this it is necessary to develop the distinction between fact and opinion, relevance and irrelevance, validity and truth.

This, then, involves a complete reversal of the view (widely held at all levels) of economic theory as a body of doctrine to be digested and interpreted in much the same way as the Law. It suggests that a student is likely to learn more about industrial problems and behaviour by examining the existing structure of industry and by trying to analyse and simplify the competitive set-up in a specific market than, for example, by starting in an abstract situation created by making a lot of 'simplifying' assumptions to understand the behaviour of firms under perfect competition.

Most of the propositions and arguments I have advanced lie between what in the field of economics might be described as 'armchair theorizing' and 'casual empiricism'. There are doubtless many who would class my (implicit) assumptions on the ability of students and (perhaps more justifiably) of teachers as overoptimistic. Whether or not this is justified can only be decided by analysing carefully gathered evidence, and I hope that it will be possible in the future to test some of the views advanced here. To my mind, this kind of approach to the teaching of economics widens the teacher's scope and is not only more scientific but it is likely to demand less from pupils by way of memorizing difficult pieces of economic theory, the value and relevance of which they are in no position to begin to appreciate.

VII: A CURRICULUM INNOVATION: THE BUSINESS STUDIES PROJECT

14: Lessons from the 'A' Level Business Studies Project

RICHARD BARKER

This paper will be divided into three major parts. Firstly, it will consider the background to the Project and the main stages of its development. Secondly, it will look at the objectives and methods used in 'A' level Business Studies and its supporting Project. Lastly, it will highlight some of our major findings to date. This is an extremely wide area of coverage for a short paper. Of necessity, issues are tackled in outline and only general interim findings are given. However, I hope that you will be able to grasp the fundamentals of the Project and make some judgment on its progress and possibilities.

Stages of the Project's Development

The 'A' level began in September 1967. It is useful to examine the feelings and events of that period for these were influential in the birth and structure of the new subject. It was a time when some flexibility was creeping into sixth form curriculum (syllabuses, materials and examinations) whilst there was considerable talk about the advantages of broader, interdisciplinary, courses. Relevancy was an over-used phrase, but many students were showing their own desire for this through the patterns of their subject options. Businessmen and educationalists continued, at least in discussion, to see the need for greater links at sixth form level, whilst in management education our two major Business Schools arose, along with a wider acceptance that there was business material which could usefully be taught. Even the nature of the business material suddenly became a topic of great interest and clearly defined areas were emerging.

Around our own subject area, 'A' level Economics was growing apace and suggested the possibility of developing educational courses even more closely affiliated to subsequent pursuits. Some sixth forms were also offering Law and Accounting 'A' levels, usually to their less-able students, as vocational courses, whilst across the fence there was the O.N.C./H.N.C. in Business Studies made up from a series of isolated functional disciplines. Lastly, sixth form General Studies was being introduced with some emphasis being placed on an understanding of business behaviour.

It was in this environment that John Dancy (then Master of Marlborough College) started to explore the possibilities of building an extended sixth form course to explain something of business behaviour. He envisaged the possible educational advantages of such a programme and felt that the time was ripe to experiment. By good fortune, at the same moment the Wolfson Foundation decided to give money for a suitably designed sixth form business programme and the two parties met. Both found agreement on the need to examine the possibilities of giving boys and girls a good understanding of the nature and problems of industry and commerce. Both saw the need to prepare the ground carefully before any programme was begun. So they set up a feasibility study, Wolfson generously providing the finance and John Dancy the educational ideas and day-to-day control of the Project.

This *feasibility study* was conducted by a businessman and a teacher. For six months they sought the views of influential educationalists in schools, technical colleges and management centres, and from businessmen in major companies, business organizations (C.B.I. and B.I.M., etc.) and the professions. They aimed to find out whether a sixth form business course was widely felt to be desirable and, if so, how it might best be fitted into the school curriculum. They found a widespread desire that a course should be attempted at this level. They found far less agreement on which materials and approaches could be used; in fact, it became evident that little careful thought had been given to this by anybody. On the strength of the report the Wolfson Trustees then authorized a five-year experimental programme to see if a useful Business Studies programme could be run in schools at 'A' level.

The *experimental programme* was initially conducted in two main schools, Marlborough College and Lawrence Weston Comprehensive, along with a small number of affiliated schools. Before the course started, the Cambridge Local Examinations Syndicate agreed to examine and a syllabus was produced acceptable to all parties (including the Schools Council). So teachers and students set sail into the new area with a syllabus, materials, teaching ideas and an examination structure which even today would make us quail. It is perhaps surprising that many boats did not sink with all hands.

Much was learnt from these early courses. As each successive group of centres embarked on the programme it became more purposeful, feasible and coherent, until in 1971 the Social Sciences Committee of the Schools Council were happy to give their blessing to an expansion of centres to around 50 for the 1975 examination. At that point, they said, they would examine the possibility of throwing the examination open.*

So the experimental programme† finished in 1972 and the *development phase* started in September of that year. A wide range of business organizations and charities generously gave financial support; many others offered assistance with teachers' training and the students' practical projects. The number of centres reached 40 (so that the additional centres entering in 1973 could bring the total up to 50) and about 400 students began their 'A' level course that year.

In this phase the Project aims to expand the support available to all affiliated schools and to write up the programme and its materials. In 1975 the Project, in its present form, will disband, having first set up any new structures needed to assist in the long-term administration.

The Objectives of the 'A' level Business Studies Project

The main objective of the Project was to see if an 'A' level in Business Studies could usefully be developed in schools. This meant that there were three interdependent sub-objectives. Firstly, a body of material, suitable to the educational needs of the 'A' level student, had to be isolated and appropriate methods of teaching and examining developed to enhance the educational value of this material. Secondly, the material had to be drawn

---

* 1976 examination (1974 entry) is open to any school or college.
† For some additional statistics see Appendix II.

together in a way which could, at this level, provide a student with an understanding of the nature and problems of organizations and, in particular, business; this understanding should be, so far as was possible, of a type which the student could further develop himself rather than being centred on specific data that was an end in itself. Thirdly, if the above two sub-objectives were found to be feasible and desirable, the Project Office needed to support the development of such a programme in a small number of schools across the educational spectrum. Further it would be required to leave the subject in a state from which it could both maintain and further develop its programmes.

The course was not designed to prepare the students for any specific career, profession or discipline. Although apparently providing a specialist 'A' level, in practice it seeks to provide an interdisciplinary general education. It is hoped that the course will not be taken as one of a cluster of commercial subjects: it is rather expected to form a bridge subject for students who are otherwise engaged in the sciences or in the arts. It is also hoped that courses will contain a spread of student ability, some students hoping to go through university and others, for academic or other reasons, wishing to move straight into professional training, whether within or outside business.

The Methods of 'A' level Business Studies

The syllabus, the teaching methods and the structure of the examination have been planned as an integrated whole. Bearing this integration in mind, we will look at each of these aspects.

*The Syllabus** considers various aspects of four areas where stress needs to be laid in any organizational decision-making:

(i) The significance of finance and accounting;
(ii) The planning and interpretation of quantitative data;
(iii) The study of human behaviour and organizational objectives;
(iv) An understanding of the effects of the environment on business.

It aims to balance and integrate their relative contributions and to apply these to certain decisions, particularly within the areas of marketing, production, personnel and financing. Such

* An abbreviated examination syllabus appears in Appendix I.

a broad but purposeful analysis can provide a marked and useful contrast to the other 'A' levels the student may be reading in parallel. In addition, knowledge within the quantitative areas of statistics and accounting can help subsequent study in the Social Sciences and allied fields; the examination of individual and organizational behaviour can assist the student in understanding himself (or herself) and some of the human problems around him; overall understanding of organizations may assist in career choice.

This syllabus is examined through the Cambridge Local Examinations Syndicate under our Chief Examiner, Professor E. A. G. Robinson, and our Chairman of Examiners, Professor R. H. Barback. They and the Syndicate have combined with the Project to set an examination which both assesses the student's ability within the different skills and materials outlined and is in line with the course's general philosophy. They have also encouraged a form of examination which can help to guide the teacher within this new syllabus, for we think that this is one of those rare cases where the structure and style of the examination exerts a beneficial effect upon the teaching methods.

Basically the examination is now (after experimentation in parallel with the syllabus) divided into four equal parts, papers 1, 2, 3 and a practical project. Within these the student is forced into each major area of the syllabus and required to show different general skills. Papers 1 and 2 are of fairly traditional design, one largely quantitative and the other verbal; plenty of choice is available in the questions. Paper 3 is a case study within some central area of the course and demands quick clear thought about a business problem. The practical project is written on a small problem individually studied within an organization. It is presented for the examination in about 5,000 words. The student has control over the subject area and the time available for his work. The examiner, in reading and viva-ing each, is more concerned with the way the problem has been tackled than with the actual conclusions reached.

The teaching methods encourage an objective and critical approach to material as is normal in any 'A' level. Emphasis is placed on participation and on the application of ideas. Four particular teaching methods are encouraged. Firstly, both small and interdisciplinary case studies are used, which force the student to analyse and apply his knowledge as well as indirectly providing a way of introducing reality into situations and allowing the student to assimilate descriptive background material. The inter-disciplinary cases, often used towards the end of the programme, can also give students practice in using a decision-making approach.

Secondly, limited use is made of Business Games. They can give understanding of particular factors (break-even analysis, auction bidding, the need to keep and use relevant information). They can act as a general motivator. Thirdly, the course exhibits its empirical approach (and the need for an understanding of decision-making) when it compels each student to consider a problem within some organization. In this, his practical project, the student is made to plan the whole operation, choose the approach, the type of material required, the method of collection and presentation, the structure and the overall presentation of his findings.

Fourthly, some emphasis is placed on the ability to interpret data, particularly of a quantitative nature. Hence within areas like Final Accounts, Cash Flows, Quality Control, Decision Trees or Investment Analysis the student is seldom asked to construct any but the simplest model: he is often asked to use information within a general problem.

The Project's Support for the Programme

So much for the basic structure of the 'A' level. Whilst it is in line with much that is now being done within the sixth form there are several areas of departure. Because of these departures and the additional load of establishing any new 'A' level there has been a need for short-term support outside normal teacher activity. The Project Office plans and co-ordinates a number of activities to provide this support. Together these activities have placed a substantial load on the Project Office. The tasks go beyond normal course planning, advisory and publicity services for those within or outside the programme; they include assist-ance with the materials, teachers' training, practical projects and student experience.

The special materials for the student and teacher were developed slowly. Initially they were written to supplement published texts, but with the change in the syllabus it was found necessary to produce our own tailor-made and inter-linking materials right across the course. First drafts of the basic material are nearly complete and have been collected in a file which is available to all affiliated schools (along with a subsidized copying service so that this material can easily move into the hands of the students in any centre). There are now about 300 articles in the file varying from one to a dozen pages each. They are arranged in line with the 'A' level syllabus. Material for each topic usually includes: (i) a General Teachers' Guide to the area with solutions to any problems or exercises; (ii) a number of Fact Sheets for the student; (iii) some exercises and case studies (according to the area); (iv) a small number of further articles for the teacher or brighter student.

As the programme has progressed more and more materials are being evaluated and written by experienced teachers throughout the Project. They have brought materials into a form which can easily be employed by new teachers snowed under with the demands of a new programme. These materials, to which many centres have contributed, will form the base of Project Books. It is hoped these will be published in 1975.

Teachers new to the Project may gain further support through attendance at an introductory teachers' course run annually, since 1971, in conjunction with the Cambridge Extra-Mural Board. It is organized by the Project and uses its materials and many of its experienced members. These courses will continue for at least the next three years and are available to teachers from new* or existing centres. Where numbers allow we welcome teachers who just want to examine the new programme.

In 1972 there was also a Senior Teachers' Course, but this will not be repeated this year. Instead the Project will heavily subsidize many of its members on carefully selected Management Courses, thanks to a generous gift we have just received. Thus for induction and for more advanced learning there are opportunities for a teacher moving into the Business Studies area.

This year, for the first time, there will also be a purpose-built Student Course for those who wish to extend their experience beyond their formal programme. It will be run by David Dyer and take place for a week at the end of the Summer Term. It aims to provide an opportunity for carefully prepared case study work, both within and outside firms, and to teach the students

* The Schools Council has asked that new schools/colleges send a member on this course before they can be accepted to take the present 'A' level.

more about how to tackle their individual practical projects. Once more it will be staffed with Project teachers calling on extra expertise where necessary.

Lastly, thought and support has been given to the *organization of the students' practical projects.* This aspect of the course is of supreme importance to the educational value of the whole programme (as teachers, students and examiners have often noted), but it is ambitious and relies on the goodwill and active co-operation of those in the business world. Although already 600 students have completed their projects by individual approaches with or without the help of teachers, parents, etc., we feel that this does not provide a secure base for the future. As numbers increase so it becomes desirable to provide simple machinery which can dovetail the demand from students with those in the business world who generously assist this initiative. After a small experiment with Shell-Mex and B.P. Ltd in 1970, Jim Clifford (the Project's Deputy Director) organized a full scheme last year. It was based on London. The students stayed in one centre for the fortnight and went out to their five host firms for their practical work. The scheme worked well and this Summer there are plans to run two centres linking about 18 firms with over 60 of the 'A' level students.

Some Major Findings at the Interim Stage

The project covers a wide field. Much of its initial work has been within broad strategic areas of Curriculum Development. Thus it seems most appropriate, at this stage, to highlight one or two of the broader findings.

In general, there does seem to be a place for a Business Studies 'A' level along these lines. With the minimum of promotion, the special requirements for Project schools, the dearth of published material (indeed any comprehensive material in the early days) and initial doubts about acceptability, many schools and colleges of widely differing types have joined with considerable enthusiasm. However, it is not a soft option.

Acceptability

There is always a problem of academic acceptability for a newcomer within the 'A' level field. This is particularly true where some other subjects in nearby disciplines have not wanted or sought this. Hence it was necessary to convince the universities of the educational value and standards of this 'A' level. The Project tackled this in three main ways and I believe has been very successful.

(*a*) It only began the first course after seeking advice from many of the potential users of the programme; in particular, the universities and the professional bodies.

(*b*) From the beginning it concentrated on the educational side of the programme (the 'studies' rather than the 'business').

(*c*) It tried to prepare the ground in one or two initial centres so that the subject grew up in the right atmosphere. Thus it immediately became considered as an academic programme by the students, their parents and their teachers.

Undoubtedly this Project suffered through being established outside a national educational organization. At the time opinion within the educational world demanded the freelance approach. If the Project were to start now I should seek to place it under such a sponsorship at an early stage.

Material

We have found no evidence that business material is either too sophisticated or too remote for sixth-formers—given that it is suitably chosen and presented. We are equally certain that there are useful principles to be taught which can be used to provide analytical and interpretative experience.

We also feel that business material can be presented in a form which is at least as educationally viable for sixth-formers as that employed by other subjects. Not only has it the natural advantages of an interdisciplinary approach, but it indirectly provides some understanding of man in society, of man's scientific environment, of numeracy and literacy. The one area in which it fails badly is its lack of aesthetics; for this a student must choose suitably from his other 'A' level subjects.

Whilst stressing the suitability of material I do not want to leave the impression that all material is now in ideal form for this course. It is not. We have made a beginning but there is much more to do. I hope some worthwhile steps can be taken in the development phase.

Syllabus

In our early years we completely failed to provide a meaningful or workable syllabus. Placing side by side some functional disciplines close to the business area (Economics, Mathematics, Accountancy, Social Psychology and Law) is not the answer. Our experience within the field of 'A' level Business Studies has led us firmly to the view that there is little educational future here for the non-integrated course. Business material is naturally diverse and it needs to be presented and taught around a core which is meaningful to the student. Ideally this core should both assist the educational process and help to explain the material. We suggest that decision-making is one such core. Where we had no core (the first two courses) the students only gained rather shallow knowledge in the functional disciplines: they did not appear to arrive at an understanding of business; *nor* were they able to draw together and relate the different parts of their material.

Practical Experience

We believe that the practical project is a central experience— indeed the examiners might say that this is *the* central *experience* of the course. (*a*) It allows each student to take a purposeful glimpse at the complexity of organizational problem-solving and hence to integrate theory with practice. (*b*) It provides the experience of an extended piece of simple research. (*c*) It makes a purposeful bridge between school and life beyond: a bridge built in the natural course of academic studies.

In terms of logistics from the differing viewpoints of the schools, the students, the firms and the examiners, the projects have worked remarkably well on a small scale. We have yet to see if we can maintain the benefits with larger numbers, but are now planning for this (see above).

Teaching Methods

We certainly feel confident that three types of approach are worth further development. Firstly, the extended practical project as previously mentioned. Secondly, the use of various types of case-study work. Thirdly, the empirical approach to new ideas.

The Examination

We feel that we were right to stress the integration of the examination with the total course (and many thanks go to the Cambridge Syndicate for allowing this). The links which ensued between the Project and the Examination have, it is hoped, produced a viable method of assessing the student and of supporting the teacher. Much more work needs to be done, but it is an exciting partnership.

Overall Project Planning

We failed to appreciate the work and resources that would be needed by the Project if our initial foray was successful. In the early stages, the Project team were too bound up with the problems of initiating and developing the course in their own centre and gave insufficient support to affiliated schools. We also failed to gain the necessary ancillary staff to service the needs of a programme within this new area of school activity. We hope that the new structure initiated in September 1972 will cure this.

We have only made a beginning and are very willing to hear comments and criticisms. There are left nearly three more years to tidy up and develop the programme before leaving the subject in a form which could enable it to continue and mature.

Appendix I

'A' LEVEL BUSINESS STUDIES PROJECT

ABBREVIATED EXAMINATION SYLLABUS

The course is designed to introduce, over a two-year period and at a level suited to the needs of sixth form students, the principles governing business decisions and the solution of business problems. It investigates four elements in the analysis of such problems:

(i) the significance of finance and accounting;
(ii) the interpretation of quantitative data;
(iii) the study of human behaviour;
(iv) the understanding of the economic environment's effect on business.

The course aims to balance and integrate the relative contributions of each of these four elements into a final process of business decision-making.

The abbreviated syllabus that follows is also illustrated in the accompanying diagram.

I The Development of a Decision-Making Theme

1. *Background:* Variety of organizations in industry; some pioneers.
2. *The Decision-Making Process:* Basic phases; differing applications.
3. *Objectives:* Value and problems; the nation, firm and individual.
4. *Constraints on Decisions:*
   (a) *Human*—perception; attitudes; groups; problems of change.
   (b) *Legal*—background business law; legal identity; accountability.
   (c) *Financial*—sources and methods of raising finance; implications.
   (d) *Macro-economic*—influence on business decisions of employment levels, international trade, inflation and State intervention.
5. *Information:* Interpretation of statistics (national and specific); random sampling; market information and research; use of computers; production information and costing.
6. *Innovation:* Creativity; creative groups; research and development.
7. *Alternative Choices:* Model-making; introduction to operational research; capital investment alternatives; D.C.F.
8. *Planning:* Types and structure; critical path analysis.
9. *Communication:* Problems, methods, media; techniques of persuasion; committees, public speaking, report writing.

10. *Review:* Budgetary control; problems and principles of final accounts; analysis through ratios and cash flow.

II The Theme in Application

11. *The Marketing Mix:* Selling, distribution, promotion, diversification.
12. *Pricing:* Price theory; cost structures; market influences.
13. *Productive Efficiency:* Location; scale; work study; quality control.
14. *Formal Organization:* Delegation; hierarchy, etc.; optimization.
15. *Motivation:* Individual and group; financial and non-financial.
16. *Collective Bargaining:* Participants; wage negotiations; State role.
17. *The Decision-Maker in Business:* Methods and roles of leadership; the shop steward, supervisor, manager, director.

III The Practical Project

As part of the examination, each candidate presents a 3,000–5,000-word report on a practical project normally covering about one month's work on some mutually agreed problem in an outside firm.

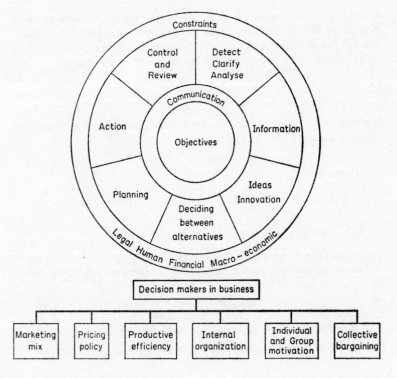

BUSINESS STUDIES 'A'–LEVEL a decision-making framework

Appendix II
SOME PROJECT STATISTICS

1. *Scale*

	1967	1968	1969	1970	1971	1972	1973
Project schools starting each academic year	4	8	11	12	25	40	48 (accepted)
Students starting each academic year	43	72	108	136	260	400 (approx.)	

2. *'A' level Combinations*

Other 'A' levels combined with Business Studies, in order of their popularity, for students examined in 1971 and 1972: History, English, Geography, Mathematics, French, Economics, Physics, Biology, Art and German (others were read in less than 5% of the cases).

3. *Examination Grades*

These were given by the Cambridge Local Examinations Syndicate on the examinations of 1971 and 1972.

Cumulative %	A	B	C	D	E	O	F
1971	10	22	26	42	75	93	100
1972	10	23	36	57	72	93	100

4. *Qualifications of Teachers*

An idea of the teachers' qualification subjects is gained by looking at those of the teachers who attended the Junior Teachers' Programme in 1971 and 1972. They were as follows:

	%		%
Economics	69*	Law	9
Politics	14	Philosophy	8

* Many teachers read more than one subject for their first or second degree.

	%		%
History	11	Business Studies	6
Commerce	11	Accounting	6
Mathematics/Statistics	9	Remainder less than	5

5. *Student Movement*

An analysis has been made of student movement after the 1969, 1970 and 1971 'A' levels. A 73% reply rate was received from the questionnaires; a slightly higher proportion of those not replying were in the failure bracket of the examination.

39% Are at or firmly accepted for University
11% Are engaged in professional training
10% Are at or firmly accepted for a Polytechnic
8% Are at or firmly accepted for a Technical College
8% Went straight into business or commerce
5% Joined the Armed Forces
19% Were still at school or followed other pursuits.

6. *Subsequent student opinion*

In the above questionnaire each student was asked whether he was pleased or sorry he chose to read 'A' level Business Studies. The replies were:

125 said pleased
16 had mixed feelings
12 were sorry
4 made no reply.

Appendix III

MAJOR DIFFERENCES BETWEEN 'A' LEVEL BUSINESS STUDIES AND 'A' LEVEL ECONOMICS

1. Business Studies explores man's behaviour from the standpoint of organizations (and in particular, firms). Economics spends part of its time in the same area but as much, or more, in the macro area. Thus one course tends to look entirely through the eyes of managers, supervisors and men: the other considers these whilst frequently exploring matters from the Chancellor of the Exchequer's viewpoint.

2. Business Studies places an emphasis on decision-making. In particular, it considers the way that businessmen tackle their decisions, and some of the general tools available to them. Economics uses a more theoretical model and, within this, attempts to probe the workings of the system (both in the macro and micro area). Thus relatively, Business Studies is more empirical and Economics more abstract.

3. Business Studies was planned for educational purposes, as an integrated interdisciplinary course in the social science area. It took and drew together 'hard' material from Statistics, Accounting and Economics itself as well as 'soft' material from the areas of human behaviour. Economics chooses a slightly smaller range of materials not going so far in its requirements in either direction; it does not set out to be interdisciplinary.

4. Business Studies selects and presents material in a manner which can help to inform the student of the processes and problems of decision-making. All material is related to this conceptual core. Economics sometimes employs this approach but has chosen to give it far less emphasis.

5. Business Studies is more vocational in that its educational and knowledge base have wider common applications after school. Economics is more concerned with providing a specific base for subsequent university economists or those who wish for an understanding of this discipline. Neither is vocational in that they teach skills of immediate commercial value.

6. Business Studies has an important part of the course which takes the student outside the classroom into industry and commerce. It compels him to deal with primary data. Economics does not.

7. The Business Studies 'A' level Examination has been designed both as a tool for assessment and as an educational target for the teacher. The student has to show his ability in a number of totally different skills carried out under very different conditions (case study, practical project and viva). The examination is as much concerned to see whether the different educational skills have been learnt as to test the student's knowledge and understanding of the subject material. Most Economics 'A' level examinations appear more restricted in their aims and concentrate on the understanding of concepts and other general syllabus material. The economists use multiple-choice questions which are not employed in Business Studies. Economics is able to hold a significantly shorter examination.

N.B. All through these comparisons I only seek to compare the 'A' levels (not courses outside these). No value judgment is implied in any of these differences.

VIII: ECONOMICS FOR CIVIL SERVANTS AND STUDENT TEACHERS

15: Teaching the Essentials of Microeconomics to Managers in the Civil Service

GORDON HEWITT

Introduction

Getting to the core of economics and isolating its essentials is often regarded as a popular sport. It makes a fascinating pastime in which to indulge on a 'one-off' basis; a subject which, as E. J. Mishan says of welfare economics, 'one dabbles in for a while, leaves and, perhaps, returns to later in response to a troubled conscience'.[1]

This paper deals with yet another attempt to expose the essentials of economics, and it reports on the way in which these essentials have been taught to a particular group of people. It should be stated clearly at the beginning that I make no claim to have discovered *the* essentials of economics—the Aladdin's lamp which people need only mentally touch for the whole structure of economic analysis to unfold suddenly before their eyes.

Whether or not common agreement could ever be reached on *those* essentials is a matter for argument elsewhere. It will be a common theme of this paper that the way in which I approach the problem of teaching the essentials of economics is shaped by the work which the Civil Service College does, the needs of the people it teaches and the constraints under which it operates. So I begin by outlining these background features.

Background

The Civil Service College was set up following the Fulton Report,[2] one of whose recommendations was the establishment of a management training centre for civil servants. The College is organized around five major academic subject areas—Economics,

Statistics and Operations Research, Public Administration, Social Policy and Administration, and Personnel Management. Civil servants from many strata—from quite junior management grades to Heads of Government Departments—attend courses run by the College which are considered relevant to their pattern of career development.*

Sometimes the courses are based on a single discipline—e.g. a number of courses on particular aspects of economics are run for people doing certain types of work for which this specialized knowledge would be an advantage (International Economics, Government and Industry, etc.). Occasionally, courses combine all the subject areas, with the intention of showing the contribution of various disciplines to the business of management in the public sector.

Already, however, the first constraint has arisen. To state that we teach *relevant* economics is very laudable, but there are different *purposes* or *aims* which a knowledge of economics could serve, all of which are relevant to civil servants for quite different reasons:

(a) Should we be teaching mainly descriptive-type economics, e.g. informing civil servants about the composition of national income and public sector expenditure, the structure of trade unions and business organizations, the banking system, etc.? In other words, is economics relevant by way of plugging information gaps, in the expectation that civil servants will thereby become more 'aware' of the 'facts' when they suggest and implement policy?

(b) Should we be teaching extracts from the standard undergraduate syllabus in economic analysis, perhaps with the emphasis more on the applied than the theoretical side? One purpose of this would be to show civil servants the kind of training professional economists have had, and therefore make them much more sympathetic, in the broadest sense, to the arguments put forward by economists in government departments. This aim, which is really an attempt at closing the communications gap between administrative civil servants and economists, is certainly a concern of the Fulton Report.[3]

* The vast majority of training programmes—concerned with 'job-related' training for specific skills—are still run by departments.

(c) Should we be concerned with the aim of showing the relevance of economics to the management task of decision-making, especially where decisions involve the selection of a course of action from a series of alternatives? This aim suggests a more practical use for economics, certainly for a larger range of people, than the previous two. It suggests that economics has some guidelines to offer any civil servant, whether or not he is engaged in fields of policy which could be conventionally described as 'economic' or, indeed, whether or not he will ever actually meet an economist in his life.

Each of these broad aims has much to commend it, but the relevance of these aims will vary from person to person within the civil service, depending on the type of work he is doing. A senior civil servant in, say, the Department of Trade and Industry, administering policy towards mergers and monopolies, would obviously be more in need of instruction which fulfilled aim (b) (and to some extent (a)), compared to a more junior civil servant working in, say, the Inland Revenue.

In constructing a syllabus, therefore, the first practical problem is defining precisely what aims are relevant to the target population. In addition, however, by far the biggest practical problem arises due to the constraint of time. Courses at the College are generally short, lasting on average a few weeks. Consequently, we have to pay great attention to the problem of translating these broad aims into content, and also selecting the most effective teaching methods. We also need to know just how effective we have been, both in terms of learning effectiveness and relevance.

These problems, then, of deciding what it is we want to do, the most effective way of doing it and the extent to which we have succeeded, are central to the business of planning, organizing, teaching and evaluating economics sessions on College courses.

The example which is discussed below illustrates how these decisions were made for one particular course. It is chosen because it is the most extreme example of a time constraint which I have so far faced at the College.

Target Population

In September 1972 the first of a new type of course was launched for civil servants in the Higher Executive Officer (H.E.O.) grade. The average H.E.O. can be described as a person in his late 20's, who has entered the civil service as an Executive Officer direct from school at about the age of 18.* H.E.O.s usually have minimum university entrance qualifications and have received promotion to their present grade shortly before coming to the College for their course.

Here are people, then, with some years' practical experience of executing government policy, who are beginning to take on (and will increasingly take on) the roles of managers in the sense of managing resources and managing people.

The course which they attend is appropriately enough called 'Introduction to Management in Government'; it lasts for four weeks and roughly thirty people attend each course. The allocation of time to the study of microeconomics is two days, comprising twelve periods of one hour. What, any self-respecting economist will ask, can be sensibly taught to people and learned by people in that space of time?

Aims

The aims of the course are defined as 'Helping develop skills in decision-making techniques and improving course members' management capacity'. At least this defines which of the broad aims referred to previously is more appropriate here. Now the problem becomes that of deciding in what way microeconomics is relevant to decision-making, and in what ways this can best be shown in two days.

Content

Microeconomics is about choice; about decisions involving the allocation of resources between alternative courses of action. One aspect of every manager's job is also precisely this; deciding whether to go for action A or B; or how best to allocate resources between them; or whether to go for action A or do nothing. In two days, is it possible to isolate, teach, and make it possible for

---

* Some H.E.O.s are graduates, and some have entered the civil service at a more mature age from other professions.

this group to learn effectively those fundamental microeconomic concepts which are relevant to the business of making choices?

The syllabus, which comprises four essential concepts and two techniques derived from them, is outlined in schematic form in Figure 1.

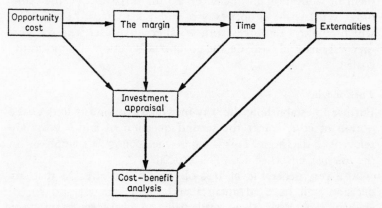

Figure 1

Opportunity Cost

In everybody's list of the essentials of economics, this concept would surely find a place. Yet what matters in this context is the way in which it is shown to be relevant to the kinds of decisions which have to be made by the course members.

The notion of 'cost' is central to many decisions made in the public sector (as elsewhere). What we try to emphasize is that 'cost' is a concept whose meaning should be examined in detail; that the economist's definition of opportunity cost may be more relevant for decision-making purposes than the traditional accountant's definition, which includes purely those financial costs which have been or will be physically incurred in some transaction.

A mature audience of this sort is only too well aware that very often the resources over which it has control are scarce and have alternative uses. So, if they are used in one way, it involves a sacrifice of something else. The notion of opportunity cost is presented to them in general as representing the cost of undertaking some action in terms of what is lost by not undertaking the next best alternative.

It is important that civil servants with managerial responsibilities should understand this concept. At the very least, it forces them, when considering a particular measure, to ask the fundamental question, 'The cost to whom?' What is the cost of raising the school-leaving age to 16? The cost to whom? To the Department of Education and Science? To the taxpayer? To the economy? What is the proper way of judging the cost of an action which employs resources with no alternative use? The straightforward financial cost? Or the economist's notion of opportunity cost?

The Margin

Further to establishing the way in which economists look at the notion of cost, comes the second question of which costs are relevant to decisions. This is where the economist's emphasis on the *marginal* effects of actions is crucial.

At a very general level, it is obvious to the H.E.O.s that any decision will have advantages and disadvantages, and so, to evaluate it properly, there needs to be an awareness of the 'marginal' returns (or 'incremental' returns, to be strictly accurate) and the 'marginal' costs (or extra sacrifices) involved.

Managers in the public sector, however, are often confronted by financial data, much of which is in the form of 'averages' usually incorporating an allocation of fixed costs. The notion of the 'margin' alerts students to the possible dangers of using such data for decision-making purposes, particularly if certain costs will be incurred irrespective of the course of action chosen. The practical problem of being able to identify easily marginal costs of actions is certainly stressed, but it is the method of approaching the problem of identifying relevant costs which is important—bygones are bygones.

Time

Quite often, course members are responsible for decisions whose effects stretch over a period of time. The most obvious example of this would be a situation where one of the H.E.O.s was concerned with judging whether action A costing £x for the next three years and £y for three years thereafter was better than action B costing £v for the next three years and £w for the three years thereafter.

The issue which the third concept—the notion of time discounting—asks students to examine is whether a sum of money of, say, £x payable or receivable one year, two years and three years from now should always be given the same weight in the decision.

It is certainly true that discounted cash flow methods of investment appraisal have been subject to criticism recently, and so it is all the more important that young managers understand the conceptual basis of the techniques first of all—why it is appropriate and under what conditions it is appropriate to discount future streams of costs and revenues to present values.

Externalities

The concept of externalities, looked at as a divergence between private and social costs and benefits, is classically defined and expounded in A. C. Pigou's *The Economics of Welfare*.[4] The course members are certainly aware, especially in our environment-conscious age, that smoky factory chimneys pollute the atmosphere, but that such pollution is an external cost imposed on society but not necessarily borne by the organization which is the source of the pollution. As civil servants, they are intuitively aware of the fact that the central characteristic of many government programmes is the extent to which they generate 'externalities'.

However, the definition of this concept goes further, to embrace the important idea that if activities in one part of a system or organization have 'spillover' effects on other parts of the system, then these effects should be identified and evaluated. Professor Nove[5] has christened this activity 'Internalizing Externalities' and it is of particular concern to those working in the public sector.

Conventional wisdoms like 'every activity must pay its way' may well go wrong if operations, looked at purely in isolation, are reported to run at a financial loss and are axed on the grounds of being 'uneconomic'. Some projects, however, may impose external benefits on another part of the system, and conventional accounting information may not attribute these benefits correctly to their source. There can be, therefore, a danger that managers are often given financial information which evaluates activities in isolation from the main purpose which they serve.

These, then, are the four microeconomic concepts selected for this particular course. They are presented to the students as ways of thinking clearly about the issues involved in choosing between alternative courses of action. What do we mean by the 'cost' of doing something? What costs are relevant to this decision? How should we allow for the effect of time on the costs and revenues associated with this decision? Does this activity impose any external benefits elsewhere, and if so, are they being attributed to the activity itself? These are methods of approaching and analysing problems in order to reach more rational decisions.

In selecting the essentials of a subject for teaching purposes, the question obviously arises, 'Why pick on these particular concepts? Are they chosen at random, or is there some logical reason behind their selection?' As suggested in the previous paragraph, the concepts form a logical chain of reasoning in any analysis of alternative courses of action.

Further, in an article dealing primarily with military planning, but which has more general application, Hitch and McKean[6] noted that 'The essence of economic choice . . . is not quantitative analysis; calculation may or may not be necessary or useful, depending upon the problem and what is known about it. The essential thing is the comparison of all the relevant alternatives from the point of view of the objectives each can accomplish and the costs which it involves; and the selection of the best (or a "good") alternative through the use of appropriate economic criteria.'

The authors go on to state that the elements of economic choice are as shown in Figure 2:

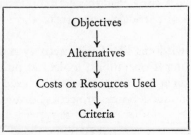

Figure 2

First, what aim is the decision-maker trying to achieve? Secondly, by what alternative means can this aim be achieved?

Thirdly, what are the costs of each alternative? Fourthly, by what test is a selection between the alternatives made?

If these are considered the stages of economic choice, then the four concepts we have isolated are certainly crucial to a proper analysis, as suggested in Figure 3:

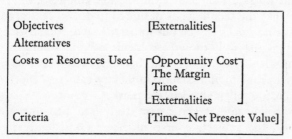

Figure 3

The notion of externalities is central to the evaluation of objectives in many public sector programmes. In assessing the costs of alternatives, opportunity cost is the appropriate measurement, and marginal opportunity costs are the relevant ones. It may also be the case that external costs should be identified and evaluated. If the alternatives involve costs or revenues/benefits over time, they should be weighed by discounting procedures. By so doing, we derive a criterion, net present value, which indicates the relative desirability of each alternative.

Hitch and McKean appropriately conclude, 'It cannot be stated too frequently or emphasised enough that economic choice is *a way of looking at problems* and does not necessarily depend upon the use of any analytic aids or computational devices'[7].

These four concepts are basic to the presentation of the next part of the syllabus. We consider two particular appraisal techniques which are used regularly in government departments to assist decisions between alternative courses of action—namely investment appraisal and, in its wider form, cost-benefit analysis.

One of the great advantages of having students acquainted with the conceptual basis* of these techniques is that they more readily examine the purpose of the techniques, play down the

* To be strictly accurate and apply the jargon, these four concepts are a necessary but not sufficient basis. Others, such as consumers' surplus in the case of cost-benefit analysis, are needed.

number-crunching aspect, and spend more time discussing their scope and limitations.

This is particularly important in the case of cost-benefit analysis, whose influence as an appraisal technique seems to be growing, yet whose purpose is still widely misinterpreted both inside and outside Whitehall. Considerable emphasis, therefore, is put on what the technique is designed to do, so that arguments about its drawbacks can be put in perspective. Acknowledgment is given to the well-known problems of establishing a cut-off point in identifying costs and benefits, and the occasionally emotional problem of attaching monetary values to effects which are not customarily valued in the market.

After having undertaken a case study (see Teaching Methods below) on the subject, course members consistently raise the point that they find the technique at least begins to make explicit the value judgments which decision-makers would make implicitly. From the practical point of view, it may be that the limitations of the technique, according to one leading practitioner, 'are as frequently problems of cost estimation, forecasting and basic data requirements as they are of failure to derive acceptable values for those effects for which no monetary equivalents exist'.[8]

Teaching Methods
The College has been devoting increasing attention to methods of teaching and learning. Course members are highly motivated,

Day 1	*Day 2*
1. Introduction, and Presentation and Discussion of Opportunity Cost and the Margin	1. Presentation and Discussion of Investment Appraisal Techniques
2. Group Exercises	2. Group Case Study
3. Report and Review Session	3. Report and Review Session
4. Presentation and Discussion of Time and Externalities	4. Presentation and Discussion of Cost-Benefit Analysis
5. Group Exercises	5. Group Case Study
6. Report and Review Session	6. Report and Review Session
Each session lasts for 1 hour	

Figure 4

and bring considerable practical experience to the classroom situation. These are assets which are particularly suited to participative forms of learning, designed to let the student monitor his own understanding and to apply the concepts and techniques to real-world or simulated situations.

The breakdown of the syllabus by time allocation and teaching method is shown in Figure 4.

This breakdown reflects a 'cycle' approach to teaching and learning. Very broadly, this involves a presentation of the concepts/technique to be mastered, followed almost immediately by a session of group work on an exercise or case study, followed by a report and review session back in the classroom.

Presentation and Discussion

The first presentation session, for example, is concerned with the concepts of opportunity cost and the margin. I refrain from calling it a lecture, because a high degree of student participation is solicited throughout. This is attempted by using a problem-solving approach in which the identification and explanation of each concept is built into a consideration of a particular case— e.g. assessing what is the 'cost' of raising the school-leaving age to 16.

Exercise/Case Study Session

Like most management training centres, the Civil Service College puts some emphasis on the use of case studies by which students can apply concepts to real-life decision-making situations. This emphasis on giving students the opportunity to apply theory to practice is particularly important in demonstrating the *relevance* of economic analysis to decision-making problems.

We have found in practice that the greatest care is needed in preparing such case studies. To be effective in achieving their primary purpose, which is surely to reinforce students' understanding of the concepts being considered, the case study has to be tailored to highlight the central role that these concepts play in defining, analysing and solving the problem. As in all good economic models, there may have to be a sacrifice of reality in order to focus attention on the critical variables.

Report and Review Session

The third stage in the cycle involves each group presenting in open forum their solution to the problem set. This usually gives way to general discussion of the case under consideration. There is no doubt that in such sessions, reasonably unstructured and flexible as they are, the role of the teacher is of paramount importance. Indeed, the conduct and success of this type of session can be analysed using Flanders' social-interaction model of teaching.[9] He has to act as the focal point of the meeting; assess the points being made; decide whether to become a lecturer for a few minutes to reinforce understanding of the concept; or introduce a further application; or question a particular group's line of argument; or rather raise some general doubt in the hope that someone in the meeting will pose the precise question and furnish the answer; but always keep some sense of direction and purpose in the proceedings.

Evaluation

The approach to planning, teaching, and evaluating these sessions does not conform to a pure definition of educational technology. There has been no definition of precise instructional objectives, and no definition of entering behaviour. An educational technologist would argue that we cannot objectively evaluate learning achievement, since we have not carried out the prerequisites. And perhaps rightly so.

Still, we do attempt an evaluation, albeit of a very subjective nature. First, students are given an evaluation form which asks them to grade sessions on a five-point scale under a number of headings, including 'Quality of Presentation, Relevance of Subject, Time Allowed'.

At best, these forms can be no more than a rough indication of students' attitudes, rather than an objective assessment of learning achievement. But they can often give useful guidelines to the need for change, for example where a session is rated high on quality of presentation but low on relevance, or vice versa.

Secondly, the students and the teacher can make some subjective evaluation of the learning achievement with respect to the four concepts, since mastery of these is needed to solve correctly some key problems in the case studies. During the case study periods, the teacher visits the groups in the role of consultant and observer, and so is in a position to assess to some extent how far students have understood the concepts.

Conclusions

Three courses of this type have been held so far, and the results have been extremely encouraging. Each group of students has reacted enthusiastically to this programme and rated it highly. This is all the more pleasing since these civil servants are looking for practical value from the subjects which they are taught, and are in a position to assess the relevance of what they are taught.

From the author's point of view, it is amazing to watch the change in the students' approach to analysing problems even in this short space of time. Perhaps it is in the affective domain that the value of this approach to teaching economics really lies. As stated at the beginning, there is no claim being made for having discovered the essentials of microeconomics, but the ones we have isolated seem to work for this particular group—which was the object of the exercise.

References

1. Mishan, E. J., 'A Survey of Welfare Economics, 1939–59', *Economic Journal*, June 1960.
2. *The Civil Service*, Report of the Committee 1966–68 (Chairman Lord Fulton), Vol. 1, Cmnd. 3638, H.M.S.O., 1968.
3. Ibid., par. 32, p. 16.
4. Pigou, A. C., *The Economics of Welfare*, 4th ed., Macmillan, London, 1932.
5. Nove, A., 'Internal Economics,' *Economic Journal*, December 1969.
6. Hitch, C. J. and McKean, R. N., 'Economic Analysis for the National Defense', in Watson, D. S. (ed.), *Price Theory in Action*, 2nd ed., Houghton Mifflin, Boston, 1969, pp. 391–2.
7. Ibid., p. 393.
8. Harrison, A. J., *Techniques of Appraising Public Sector Transport Expenditures and Policy: A Review*, unpublished paper, Strategic Planning Directorate, Department of the Environment, March 1971.
9. Flanders, N. A., *Teacher Influence, Pupil Attitudes and Achievement*, University of Minnesota Press, Minneapolis, 1960.
   — 'Some Relationships Among Teacher Influence, Pupil Attitudes and Achievement', in Biddle, B. J. and Ellena, W. J. (eds.), *Contemporary Research on Teacher Effectiveness*, Holt, Rinehart & Winston, New York, 1964, pp. 196–231.

16: Economics in Courses for Teachers in Colleges of Education

DUNCAN HANCOCK

To understand the role of economics in Colleges of Education it may help if the curriculum of a typical college is briefly outlined, ignoring the James Report and the substantial changes which may soon flow from it. There are, of course, very great differences between colleges, but most of them share certain characteristics which strongly influence the way in which they conduct their courses. In the first place many of them are mainly concerned with the training of teachers for primary schools and this concern carries with it the implication that they are training general, as opposed to specialist, teachers, capable of dealing adequately with most of the subjects they will find in schools for young children.

Secondly, the curriculum in a college is seen to have three overlapping but distinct elements: (*a*) the disciplined study of education involving the philosophy, psychology, sociology, history, etc., of education; (*b*) the professional element embracing practical experience in schools, the methodology of subjects, and courses designed to help future teachers to cope with a variety of subjects or topics of which they have no specialized knowledge but which they must teach in primary schools; and (*c*) the study of one or more academic disciplines which are not necessarily seen as the special subjects of the future teacher. Although there is clearly much overlapping, the first two elements are seen as the essentially professional aspect of college work while the academic study is devoted to the continued education of the student. That this dichotomy is in part unreal is acknowledged. When the student becomes a teacher he will make use of his understanding of child psychology, of the techniques he has acquired in the professional courses, and of the knowledge and insights he has gained from his academic study, to mention only one item from each element, when he is deciding both what, and how, to teach. But the distinction is still valid. Study in depth of the constitutional problems of eighteenth-century Britain can only be seen as indirectly helping the teaching of history to 7- or 8-year-old children and must be viewed as primarily concerned with the personal education and development of the student. This, with little further explanation, has been taken to be an end in itself, desirable not because studying a subject will make the student a better teacher in a specialist area, but because it is assumed that advanced study will benefit the student no matter what he is going to teach.

The immediate reason why economics is introduced into a college may have little to do with educational principles, but the justification which can be made is that economics is admirably designed to provide the third element of the curriculum, the personal education and development of the student. One can go further and attempt to define the particular ways in which a student will benefit from the study of economics. In common with other social sciences it uses both deductive and inductive reasoning, and practice in the use of these processes will help the student to apply them elsewhere. Economics is again not unique in helping to distinguish between normative and positive matters, but it is so rich in examples of confusion between the two that it can claim to sharpen the students' appreciation of the distinction. For example, it is often assumed that policies designed to reduce frictional unemployment ought to be pursued with vigour because it is taken as self-evident that such unemployment is evil. It has been pointed out, however, that a rational response to improved unemployment benefit is for a worker seeking employment to spend some little time making sure he gets the job that really suits him instead of rushing into the first one he finds. Thus some frictional unemployment may be a sign of improved resource allocation and not an evil.

Study of economics also stresses that the use of the scientific method is not confined to the physical sciences and gives opportunities to become familiar with framing hypotheses and with seeking ways of testing the predictions which follow from them.

In his inaugural lecture in 1967, Professor Harry Johnson pointed out that 'the concept of an interdependent system . . . is a powerful engine of classification and understanding of economic relationships and phenomena and its usefulness extends well beyond the confines of economics proper. In relation to social questions it has two important implications: that things are the way they are for some powerful reason or reasons, which have to be understood if effective social solutions are to be devised, and that any solutions so devised and applied will have repercussions elsewhere, which will have to be faced and which ought to be taken into account.' Economics abounds in models illustrating the importance of the interdependence of many factors, of which the simple market mechanism of supply and demand is but one.

Lastly economics is closely concerned with the handling and understanding of concepts. As K. Dunning has argued in 'To Know Economics', in the Summer 1972 issue of *Economics*, someone who 'knows economics' is capable of 'conceptual thinking' in a particular sphere. The acquisition of skill in the handling of such concepts as demand, perfect competition, elasticity, etc., can be looked upon as desirable for its value in understanding economic problems but also for its use in the development of conceptual thinking in general.

If the benefits outlined in the previous paragraphs are sufficiently great it could be argued that not only is the introduction of economics into a college course well justified but that many more students than currently study the subject should be encouraged to do so. In addition it needs no stressing that the development of economic literacy and numeracy, which is closely tied up with the study of economic concepts and their interdependence, is, of course, of great importance in a democratic society in which many of the matters of public concern are economic in character. The case for the more widespread study of economics has been made elsewhere, but it can be argued that teachers, holding, as they do, a unique position of influence, are as much in need of an understanding of economics as they are of the ability to express themselves clearly in the English language.

Let us assume that the case has been made for the introduction of economics on a much bigger scale into Colleges of Education. Can a similar case be made for the extension of the teaching of economics in schools, particularly for the younger and less-able children, many, if not most of whom will be taught by the products of Colleges of Education?

There is much agreement about what constitutes a course in economics. T. K. Robinson, in an article in the Autumn 1971 issue of *Economics*, has given clear criteria by which we may judge the validity of a course in economics, and accepts the view expressed by Professors Lumsden and Attiyeh in *Economics* for Summer 1971 that there are four fundamental concepts in economics—scarcity and choice; economic efficiency; income distribution; aggregate output and income—which 'form an important part of the core material of a basic economics course'. Judged by these criteria, courses which are essentially of a descriptive nature, outlining what is, rather than attempting to explain why, cannot be accepted because they do not provide any worthwhile economics understanding.

Can the conceptual approach be successful at a level appropriate for the 'Newsom' child? The work of Piaget and Bruner, in particular, would suggest that there should be no problem in helping pupils in the lower and middle ranges of secondary schools to grasp the meaning of the concepts involved, provided that the approach is sufficiently elementary in the first place, and time is given for practice in the handling of the concepts, so that their meaning becomes embedded in the mind of the child. To teach these concepts at an elementary level it is not necessary to distort their meaning; the appeal must be to comparisons with the real experience of the children. Let us take the problem of aggregation as an example. As we know, action taken which may be appropriate or beneficial for an individual if taken in isolation, can frequently be totally inappropriate when taken by all people together, for instance an increase in the propensity to save during a slump. The essential differences between individual and mass action can be illustrated by at least two examples both easily grasped by the young mind. In the first, the contrast can be made between the successful escape from danger of a man sitting alone in a large hall who leaps to his feet and runs for the nearest door when a fire begins, with the carnage which would result if the hall had been crowded and the whole audience had attempted to rush to the exit doors. A second example can be found in everyday experience of the motor-car, which bestows freedom of movement on its owner until everyone owns one, when the resulting congestion destroys that freedom. From these homely illustrations it is possible to move on to more directly economic examples.

It is not difficult to find examples of this nature for most of the concepts required in an economics course, but it is equally important for the pupils to learn to handle them so that they become familiar and recognizable when seen out of the context of the text-book or classroom. Too often pupils can handle a problem when told what concept it involves, but are incapable of identifying the concept for themselves. Changes for the better in respect of this shortcoming are taking place in the teaching of economics. The proliferation of workbooks with problems to solve is an illustration of better techniques, but still too much teaching involves the pupils only as passive listeners. It is as if a teacher of mathematics, having explained how to multiply, moves straight on to an explanation of division, without giving his pupils an opportunity to practise multiplication. With younger or less-able pupils the need to use the knowledge and under-standing they are acquiring in order to strengthen their grasp of it, is even more important than for academically inclined pupils in a sixth form, and it is just as important for economic ideas as for those of mathematics.

One obvious conclusion emerges from this point, that a good economics course must take time. 'A' level courses traditionally cover a great deal of ground in a comparatively short time, and while the really bright sixth form pupil may be able to grasp the essential concepts and make use of them in solving problems in the time available, the weaker ones fail to do so. Time and again the average student who comes to a College of Education, having reached a low level of achievement at 'A' level economics, shows that he has not absorbed the ideas he has been taught at school. To take the recent case of rapidly rising house prices, few of our latest intake of students have been able to use an analysis of market forces to give at least a partial explanation. There was clear evidence that they had heard of supply and demand, of equilibrium prices, and of shifts in demand and supply curves, but were quite incapable of using these tools to solve the problem. Examples of the shortcomings of much traditional sixth form teaching can be multiplied indefinitely and are an indication that merely simplifying an 'A' level course is not the answer for less-able pupils. To understand fully the price mechanism, the pupils will have to build up curves, study shifts in them or movements along them, appreciate the significance of slope, and solve dozens of different problems with the aid of market models before we can feel confident that the concept is really absorbed.

So far, aspects of one problem concerning courses for pupils below 'A' level have been focussed upon, namely the need to develop conceptual thinking by constant practice on the part of the pupil. The second major problem is that of developing an understanding of the relationships between the concepts of economics. It has often been noted that economics is a circular subject with no obvious beginning or end, in which no one part can be fully understood until all have been covered. Put another way, economics resembles a jigsaw puzzle in which the picture only becomes clear when the final pieces have been assembled. In the case of the rise in house prices previously cited, it was stated that a partial explanation could be given by analysing market forces, but the underlying inflationary rise in prices requires an explanation from the field of macroeconomics. Is there any justification for giving only a partial explanation, or is there a danger that partial knowledge can be misleading? If this view is taken, the need to show the full interdependence of economic concepts carries with it the implication that short courses in economics will have little value. Both for less-able pupils and for minority time in sixth forms, short courses in economics dealing with a limited area of the subject have often been proposed. They have had titles such as the economics of housing, the economics of retailing, or the economics of the motor industry. As a means of concentrating attention such devices have their uses, but they can also be dangerous. Would a study of the car industry undertaken by pupils in Dagenham have very much value without noting the effect of foreign competition, and could the influx of French, German, Italian and Japanese cars in recent years be understood without a grasp of the essentials of international economics? Short courses of this nature can hardly be called courses in economics; some concepts may come across but the interdependence between them cannot possibly be made explicit.

If these points are accepted, the form and content of a course for the 'Newsom' child become clear. To summarize, it must concentrate on bringing out the fundamental concepts exclusive to economics, ensuring that the pupils can handle them with ease and familiarity by constant practice. The intricate relationships between the concepts must be brought out by having a course long enough to cover at least the major fundamental concepts outlined by Professors Lumsden and Attiyeh, and to facilitate the study of the connections between them in some depth. Such a course could not be treated as a minor one, squeezed into a lesson a week; it would have to be a major course, a significant part of the school curriculum.

Colleges of Education can provide the teachers for this type of course. They have the advantage that a substantial part of their courses is devoted to the methodology they will need to have as teachers. Because the demands for economics teachers for younger and less-able pupils has not been great, some colleges have concentrated more on the educational aspect of their courses in economics. If the demand increased, it would not be difficult to change the emphasis. Already a wide variety of techniques is used to teach the students. All that would be required would be fuller discussion of the relevance of the methods used in colleges to the teaching of economics in schools. Problem-solving techniques, participatory exercises involving the calculation of price indices, investment on the Stock Exchange, or the analysis of local economic problems, etc., are already in use. The provision of suitable audio-visual aids is beginning, and students are taught how to handle the equipment and to discriminate between useful and useless material. Field courses are undertaken and direct contact made with sources of economic information and activity. If the colleges can be successful in teaching economics to their students, the same students can become successful teachers of economics in the schools.

One final point needs to be made. Few economics teachers doubt the wisdom of the introduction of their subject to a much wider school population and seem clear about why they wish to do so. The usual explanation has been mentioned earlier in this paper, that in a democratic society deeply concerned with economic problems, economic literacy is essential if the electorate is to make sensible decisions in its choice of economic policies, and is to be able to interpret with some insight the news of, and comments on, economic events as they appear in the mass media. But it is surely disingenuous to believe that economics teachers are only trying to increase understanding and have no wish to influence their pupils. A television set is a vital part of the life of most people today, but we do not seek to introduce courses in TV maintenance for all children, because to know how it works is only of concern to the repairman who will deal with it when it goes wrong. By analogy, are we not seeking to introduce economics on a wider scale so that the population at large will be better equipped to deal with the things that are wrong with the economy, and by implication, with society?

The only other interpretation of the desire to increase economic understanding is that it is an exercise in the pursuit of knowledge for its own sake. However suitable this may be for the academic élite who will go on to study in universities, it is doubtful if this is what most pupils themselves want, and it is not the way the current of educational philosophy is flowing today, with its cry for greater relevance. Even if teachers believe that they will not seek to influence, but only to explain, it is doubtful if the distinction between the two can be sustained in practice. It is surely naïve to believe that a teacher dealing with the causes and consequences of economic growth can avoid value judgments about the 'quality of life'. This is not to suggest that all economics teachers will become blatant propagandists, but to emphasize that the type of course discussed in this paper will inevitably place the teacher in an exposed position where the authority he derives from his superior understanding could be used to lend weight to his own value judgments. Teachers have always derived authority for their moral judgments from their position as adults and teachers, but the serious study of a social science in schools introduces a new element which places the teacher of economics in a category, shared only by the teacher of religious studies, where his opinions appear to be supported by the subject he teaches.

Mathematics, the sciences, geography and languages can be assumed to be morally neutral in schools. History teachers take sides, but as they concentrate on the past this may be unobjectionable. Literature and the arts deal with moral values, but usually those applicable to individuals only. The social sciences, by contrast, can hardly avoid discussion of the moral values of society as a whole. In the classroom, as in the lecture room, it will be very difficult to retain the classic posture of the amoral positive economist concerned with means and not ends.

IX: DIGEST OF SEMINAR DISCUSSIONS AND CONCLUSIONS

17: Digest of Discussions*

DAVID WHITEHEAD

The Classification of Educational Objectives in Economics

Most of the discussion centred on the question of the usefulness of Bloomian-type taxonomies (see Chapter 1). Although it was asserted that teachers might find such a taxonomy a useful reference, there was no evidence at present that they did so. Nevertheless, the most valuable use of Bloomian objectives had been the way in which they had made curriculum developers and teachers think and talk about the subject. In particular, consideration of such objectives had made teachers, and especially examiners, more aware of higher domains than such easier ones as recall of knowledge. Too many courses, which were open-ended, tested only simple knowledge levels, and the whole exercise of trying to construct a Bloomian taxonomy of educational objectives for economics seemed to make people far more aware of higher domains. Following this awareness, they would try to introduce such higher domains into their courses. A useful exercise would be to try to categorize examination questions in Bloomian or some other taxonomic terms; examiners would be shocked to realize how low are the domains tested.

Another defence of Bloom began by emphasizing that works such as his were statements of educational, not teaching, objectives. As such, they at least give the teacher a guide as to how he might proceed. Bloom could be regarded as a kind of card index, against which the teacher could check what he is doing. (As with

* *Editorial Note.* It was decided at the Conference, in the interest of vitality of discussion, that remarks would not be attributed to individuals by name. It is hoped that the dullness of anonymity is to some extent offset by couching much of the digest in the present tense. The reports of discussion follow the same order as the papers in the body of the text, with references to particular papers where appropriate.

the objectives stated in Maciver's paper from the Scottish S1 units.)

Several speakers raised doubts as to the validity of Bloomian classifications. One alleged that perhaps the development of a taxonomy of educational objectives was no more than an academic exercise. To adapt Keynes, were practical teachers today to be the slaves of some defunct educationist? The notion of behaviour that underlay Bloom and much behavioural psychology in the U.S.A. was both naïve and more related to animal than to human psychology. There was a feeling that teaching might become 'over-planned' and that such planning might distort education rather than aid it.

Some argument took place on the value of taxonomies to curriculum developers. One participant opined that statements of course objectives were often an old-fashioned syllabus with behavioural prefixes, such as 'A knowledge and understanding of . . . .'; such statements made very little difference to teaching or to the kind of curriculum that one might want to adopt. To state that it was an objective 'that the pupil knows that any output is made up of several inputs' was no different from specifying a list of syllabus topics as in the past. If teaching and curriculum development were creative processes, which were not capable of being described in simple how-to-do-it models of the objectives/content/method/evaluation type, then a much more open-ended approach would be more helpful than such attempts to develop taxonomies.

Against this, another participant took the view that if there was going to be any kind of curriculum development, one had to set out with a fairly clear idea about what one was trying to achieve. Some statement of objectives was therefore necessary, so that assessment procedures could be based on such objectives, to ascertain to what extent they had been achieved, using the materials of that particular curriculum development project.

One participant entered the caveat that it was important to appreciate the limitations of Bloomian taxonomies, and to avoid the temptation to use them for purposes for which they were not designed. Although taxonomies might help to clarify what was meant by the content of economics, they did not necessarily carry any implications as to how that content should be learned. Also, even if one could devise a taxonomy, categorizing under knowledge, understanding, etc., this would not take from teachers the decision about which of those categories ought to be 'exposed' to particular types of pupils or students. Moreover, any scheme of objectives was only likely to be successful in so far as it convinced the teacher in the classroom. Would not the teacher using Bloom's taxonomy end up a nervous wreck?

In defence of the Scottish course objectives (see Chapter 2), it was felt that if the teacher could be provided with a framework whereby he could get his pupils to perform certain activities, then he would be in a much better position to see some positive learning taking place. But doubts were expressed about the criterion objectives as stated in the S1 unit, with respect to the level of attainment which was regarded as sufficient. Why should 100% attainment be required for some subjects, but only 50% for others? If only 50% was expected, for example, for comparative costs, to what extent was this really a measure of success at all? It was agreed that there was some degree of arbitrariness about the statements of success gained in achieving particular criterion objectives, and that this was a problem which had not yet been resolved.

Two final points were made by Ryba and Drake. First, if a Bloomian taxonomy was used as a basis for planning a syllabus, was there not a danger that economics teaching was missing out on certain very important areas which reflected central activities of economists, for example, the activity which was involved in recognizing a particular problem, or in recognizing that there *was* a problem in a collection of data which was presented to the student? Problem-solving cut across all the categories of the cognitive domain. Practice of this type of activity was not encouraged by present methods of assessment. There ought to be a third mode of examining, as well as essays and objective tests, to assess and take account of this central activity of problem-solving in economics.

Secondly, it should be stressed that the usefulness of Bloom came from reading his work, criticizing him, and seeing what conclusions could be drawn from trying to construct an educational taxonomy for economics. It was important that such criticisms as were made of Bloom's work should not lead teachers to abandon him before having even considered his approach.

Values in Economics Teaching

Lee's paper had a significant impact throughout the seminar on participants' awareness of the value-loaded implications of many economic statements (see Chapter 3). In the light of the kind of tasks it had been suggested (in the previous papers) that the teacher should perform it was the view of one speaker that the 'special challenge' of coping with the elucidation of values in economics would be likely to cause the teacher to collapse!

Lee's argument that the reinstatement of ends within economics courses did not involve the abandonment of the positive/normative distinction was held by some to be invalid, since it had been shown in the last twenty years that many of the ends (especially of macroeconomic objectives), were conflicting, and that there was a trade-off between them. We were finding that ends themselves had to be questions, and it was argued that perhaps this was endemic to the subject. Against this, the view was put that for example macroeconomic objectives were lower-order aims, and that what economics courses were in fact about was optimal resource allocation, which was really value-loaded.

Although Lee emphasized bias in the subject matter of economics, which was admittedly important, another aspect of bias which should not be ignored was that which emanated from the teacher, and indeed from teaching methods. Little work had been done on assessing the significance of such bias.

Another participant stressed that there was a semantic bias in positive economics. For example, 'free' enterprise: freedom has overtones of something certainly to be desired. 'State interference' is itself a loaded expression. 'Perfect' competition has connotations of excellence and desirability. Monopoly is not called perfect, although it could be, in the same sense in which competition is called perfect. It was agreed that the tendency here was conservative, but what was the evidence to suggest that it was strongly so?*

It was pointed out that Lee's paper did not mention the demand from sixth-formers to discuss ends. If it is agreed that it should not be the teacher's job to deal with value judgments

---

* For more extended treatment of these points see R. Szreter, 'The Teacher of Economics and the Problem of Political Bias', *Economics*, Vol. IX, Part 6, pp. 353–7.

(which is questionable) then it is important to obtain reading suggestions for thoughtful sixth-formers in this area. It is difficult to see how, in the classroom, one brings out the techniques of *constructive* criticism, which is the sort of criticism one participant wanted to hear. There is still much to learn about how the attitude of criticizing in a constructive way can be developed in children.

Many Advanced Level questions were couched in the form: '*Should* we do so-and-so . . .?'; this tended to provoke the more emotional into boldly stating one or other extreme of the argument, under the strain of examination conditions. In how many such questions was the evaluation ultimately a question of values? There had been little thought about ways in which it might be possible to *assess* how pupils handled values and ends. Usually, all teachers got were a few pejorative phrases in examiners' reports.

Finally, it was noted that in Australia there had been a very strong movement from secondary school economics students, concerned that economics as a subject was not value-free. We might be forewarned that teachers there were being accused of having bias built into their methodology and content.

Some Research Problems in Economics Education

Two main questions were examined in the light of Scott's paper: first, the meaning which should be attached to the concept 'core of economics', and secondly, the problems associated with assessing the 'teacher variable' in the Project (see Chapter 4).

Although there might be agreement between economists about what constituted the 'core of economics', there might just as well be a conspiracy as an agreement! In any case, agreement is not a valid criterion for judging whether what is regarded as the 'core of economics' really *is* the 'core'. Is there any empirical evidence about what constitutes the 'core'? It is important to be quite clear about what is the status of an *asserted* 'core', or a 'core' which is the product of casual empiricism. Against this view, however, it was argued that there could never be proof of what constituted the 'core'. How might an experiment be set up to test what the 'core of economics' was?

It was emphasized that the Project was only concerned with

knowledge of fundamental concepts which constituted *basic* economics, as opposed to assessing what 'an economist' should be considered as having a duty to know. Perhaps it might suffice to teach pupils only one half of the basic knowledge that they at present learned, because all one wanted to do was to give them an inquiring approach to the subject. In which case the main problem would be to decide which half of the content to jettison!

The nub of the criticism of the Economics Education Project was perhaps that, although it alleged that economists were being unscientific in relation to examining economic understanding, and what would be the most efficient way of increasing it, in fact the Project itself set up a 'core' for output measurement which was irrefutable.

The second main area of discussion centred around the questions of the 'teacher variable', and the use made of the Project's results. One participant felt that, although he welcomed the exploration by the Economics Education Project, it was worrying how the results were being used by other people, as if such results were of the kind upon which decisions could be based. One particular result in this context was the finding that those who combined geography and economics at Advanced Level did less well at economics than those who did not take geography. Nothing necessarily follows from such a result. It was stressed that practically nothing was known about the teacher variable, and that variations in teachers' abilities were not really accounted for in the results. Despite such caveats, there was real evidence that the results were being used in a way for which they were not intended.

It was important that the Project's results should not be used by some sorcerer's apprentice, without reading all the caveats. The value of the Project, which was real, was to put weight behind certain questions, such as whether 'economic thinking' could be differentiated in any way. But the questions of curriculum development in the sixth form, and of what combinations of subjects should be recommended, were not predicated on the kind of results that had issued from the Economics Education Project.

The second area of discussion on research problems in economics education centred on audio-visual aids (see Chapter 5).

Participants were mainly concerned with how such audio-visual materials as were on the market could be tested. It was generally assumed that they would be used in conjunction with traditional teacher exposition; their role in heuristic techniques of learning has not yet been investigated.

Many audio-visual materials have recently been produced, and the education industry is selling them very hard. This makes the question of how audio-visual materials help in the learning of the subject very important. The problem of choice faces the teacher (with a definite expenditure constraint). There is such a range of materials available, as well as a variety of ways in which they can be used. What criteria should teachers use to assess the effectiveness of particular audio-visual materials or media as against others? This area needs urgent investigation. A further important investigation would concern whether learning with audio-visual materials, or through different media, is communicated more effectively at some ages than at others. For example, would it be more useful to give a visual representation of economics to younger pupils?

There was a general consensus that very little of the work done in this field had been related to economics. Such American work as had been published was extremely imprecise about what audio-visual aids had actually been used, their quality, and how the control group had been set up. Despite the advanced statistical procedures used, most of the research appeared rather unconvincing.

However, one should not underestimate the considerable problems of experimental design involved in trying to set up any kind of project to test an individual audio-visual resource. Any particular resource would usually be part of a package, and it might be more or less effective with a package of a different composition. The way in which the teacher used the materials was especially crucial. American research to date had been very inadequate in trying to standardize for the student variable.

One sceptic felt that audio-visual aids had been oversold to teachers, that although they might create and sustain interest, it was already being accepted that they could aid and increase understanding, whereas the evidence for this was lacking. Against this view, it was argued that a false sense of conflict was created by suggesting that the utility of any particular audio-visual resource had not yet been proved. A visit, or a piece of audio-visual material, was after all one of many experiences to which pupils were exposed. It was not a question of whether one experience was more effective than another; rather, the aim was to expose the pupils to as many relevant experiences as possible. So little was known about the process of learning, that at least one might hope that exposure to a variety of experiences would enable the pupils to learn one way or another.

It was felt by another speaker that the degree of concreteness did not reside in the medium itself. For example, playing a tape recording of an abstract exposition of diminishing returns was different from hearing a tape of a manager talking about how diminishing returns were relevant to the decisions that he had to make in his factory. In other words, the tape conversation had to be capable of being visualized, in order to be concrete.

Another suggestion was that some people felt that audio-visual aids, visits, etc., were anti-intellectual, that they were acceptable for young children, but that it was not academically respectable to indulge in their use. In fact, once the academic teacher overcame this initial blockage, he would appreciate their use, and indeed realize that a good deal of professional skill was needed to use such aids properly. It was implied that perhaps some teachers had not given sufficient thought to how these skills might be developed.

For example, any changes in the teacher's role in the classroom, precipitated by the use of audio-visual aids, might prove a stumbling block to their introduction. Teachers might not be aware that the use of such materials might necessitate a change in their classroom behaviour. Were they to conduct lessons traditionally, with the audio-visual material used purely incidentally, or should the whole situation be differently structured? One participant suggested that such 'software' as existed could be used in conjunction with a wide variety of classroom styles, from pure didactic to problem-solving. For example, the Economics Association filmstrip entitled 'Location of Industry' might lend itself to the latter, the 'City of London' filmstrip to the former.

Finally, various practical questions were raised. Despite a teacher's desire to use audio-visual aids, he might be hindered by not having the necessary equipment readily available, nor ancillary staff ready and willing to set it up. Now that schools were moving towards resource centres, one of the most important developments ought to be the appointment of ancillary staff to assist in the setting up and preparation of materials. Another constraint was imposed by the teacher's allowance for purchasing equipment and materials. It was suggested that teachers ought to ask more strongly for what they thought was necessary. If the demand were from a large number of teachers, the schools would find it worth while to provide such equipment. Science departments seemed to have no difficulty in obtaining materials and assistants.

One last comment: compared with what children saw every day on television (especially colour television), the sort of things to which they were subjected in schools were often a kind of museum experience!

Economics and Social Studies at School

There was little consensus in this field. Argument was concentrated in two main areas, revolving around whether economics should be 'integrated' at sixth form level and at lower levels.

Holley argued for an integrated social science course at the lower end of the secondary school. Since we could not teach everything we wanted to teach, and given the opportunity cost of teaching economics at that level, it would be preferable for economics to make its contribution below the sixth form through some interdisciplinary or integrated course in social science (see Chapter 6).

One participant also suggested that the opportunity cost argument applies equally at the sixth form level. Doubts are now being expressed about the content of sixth form economics courses, especially for the majority who will take the subject no further. When pupils leave school, they should have *some* knowledge relevant to what they are likely to face in the world. If a course is to be of practical as well as educational value, then it must be really integrated, in the sense that the material is brought together in a new way for a new purpose.

Various problems could nevertheless be foreseen in any attempt to construct a sixth form integrated course. One basic objection is that the most cogent arguments are for discipline-based courses. But another major problem concerns whether the teachers would be able to cope with such a course. There is already so much confusion of aims within subject areas at school level. Considerable criticism could already be levelled at the teachers' lack of sensitivity to the subject and to the pupils. Any kind of integration in which the teacher has not got the support of a discipline with which he is thoroughly familiar, is likely to be faced with enormous problems. Society is making increasing demands on the teacher, and today he is called upon to perform a vast number of tasks which in the past he was not expected to do. If we are expecting teachers to be almost superhuman already, are we not now expecting them to do an increasingly impossible job? If we add the need for the teacher to be a polymath, even if just within the social science field, it is an unrealistic hope. However, it must not be overlooked that team teaching might go some way towards solving some of these problems.

Still at the sixth form level, another problem concerned the proliferation of social subjects such as psychology, sociology and anthropology pressing for a position within the curriculum. If we are expecting pupils to absorb the particular thinking of all these different disciplines (which would be compounded within an integrated social science course), then we are expecting a very great deal from them.

The second area of discussion focussed on possibilities below the sixth form. One question which needs to be explored concerns the teaching of individual social subjects in relation to children's learning capacity. What was the educational rationale for the teaching of history and geography in the early stages of secondary schooling, and for admitting other social subjects only at some later stage into the curriculum? (see Chapter 7).

Secondary education might either start with a grounding in the various disciplines, then broadening out into an interdisciplinary or integrated course at a later stage (by which time pupils will have got some understanding of the basis of the discipline), or, at the start, one might use a thematic or topic-based approach, cross-disciplinary in nature, and only at a later stage in the learning capacity of the children, expose them to a really serious examination of the individual disciplines.

Another speaker suggested that if we are going to start introducing economic concepts to children aged eight, then might not an approach which starts in an integrated way, then splits up into individual disciplines for the early secondary years, and finally concludes with integrated studies, be a possibility? Doubts were however expressed about the theoretical basis for such a sequence. Could it be justified on Piagetian grounds? If not, what would be its rationale?

A further problem concerned whether there would be enough economics teachers to cope with the extension of the subject, even if only contributing to part of an integrated course. This led on to discussion about whether an early secondary level integrated social studies course *should* be taught by an economist!

On a practical note, it was suggested that when we actually try to integrate the social sciences, we immediately turn up our taxonomies, to seek guidance from them. The result is usually that it is the very low levels of the taxonomies of the subjects (knowledge-centred) that we end up by integrating, and we do not in fact achieve integration of the kind of techniques which we want the pupils to learn.

If it were accepted that integration ultimately takes place within the pupil, then ideas like co-operation should not be ignored. It is possible to design such choices within the school curriculum that, given wise guidance, the pupil can select a spread of subjects that enables some kind of integration to take place within him rather than for teachers to try and integrate subjects for him to take. One sceptic regarded that as wishful thinking; such choice might often result in confusion rather than integration. Should general education be structured so that it becomes nothing in particular? Also, one repeatedly came across confusion in educational circles between integrated, multi-disciplinary, and cross-disciplinary studies. It was important to be clear about which type one was supporting.

Some people may regard attempts at integration as 'social slops' or 'cross-sterilization', but nevertheless there is a distinct pressure for interdisciplinary social science in schools. It would be cynical to suggest that this was connected with the large numbers of sociologists emerging jobless from universities.

Some final notes: the Tasmanian syllabuses in this area are interesting and worth consulting (integrated studies are called 'fused' in Australia!). The East Anglian C.S.E. Social Studies Syllabus B is an attempt at an interdisciplinary social science syllabus.

Economics Below the Sixth Form

One participant sought clarification of the teacher's role in the Scottish Curriculum Development Project. Was he left with any initiative? In fact, he is left with considerable freedom in the way in which he presents and uses the materials of the Project (see Chapter 8). He is actively involved, to a much greater extent than in many formal lesson situations. The Project involves much group work, where the teacher is occupied in moving around the groups, setting up the projects, working with individual pupils, answering their questions, and suggesting lines of inquiry and development. Most of the lessons are extremely open-ended, the pupils playing roles with the kit material, and it is really a very demanding role that the teacher has to play. Pupils of different abilities gain different ideas from the same situation, and the teacher has to operate on various levels during any given lesson.

Another speaker asked how widespread the pilot Project was. The scheme is operating in 15 to 20 schools, with about 1,300 pupils. It was stressed that it was still at the experimental stage, and results had not yet been received covering the first term's work. One question that would have to be looked at very carefully is whether the material would have to be graded in relation to the pupils' ability ranges.

Doubts were expressed about whether, with such a demanding scheme, there are sufficient teachers of high enough calibre to do the job that is required. Against this it was argued that there are a considerable number of teachers who do want guidance, and for whom a fairly precise statement of objectives, such as that in the Scottish Curriculum Development Project, is helpful.

While most of the discussion on Christie's paper revolved around problems for the teacher, the emphasis in Robinson's paper was on the pupil, and concerned whether economics *could* be taught to the less-able pupil (see Chapter 9).

One participant questioned Robinson's statement that the simplicity or complexity of a discipline was largely a function of the language and illustrations used to explain it. Although this might be so, was there any evidence to support it? Robinson meant that the basic ideas of economics were very simple, but that they were often made very much more complex by the language which the economist used to explain them.

Another speaker queried Robinson's statement that less-academic students were unlikely to be able to reach beyond the comprehension stage of the cognitive hierarchy (in Bloom's taxonomy). Are they incapable of performing the essential operations of the higher-order skills, and of grasping the essential ideas and relationships? In answer to this, it was explained that the statement was made in the context of trying to devise objective questions testing for example synthesis; such an operation would be extraordinarily difficult at Advanced Level, let alone in the first years of secondary schooling.

Despite the doubts expressed in some quarters about teaching economics to less-able pupils, the fact remained that the subject had been taught at C.S.E. level for a number of years. Smith's paper supplied useful background material in this field (see Chapter 10).

It was pointed out that the three main sections of the syllabus quoted in Smith's paper were entitled: 'Men as Workers', 'Men as Consumers', and 'Men as Citizens'. It seems that girls and women have no role to play as workers, consumers, and citizens! Perhaps one ought to be aware of such value implications of syllabuses when they are constructed.

Another criticism of the syllabus was that it seemed pointless to include such a large element of quickly forgotten facts. (This might also be alleged against 'O' level and 'A' level, although admittedly that would not be a defence of the C.S.E. syllabus content.) The course did not seem to be based on the 'core of economics'. Clearly elements of economics would emerge in such a course, but only tangentially, and the examination paper cited does not test any real understanding of economics. It could be passed well by pupils with good recall of facts, but without any real grasp of principles.

It was noted that the project was a voluntary part of the examination. Since the project's worth was so highly praised, why was it not made compulsory? It was pointed out that it *was* compulsory for one Board. Also, in the Middlesex scheme, candidates are seen individually for 10 to 15 minutes, and they are orally examined on their projects. It would be useful for an examiner to spend more time in the schools, interviewing the candidates to test their economic understanding.

One participant asked why Mode III had disappeared. One possible reason is that teachers are much too busy to prepare and submit their own syllabuses and examinations. Another is that Boards may have been over-critical of teachers' efforts, and have rejected syllabuses, which teachers subsequently have been too busy to revise and re-submit. The one teacher who had used Mode III had transferred to Mode I, either perhaps because he eventually decided that he liked the Mode I syllabus, or because he wanted his pupils to do the project, which is examined in Mode I but not in Mode III.

Economics in the Sixth Form, and its Relationship to University Level Economics

There was considerable argument, arising out of Oliver's paper, concerning the type of economics that should be taught at university (see Chapter 11). There was a danger of overselling the subject. Some evidence existed to show that post-school economics students were becoming disappointed with what economics actually offered them. They had been given a quite mistaken idea of the practical utility they would derive from their course. Despite the use of for example problem-solving techniques, students were becoming disillusioned about the subject. Therefore it was important that teachers should be careful about what claims they made for the subject, especially in relation to some of the syllabuses and examinations set for the professions.

Only a very small percentage of those who do economics for their first degree go on to become professional economists. Surely therefore the most important role for economics is as part of general education, not only at sixth form level, but also at university, whence graduate economists do not emerge to use the professional skills of the economist in their jobs. If this is so, then it would follow that the pressure for an increased mathematical content at 'A' level economics would be seen in a new light (see Chapter 12). It might be granted that certain mathematical techniques are part of general education, but whether they should be taught through any particular subject is another question.

Even if students do proceed to become professional economists, of what use is their first degree in economics? It is interesting to note the extent to which even people who have a specialist degree in economics, and who want to become professional economists, need to reappraise what they learnt in the first three years, when they start practising what in professional terms is known as economics. Do university graduates in other disciplines have the same problem? For example, surely graduates in mechanical engineering can use the facts and skills they have acquired at first-degree level, and build on what they have done. In this sense, economics is unique, in that most of those who come out of universities to work as professional economists are simply ill-equipped for the tasks they are called upon to perform. The training of professional economists is gradually coming to be seen as a post-graduate activity.

Other participants thought that this view was exaggerated. There was a danger in being too market-oriented in approaching what needs to be taught at university. Why should universities train people to learn for example just those skills that are needed at the Treasury, or in some large company, or by the accountancy profession? Taking the analogy of the graduate engineer, it is not strictly true that he can go out and be usefully employed straight away; he has to serve his time in training. In any case, there are several places where economics degrees can be obtained which do at least equip the graduates to 'think usefully' when they join an organization. It might however be the case that universities are so intent on packing great quantities of information into the course that graduates may not be very well equipped at expressing their own ideas.

Some courses tried to overcome some of these difficulties by providing a variety of interdisciplinary degrees, containing an economics segment. Such degrees have not to date been very satisfactory, because they have not been integrated in any way. What are the objectives of such courses, and how do you decide when they have been achieved? Some attempt must be made to bring about a relationship between different parts of the course. For example, economics lecturers should work out their course in relation to what other subject specialists are dealing with in their part of the same degree course.

Moving on to consideration of 'A' level economics, the educational value of much of its content was questioned. The divorce between economic models and statistical techniques at this level was unfortunate. If one looked through any traditional school economics text-book, a large part of the economist's way of thinking and way of testing would be missing. The standard text-books, full of deductive argument, present a rather bogus view of what economics is. On the other hand, there are difficulties in trying to introduce empirical research at this level. For example, the Phillips Curve has been taught for some time as though it were a received truth, whereas the original article was tentative and full of provisos. There is a real problem as to whether we ought to try to introduce that kind of work (as Lipsey has done) into 'A' level courses.

Examinations in economics were discussed in relation to most of the papers presented; the argument has been synthesized below. The main area of controversy concerned the effects which examinations have on the content of economics syllabuses and on methods of teaching (see Chapter 13).

On content, it was suggested that it was easier to add to examination syllabuses than to cut topics out of them. For example, on committees for revising examination syllabuses, most members might well have wished to reduce syllabus scope and content. But it was very difficult to reach any agreement about what should be left out.

It was agreed that Chief Examiners cast a long shadow. If a question were set for example on cost-benefit analysis for the first time ever, the following winter all the teachers would be teaching that subject. But it was doubted whether Chief Examiners should arrogate to themselves the right to manipulate what the schools were doing in this way. On the other hand, nothing would change if they did not do so.

Further, the kind of examination which takes place at 'A' level may not in fact be testing the kind of qualities which characterize an economist at all. This was suggested in relation to Scott's paper, in which he used an input/output/value-added approach to educational assessment. Might one not 'add value' in one sense (i.e. higher 'A' level grades) without more fundamentally educating the pupils? Many teachers taught their pupils how to deal with economics examinations very successfully, without the pupils understanding any of the techniques in which they had allegedly been trained. (Even more alarmingly, there were a large number of students graduating with degrees in economics, who did not basically understand how to use the subject, and what it was about.) Large numbers of 'A' level candidates are able to produce plausible answers, at the same time clearly revealing that they do not understand what they are doing. Nevertheless they succeed, because they can put the right responses in the right order.

From the teacher's point of view, it was asked why examiners did not publish the marking schemes for economics. The normal response was that such a publication would most likely be misused, with pupils being drilled in the way a particular marking scheme suggests a question ought to be approached. However, one participant felt strongly that a marking scheme *should* suggest the way in which a question should be approached. Hence, surely it would be commendable for pupils to approach it in that way? Against this, it was suggested that a published marking scheme might in the long run penalize pupils who approached a question in an original way. In any case, examiners always had the opportunity to state in their reports how they thought particular questions should be attempted.

The approach of the Business Studies Project to examinations was somewhat revealing in the light of the above criticisms of the orthodox economics examinations. Each year an examiner's report is produced, together with a series of the answers that candidates have actually presented typed out in full, plus comments from the examiners about what they think about those answers. There is also a meeting where participant schools can talk about any aspect of examining. This procedure does not seem to have created any examination problems.

The final area of discussion focussed on the feedback effects of examinations on teaching methods. Was it true that the syllabus was a constraint at 'A' level on the teaching method? It might be accepted that pupils needed to spend more time on the elementary aspects of the subject, on concrete elements, before moving on to the stages of abstraction and concept-building. If so, could it not be argued that the normal syllabus was so large that the teacher was being prevented from spending as much time as he should on the more fundamental stages? This problem also arose at university level, where courses were trying to do too much. If one wished to develop 'economic thinking', the appropriate teaching methods would take much more time, so this would necessitate a reduction in syllabus content.

On one occasion, in Australia, the fifth-year economics examination was used to bring about change. One section of the syllabus was on industrial relations. Students had become completely wrapped up in the minutiae of industrial disputes, learning every insignificant detail. So in future examination papers, great slabs of detail were printed, and simple questions were asked about the basic economics of the situation. The students found this most disconcerting, but it had the desired effect of stopping the teaching of too much factual detail.

The Business Studies Project

The main areas of debate concerned the content of the 'A' level Business Studies course, how it fitted into the sixth form curriculum, the methods used to assess achievement at 'A' level and whether it was value-free (see Chapter 14).

One element of the syllabus which was singled out for praise was the treatment of 'cash flows'. Whilst one might go right through an 'A' level Economics course without coming across this concept, the Business Studies syllabus really covered such relevant ideas. Another praiseworthy aspect of the Project was the support which the Project Office gave to the programme in the schools; it was suggested how useful this arrangement might have been in the early stages of economics teaching in schools.

One participant was surprised that it was possible for pupils to take both Economics and Business Studies at 'A' level. Was this not an over-specialized curriculum? It appeared that the combination was taken by 15% of those taking 'A' level Business Studies. Originally it had been a forbidden combination; even now the Project would prefer the two subjects not to be taken together. Universities accepted Business Studies as an 'A' level, for purposes of matriculation, but not with Economics as two 'A' levels.

Another problem concerned whether Business Studies is bringing anything worthwhile to the sixth form curriculum that is not already there. One must consider whether it could be justified when some other subject must be forgone. In response to this, it was suggested that in the last resort, it was still up to the school or college to decide whether or not to provide the course. The 'A' level Business Studies course is rigorous (not a soft option as might originally have been expected by some schools), and less-able sixth-formers may not reach a passable standard at 'A' level. Nevertheless, a weaker student might get more out of Business Studies than out of an Economics course (even though he failed in the end), because of the range of material to which he was being exposed, which could perhaps be used again by him later. The weaker student would have some foundation on which to build when he left school.

Various problems were posed in relation to the project part of the course assessment. Such projects would normally perhaps present a multi-disciplinary approach, which would make it very difficult for discipline-based examiners to judge them. However, the Project team did not regard this as a real problem. In fact, examiners had clear criteria for judging projects. Had the student carefully defined the nature of the problem? Had he analysed it correctly, setting himself reasonable constraints? Had he obtained reasonable data to deal with the problem? Had it been well presented? Had he drawn logical conclusions, according to the data he had gathered? One practical problem was that if a project was to be done, the students would need access to actual data, but perhaps firms would cease to co-operate when the 'A' level became a large-scale exercise. Pilot plans are however already being made to overcome this difficulty.

Finally, concern was expressed that the course might implicitly be normative, even if this was not intended. It *could* result in turning out students who were happy to fit into a modern indus-trial organization, satisfied with the economic system. Or it *might* breed a new race of industrial radicals, by dealing with a critical examination of the aims and structure of firms. What are the concealed or revealed values of this type of course? It was stressed that the way in which the material was approached was left to the teacher, who might for example decide to go through the whole course dealing with nationalized enterprises rather than capitalist firms. Decision-making is just as relevant to the former as to the latter.

Economics for Civil Servants and Student Teachers

Unfortunately, little time in discussion was devoted to Hewitt's very interesting experiment (see Chapter 15). One participant asked what effect the shortness of the course had on methods of teaching and learning. It was found that the lecturing technique was quite redundant, mainly because of the course members' characteristics. They had practical experience, and wanted to participate. This placed considerable strain on the teacher. The course was structured around a particular problem-solving case study, soliciting responses from the participants as it proceeded. It was in fact the only course in this country known to be using solely the case-study method.

It was also unfortunate that the seminar had no representatives from the Colleges of Education present. The general feeling which emerged was that much more needed to be known about economics education in this field (see Chapter 16). Although a great deal of money is being put into Schools Council Projects, or the Scottish Project, to produce 'engineered' curricula, with plenty of materials, little attention and few resources are being devoted to the teacher. Curriculum development in the last decade has been too divorced from the teacher, although admittedly this situation is now changing. Recent projects involve much more teacher participation in creating materials and suggesting ideas. Nevertheless, there is an urgent need for more in-service training for economics teachers, to acquaint them with recent curriculum developments.

If, as Sumner's paper suggested, social studies are likely to develop in the Junior School, it was very important that colleges of education should give student teachers a deeper understanding of the *nature* of the discipline, as well as awareness of its substantive content.

It was understood that there were approximately fifteen colleges of education which ran main economics courses. It would be interesting to know what kind of economics was taught there. The type of economics that the students were being taught would obviously influence the type of economics that they would teach once they had finished their course. Perhaps 300 to 350 student teachers specializing in economics were emerging from colleges of education annually. Were they being taught just an expanded type of 'A' level course? It was thought that the emphasis on the methodology side is on teaching the subject to younger and less-able pupils.

Hancock suggested in his paper that one should start teaching the subject by using the children's experiences. One problem here is that they do not all have the same background, especially in a racially or socially mixed area, and so what one might take as an appeal to a child's experience may in fact be remote from the experience of several children in the class.

Finally, it was noted, in relation to the Business Studies Project, that it was surprising how quickly teachers could change and develop their skills, if they really wished to do so, as long as they were provided with resources which helped them to do this, and a support base to which they could refer whenever necessary. Given three or four years, one could totally change the resources a teacher possessed to help him in a new area of teaching. Pessimism therefore was unjustified.

18: The Economics Curriculum: Looking to the Future*

RAYMOND RYBA

Considerable effort has been expended in recent years on curriculum development in many subject areas. In economics, however, there is little evidence of comparable work, at any rate in the U.K. A considerable body of literature has been built up stating general views of economics in the curriculum as perceived by various 'experts'; many syllabuses, hypothetical or in use, have been described and recommended; surveys of economics education have been compiled; but no major research relating to fundamental problems of curriculum development in the subject has previously been reported.[1] Yet evidence suggested that sufficient relevant work was being done in various parts of the country to justify convening the seminar—the first of its kind in the U.K.—for which the papers collected in this volume were prepared.

In planning the seminar, Keith Drake and Norman Lee had three main overlapping areas of concern in mind: the 'A' level economics curriculum—its content and method, and its relationships both with other subjects in the curriculum and with university work; the relationships between economics and other subjects in the 8–18 age range, especially in the context of integrated courses; and problems related to the economics curriculum for those unlikely to specialize in the subject or take it further. In the event, while all these areas have been examined in several of the papers collected here, some papers have extended the scope of the discussion beyond their confines and even, in certain cases, into overlapping areas, for example, teaching methodology, examinations, and the nature of economics. In consequence, great

* The reflections contained in this concluding chapter are based on the writer's introductory remarks as Chairman of the final session of the seminar at which the papers collected in this volume were presented. The checklist of economics curriculum research needs contained in the Appendix to the chapter is also a product of this session.

diversity is evident, not only in the problems which contributors have chosen to examine but also in the approaches they have adopted and in the nature of the conclusions they have drawn.

What, then, has been achieved? And, in particular, how far has the exercise proved useful in laying down guidelines for future work and in formulating specific tasks related to the economics curriculum? The task of drawing together the many strands of thought is by no means easy and my effort to do so is inevitably personal and subjective.

In a general sense, the collecting together, for the first time, of work being done in the U.K. on the economics curriculum has been a major valuable achievement. Every individual and organization in the U.K. known to be working in the field was invited to present a paper. Virtually every one of these invitations was accepted. Consequently, the collected papers offer a representative assessment of the present state of curriculum development in economics in the country.

No less important was the possibility provided for the contributors to discuss common problems and to share perceptions. The result has been an opportunity for the cross-fertilization of ideas. The first fruits of this are clearly indicated in David Whitehead's discussion summaries. A starting point has been provided from which the course of future advances in this area of economics education can be forecast more clearly, and a more concerted and cohesive attack can be made on the problems discerned.

By piecing together the papers it is possible to assemble a map not only of what has so far been done but also of possible outlines for future work. The result, like that resulting from the work of the early cartographers, is stronger in promise, speculation and excitement than in the presentation of hard and immediately applicable data; but to say this is in no way to reflect upon its usefulness. The fact that the economics curriculum 'continent' delineated is seen explicitly as largely awaiting the kind of detailed exploration already undertaken in other subjects is itself an advance.

*　　　*　　　*

Each of the papers and the discussions which followed them have thrown up a multiplicity of research tasks which appeared to contributors to merit attention. The most important of these are listed in the Appendix to this chapter (see pp. 252–257). But in addition to these, and despite the diversities of approach, method and conclusions already mentioned, certain rather striking underlying conceptual strands may be discerned which are common to the thinking of most of the contributors. This conceptual common ground offers a basis for future work in the field.

The most striking common characteristic, in my view, has been the high degree of *future-orientation* of the papers. By this, I mean that contributors have tried to see, beyond the needs of the present time, the needs which are likely to arise in the years to come. This is not to imply that present needs have been ignored: only that concern has not been limited to them. In the consideration of objectives, for example, we have not been content to limit the discussion to the undoubtedly necessary application of Bloomian, behavioural, approaches. Instead, we have felt impelled to step further ahead, to look critically at the applicability of Bloomian taxonomies and to hazard guesses at alternative approaches.

Moving from a consideration which is essentially educational in character to one which is more directly in the economics field, the question of positive/normative distinctions has been raised. The suggestion has been made that the advantages derived from maintaining sharpness in this distinction—advantages now well understood—are not without their cost. Some contributors have clearly begun to blur the edges—perhaps more than blur them—between the positive and normative aspects of economics. They have done so, however, without returning to the *status quo ante*. The concept of a distinction between the positive and the normative is of course an important one. Moreover, it is an important one to teach thoroughly and explicitly to pupils and students in schools and colleges. Perhaps, even, the meaning and importance of the distinction is still too little grasped by many of those learning our subject. Nevertheless, the implication of some of the contributions in this volume, as well as of the discussions, is that we also think it important to bear in mind that it is not always either easy or wise to separate positive considerations from normative ones; that the one runs into the other; that the adoption of a positive economic position is itself a normative stance—and one which may not continue to dominate thinking in economics in future years as it has done in the recent past.

The positive/normative distinction is itself an example of the use of categories and categorization, a more general area about which contributors appear to have been concerned. What seems to have been implied in several of the papers is that while categorization helps purposeful discussion along particular lines, its use may well cut vital links in other directions. We are dealing after all with the seamless cloak of knowledge and, while we may need to cut that cloak into bits in particular ways—because this is the way we think—we need also to think of sewing up again—reintegrating our findings in terms of the whole cloak. This question of categorization, seen as an analytical tool—as a construct, to use Weber's language—rather than as the finished description itself, has clearly characterized several of the papers. Categorization has of course been used but attention has also been paid to its dangers.

The handling of problems related to quantification has also been future-orientated. Here it is only too obvious to the contributors, as it is to others, that courses in schools and colleges must move towards a greater understanding and practical experience of quantitative approaches.[2] Yet, looking further ahead, contributors have felt it necessary to question just what place quantification should have in economics; to ask whether limitations to its usefulness might not arise earlier than is implied by some econometric approaches at present in vogue and to consider the implications of these views for the curriculum.

And finally, in this list of future-orientated characteristics, it seems clear that we are beginning to think in new ways about methodology in educational research. Are we—in this field at least—beginning to query accepted modes of empirical research; looking more closely at the nature of the hypotheses we wish to test and at the kinds of experimental designs which might be pertinent? Here, we are particularly indebted to Alex Scott who, in his very elegant paper, led us on towards questioning the validity of currently accepted empirical approaches.

In all these matters, contributors to this volume have placed their emphasis—and, in my view, rightly so—on the future. Nevertheless, I believe a word of caution is necessary. There is a sense in which pitching one's stance in the future may not be entirely helpful to those engaged in trying to improve the economics curriculum in the present context. At a time when much effort still needs to be made to reap the full benefit of existing approaches, there is danger that readers, convinced by the future-orientated arguments we have cited, might be tempted to undervalue— even to ignore—present approaches which we have criticized. Thus, the forward-looking reader might decide to have no truck with Bloomian exercises in the identification of educational objectives, or to soft-pedal the introduction of quantitative concepts in anticipation of a reversed swing of the pendulum. Leapfrogging of this kind, analogous to procedures which poor countries sometimes adopt to hasten their development—telescoping the stages of economic growth—is superficially attractive. However, it misses the useful side-effects of slower development and leaves one exposed to potentially severe problems. The benefits of thinking ahead may easily be lost unless we distinguish this operation from the separate problem of implementing change.

So much for future-orientation. Turning now to other common strands in these papers, a second striking characteristic has been the *lack of complacency* exhibited by the contributors. There has been an almost complete avoidance of the sort of activity which, ten years ago, would have been taken for granted from any one of the contributors: that is to say, the offering of *ex cathedra* pronouncements and prescriptions, based on personal opinion and experience but on very little else. (To say this is not to belittle either personal opinion or experience.) Instead, we have had a cautious kind of consideration of our problems and a questioning approach to possible solutions; a realization that a lot more needs to be known in terms of content, in terms of methods, in terms of underlying values and assumptions.

I should like to concentrate particularly on values and assumptions for a moment because consideration of their importance and their nature seem to me to be a *leitmotif* running through many of the papers. In paper after paper, and even more in the discussions which ensued, problems related to assumed norms, judgments and criteria have constantly recurred. Contributors have concentrated our attention on their own assumptions and on those of others whose work they have been examining. They have been stressing the importance of clarifying our assumptions, of making them explicit, and of being prepared to justify them. The implication here, it seems to me, is a movement towards a repudiation of the attitude, which has been very common amongst professional academics, of saying 'I'm wearing my professional hat. Tell me the assumptions and I'll give you an answer in terms of those assumptions,' while refusing to commit oneself on their perti-nence. As in the matter of distinctions between positive and normative economics, the view has been taken that responsibility for the choice and use of assumptions and the values they state or imply should not—indeed, cannot—be shirked.

A third area of common ground to which we have been led has been an acceptance of the need for *a reconsideration of the nature of social science*. One contributor, for example, refers to Winch's book, *The Idea of a Social Science*.[3] Winch criticized, from a philo-sophical point of view, the whole notion that a social science may be built on analogous lines to those employed in the development of physical sciences. This view has certainly been prevalent, both amongst economists and amongst educationists. Yet I think it is clear that most contributors to this volume have preferred to accept the kind of relativism implied by Winch's analysis.

The view that underlying assumptions of rock-like solidity exist on which the analysis of our problems can safely be built has been challenged. Instead, we appear to be saying that we need to make up for the instability of the ground by constructing our own firm foundations—putting down concrete rafts, as it were —to counter its shifting nature. In particular, we need to take account of shifts in criteria underpinning studies, like our own, in which human intervention, with all its unpredictable non-mechanistic characteristics, is itself a factor to be taken into account.

A fourth common feature in these papers has been a tendency to move towards the consideration of what we are doing as economists and economic educators in a *societal context*. It is quite natural and proper to direct ourselves back, as we have done, to the subject itself—to thinking about the economics curriculum in terms of the subject's structure. We can't really think of curri-culum development in economics without bearing that in mind. But, at the same time, a navel-contemplating exercise—judging what economics we should teach in schools only in terms of the subject's own logic or, at most, in terms of satisfying the pre-liminary needs of specialist university economics courses—is surely not enough. We have to remember that economics is just one subject in the curriculum, that the curriculum is only part of education, and that education itself is only one sub-system of the total social system to which it contributes. And this being the case, looking simply at economics for guidance on what we should teach, without an eye to these wider considerations, would be a very partial and unsafe kind of analysis. It is therefore also right and proper that we should seriously begin to consider relationships existing between education and society which may affect the economics curriculum. A number of interesting relationships of this kind have been put before us: the world of work, for instance (by Richard Barker); examinations and their 'long shadows' (by Roy Wilkinson); university demands, and also another kind of societal pressure, the needs of underprivileged children, and indeed of special groups of children of different kinds (by Norman Lee). All these societal aspects are beginning to impinge on our thinking on what might otherwise have been thought a rather closed area of research about economics in education. There are signs in the work reported here that we are beginning to appreciate that research which is disembodied from the client—'the demand side', as one participant has put it—is not sufficient, and that a less general approach might be more productive.

The last common general characteristic in these papers on which I wish to comment has been the willingness of contributors to look at the situations which we have touched upon in a *pluralistic* kind of way, i.e. to look, not for a single solution—in fact, to doubt even whether a single solution is what we require—but to consider the viability of different solutions either as alternatives or as complementary to each other. There has been an openness in the discussion of methodological contrasts, between, for example, Pat Noble and John Oliver on the subject of visual aids; on curriculum prescription, between advocates of curricular integration (e.g. Brian Holley), at one end, and of discrete subject solutions (e.g. David Christie and Keith Robinson) at the other —and with a different position again represented by advocates of interdisciplinary approaches rather than integrated ones (e.g. Hazel Sumner). Similarly there has been discussion of pluralism in objectives. In all these areas we can see pluralistic approaches being considered. Future readers may attribute this attitude to weakness in the development of our knowledge. We, on the other hand, seem to have believed this characteristic to be a good thing: not so much a sign of being unable to make up our minds as an appreciation that there are many ways to skin a cat; that, indeed, while under some conditions some of these ways are appropriate, in other circumstances others are more relevant. This kind of view, incidentally, might well seem to observers from abroad to be a very English one, fitting in well with our empirical philosophical traditions, with our decentralized approach to educational organization, and with our tendency to delegate curricular decision-making right down to the classroom level. It is consistent with the view of one American commentator who, talking about the English education system, has said that it isn't really a system but a situation. Another has suggested that our system is one in which every classroom is an experiment, lacking controlled evaluation. We need to be careful not to push pluralism in curriculum development too close to this kind of limit.

*   *   *

So much for looking back over the papers in search of guide lines for future work. What, then, about the nature of this work? *How* should we proceed? *What* should we do?

As to the mode of procedure, it seems clear that there are three distinct aspects about which we need to think in the coming years. There is a need, firstly, for research, secondly, for what it is necessary to distinguish as development, and thirdly, for basic conceptual clarification of our problems. On the *research* side, despite the strictures and doubts which have been voiced concerning empirical research, it is important that such research should be continued and indeed developed considerably from its present very limited position. Thus, for example, there is clearly room in economics education for replication of many empirical studies already undertaken in other subject areas. Many such studies may simply confirm for economics what has already been found to be the case for other subjects. But some may not. We should not take the results for granted.

Suggestions have also been made that our emphasis might now shift from macro-research projects, as represented, for example, by the first phase of the Economics Education Project, towards more micro-patterns: towards specific in-depth studies of particular classrooms or of small segments of curricular material, for example, and even, perhaps, towards action research. Possibly, at the present early stage of economics education research, such studies might prove to be the most cost-effective. Certainly, they would be easier to mount. In this respect it has been interesting to learn that, in the second phase of the Economics Education Project, the development of work of this kind is envisaged.

On the other hand, the attitude to empirical research which seems to have emerged from our consideration of it, is one which no longer sees it simply as an alternative to making judgments—as throwing up its own judgments. Instead, we should see it as a way of *informing* judgments which, at least in part, have to be based on other criteria. Many educationists—and perhaps the same is true to some extent of economists in regard to economics —have looked to empirical research to give them definite answers to educational questions. Alex Scott's paper has amply demonstrated, in one area, that it does not do this: it *informs* us—and is valuable for this reason—but it does not of itself give us all the answers. By analogy this no doubt has relevance for other areas.

On the *development* side, of course, patient work clearly has to continue in the production of curricular materials, in the sorting out of appropriate approaches in the classroom, and in developing and refining the theory of the curriculum in the light of practical experience, at least in so far as it applies to economics education. Possibilities suggested, of considering more closely the needs of specific groups of pupils, not only in terms of different age ranges but also in terms of ability and social background, might well prove to be a particularly fruitful approach in a subject area like ours. As we have been reminded by one contributor (Luis Maciver), there is no reason to suppose that the particular mix of behavioural objectives appropriate for one age or ability group is the same as that for another, nor that the actual behaviour representing appropriate levels of achievement of particular objectives remains the same at all ages.

Equally important, and an area which demands separate attention, is the need to consider the theory of implementation of the curriculum. How does one convince teachers to accept curriculum innovation or to integrate new materials into their curricula? How does one actually get it across to be accepted in the schools? Here, our understanding is still very hazy, not only in the field of economics. Those engaged in curriculum development in economics are faced, therefore, with a general problem which still awaits solution. We will all be watching with great interest the progress of the various curriculum development projects whose work has been reported here, both with respect to their curricular proposals and in relation to this problem of implementation.

However, it is perhaps in the third aspect that I have mentioned —the area of *basic conceptual clarification*—that the need is most important of all. Neither research nor development will, of themselves, provide the answers we need without it. Both are dependent on it for their validity and usefulness. Some pretty difficult fundamental thinking is needed: thinking about the structure of economics; thinking about objectives and about other problems related to the purpose of what we are doing in economics education and the methods by which this might be achieved. No short cuts, no easy standardized procedures are available to ensure that it occurs or that it is done successfully. But the success of the seminar from which this volume has sprung—the intellectual discourse which it has initiated—suggests that the time is now ripe for a serious attempt to begin.

Turning finally to consider the actual areas in which work should be done, little needs to be added to the checklist contained in the Appendix to this chapter. The checklist includes reference only to those areas which contributors to the volume considered most important and urgent. Even so, since most of these areas lend themselves to a multiplicity of investigations, the volume of research and development implied is considerable and could take many years to complete. Among broad areas which emerge as requiring attention are those of aims and objectives, methods and materials, the structure of economics in relation to the curriculum, examinations and evaluation, pupil and student attitudes, perceptions and capabilities, and the role of economics in further and teacher education. However, in the checklist, no attempt has been made to impose any categorization, other than the ordering of the papers and discussions from which the items listed arose.

It should be remembered that the checklist derives, essentially, only from the areas explored in the foregoing papers. It is in no way intended to be a complete list of research needs in economics education, nor even in curriculum development in the subject. The coverage is not complete and any apparent weighting is accidental. Some areas, though important, hardly appear at all.[4] Nevertheless, it does represent the considered views of the contributors. Prospective researchers in the field should therefore find its contents both helpful and suggestive.

The scale and complexity of research enterprise involved in the checklist proposals varies considerably from item to item. Some implied projects are clearly of a large-scale nature. Their early initiation is obviously desirable. Indeed, in the light of the rapid growth of the subject at school and college levels, it must even be thought essential and urgent. But their viability is dependent on appropriate research grants being made available. In this respect, it has to be recognized that, so far, with the exception of the four curriculum development projects represented in this collection,* the availability in this country of large-scale funds for research in economics education has not made itself evident. Nor has there been the kind of support from industry and the business world which is such a feature of the American scene. Whatever the reasons for this state of affairs—lack of appreciation of the need, lack of researchers willing and qualified to engage in the work, even, perhaps, the failure to ask sufficiently firmly for financial support—the papers contained in this volume should provide a basis for a more favourable response.

However, not all the checklist proposals are large-scale. Many no less important suggestions are well within the scope of individual researchers working for higher degrees, or of individual or groups of teachers working at classroom or school level. Some may even lend themselves to useful exploration by students in training. It may therefore be hoped that, in one way or another, the publication of this volume will stimulate an immediate and massive effort to make up the ground which so clearly needs to be covered.

References

1. For a comprehensive list of relevant work in this country, see Fowler, P. S., Ryba, R. H. and Szreter, R., *An Annotated Bibliography of Economics Education, 1945–71*, Economics Association, 1972, pp. 14–25.
2. See paragraphs 32–33 in the joint report of the R.E.S., the A.U.T.E. and the Economics Association, *The Teaching of Economics in Schools*, Macmillan, 1973, p. 15.

* The Economics Education Project, The Scottish Education Department's Working Party on Economics, The Schools Council Social Studies Project for 8–13-year-olds, and the 'A' Level Business Studies Project.

3. Winch, P., *The Idea of a Social Science*, Routledge & Kegan Paul, 1958.
4. For example, considerations such as those explored by N. Lee and H. Entwistle in their work on 'Economics Education and Educational Theory' in Lee, N. (ed.), *Teaching Economics*, Economics Association, 1967, or by K. Dunning in two recent articles: 'What Economics Should We Teach?', *Economics*, Vol. VIII, Part 4, Summer 1970, and 'To Know Economics', *Economics*, Vol. IX, Part 4, Summer 1972.

Appendix

CHECKLIST OF MAJOR RESEARCH NEEDS RELATED TO CURRICULUM DEVELOPMENT IN ECONOMICS*

The items given below derive from a list compiled during the final session of the seminar the proceedings of which are recorded in this volume. They do not purport to be a comprehensive guide to research needs in relation to curriculum development in economics. They simply summarize those areas thought by contributors to be most urgently in need of further investigation. Seven broad areas, corresponding roughly to major sections of this book, are distinguished.

1. Educational Objectives Related to the Teaching of Economics

The absence, in the U.K., of any serious work in this area up to the present is a serious obstacle to systematic curriculum development. One need is for general behaviour-orientated work similar to that already undertaken in some other subjects. But, additionally, subject- and society-orientated approaches to the cataloguing of objectives, and the specific elaboration of objectives in relation to particular groups of pupils and students, and to the particular aims of different courses are also required.

The main suggestions are as follows:

(*a*) the detailed analysis of goals and tasks involved in curriculum development in the subject;

(*b*) the further clarification of general behavioural taxonomies of economics education objectives along lines pioneered by Benjamin Bloom;

(*c*) the development of complementary knowledge-centred perspectives on curricular objectives in economics, i.e. detailed analysis

* I am indebted to David Whitehead for a preliminary draft on which this checklist is based, and also to Norman Lee and Keith Drake for their helpful suggestions. R. R.

and categorization of educational objectives implicit in the nature of economics itself—the structure of the subject—and considerations related to the identification of its core;

(*d*) a similar elaboration of a society-orientated perspective on objectives: the identification of societal requirements which might be met through economics education, e.g. through the mastering of economic elements of citizenship;

(*e*) the development of age-specific and social-group-specific taxonomies of objectives in economic education: the identification of intended and actual behaviours illustrating levels of achievement of objectives appropriate to particular age or ability groups (e.g. less-able and younger pupils) or to groups living in distinctive environments (e.g. urban or rural);

(*f*) the detailed exploration of *teaching* objectives, as opposed to *learning* objectives: the examination of teachers' intentions in adopting particular educational strategies and of the relationship between expected and actual outcomes of specific teaching programmes.

2. Values and Economic Education

Although only one paper in this collection is directly concerned with an aspect of this relationship, important questions relating to it were also posed by several other contributors. Investigations considered most urgent include the following:

(*a*) critical evaluation of the nature and extent of overt and concealed value judgments in economics education, with particular reference to:

　(i) existing text-books and other published materials in use in schools and colleges (e.g. Hobart Papers and Bank Reviews);

　(ii) school and examination syllabuses;

　(iii) classroom teaching and formal extra-curricular activities (e.g. sixth form conferences);

(*b*) investigation of the place in economics education of the explicit and systematic study of ends within the economic syllabus and the development and evaluation of ways of doing so which might be employed and of relevant materials (e.g. resource kits, case studies, etc.);

(*c*) examination of political bias in the teaching of economics and of its effects:

　(i) micro-studies of teachers' classroom behaviour and of teacher/pupil interactions, with specific reference to the introduction of and response to overt and concealed political values (using methods developed by Philip Jackson, Flanders and others);

(ii) experimental approaches comparing effects of overtly apolitical, politically balanced and politically biased 'treatments';

(*d*) consideration of the place within economics syllabuses of related material from other social sciences, e.g. psychology, sociology, politics, etc. (how, for example, can the study of other behavioural sciences contribute to the understanding of economic behaviour?)

3. The Learner in Economics Education

The importance of the learner himself, of his attitudes, abilities and attainments, in relation to the learning of economics, is clearly an important factor in curriculum development in the subject, but one largely neglected in the contributions to this volume. In the absence of major investigations of learner characteristics specifically related to economics education, the following studies would be of value:

(*a*) examination of pupil and student attitudes to methods and context in economics education, e.g. likes and dislikes and their implications for curriculum construction and teaching methods;

(*b*) experimental investigation of learning processes in economics at different ages and in relation to different combinations and levels of learner abilities;

(*c*) investigations into the nature and development of economic thinking: the identification of fundamental economic concepts and the exploration of hypothetical sequential relationships in their acquisition.

4. Teaching Methods and Aids

The availability and use of different methods and aids conditions the feasibility of achieving given curricular objectives. Notwithstanding the importance of the teacher as the prime variable in relation to their successful use, knowledge and understanding of their intrinsic characteristics and efficiency remain critical factors in curriculum development. However, as in (3) above, investigations specific to economics education have hardly begun in the U.K. Among most urgently needed studies are:

(*a*) experimental assessment of alternative teaching methods and approaches in relation to specific areas of the economics curriculum;

(*b*) the identification of curricular areas presenting special difficulty to the learner and the development and evaluation of appropriate teaching methods and resources;

(c) research into the uses and limitations of various audio-visual aids for economics teaching, with particular reference to selected areas of the economics syllabus and to particular groups of children, e.g. regarding

(i) the value of cine-film, capable of depicting dynamic change, as opposed to filmstrips and other forms of still illustration;

(ii) the usefulness and relative merits for particular purposes of tape recordings, of film slides and filmstrip material of different kinds, and of material for use with the overhead projector, etc.;

(d) surveys of teaching methods in use in relation to specific areas of the economics curriculum, together with the compilation of a cumulative register of new approaches to particular problems, e.g.

(i) analyses of the use of fables, drama, games and simulations, etc.,

(ii) the reviewing of new resources and study kits as they become available.

5. The Role of Economics in the Curriculum

The recent rapid expansion of economics in the school curriculum has been a spontaneous rather than a planned and managed phenomenon. Assessments of its present importance, and of its contribution to the curriculum of schools and colleges and evaluative studies testing justifications of its inclusion are sadly lacking. Areas where work might be done include:

(a) surveys of economic content in primary, secondary (including lower secondary) and professional education. (What economics is being taught, in what form and at what levels?);

(b) further survey and analysis of economic syllabuses being used in schools and colleges in relation to different functions, e.g. general studies, 'O' and 'A' level examination courses, professional requirements, etc.;

(c) examination of the implications for the curriculum of the widespread introduction of economics in the 8–13 age range: the relationship of economics education in this age group to education in other subjects, especially social sciences and humanities;

(d) further consideration and investigation of the relative merits of uni-disciplinary, multi-disciplinary and integrated approaches to the teaching of economic concepts;

(e) consideration of relationships between economics and other subjects in school and college curricula, with particular reference to complementarity, overlaps, conflicts and competition, e.g.

(i) economics and other social sciences being introduced into schools, such as sociology and politics,

(ii) economics and business studies,

(iii) economics, mathematics and statistics;

(*f*) studies of subject combinations in the sixth form and in professional courses, e.g.

(i) characteristics of students selecting particular subject combinations,

(ii) educational outcomes of particular choices of subject combinations,

(iii) subject combination and examination performance;

(*g*) the development and evaluation of problem-orientated courses in economics at sixth form and other levels.

6. Examinations and Assessment

The importance of interactions between examination and assessment procedures and the articulation in the classroom of curriculum intentions makes this an important area for further consideration. The nature and effects on the economics curriculum of examinations, especially public examinations, clearly require further clarification. There is also an increasing need for the development of appropriate assessment instruments for diagnostic rather than ranking purposes and for curricular evaluation. Among urgent items in this area are:

(*a*) comparative and analytical investigation of the content, procedures and results of public examinations in economics at C.S.E. and 'O' and 'A' levels and for professional bodies, with particular reference to:

(i) comparability of syllabuses at particular levels,

(ii) evaluative surveys of different patterns of examination procedure in use,

(iii) analysis of the requirements of different examination syllabuses in terms of the knowledge, skills and levels of understanding implied,

(iv) comparative analysis of the degree to which implied requirements are actually tested by examination papers;

(*b*) the development and evaluation of new techniques of examination and assessment, e.g.

(i) objective tests in economics,

(ii) project and course work,

(iii) oral tests;

(*c*) the development of diagnostic tests for classroom use to reveal areas of difficulty or misunderstanding;

(*d*) the development of tests for lesson and curricular evaluation purposes.

7. Teacher Education and Training

Questions in this area concern what teachers of economics should know as well as what training they should receive and how this training should be conducted. Areas for early consideration include:

(*a*) study and evaluation of the content of economics courses in colleges of education, and their relationship to economics education for young children at primary and middle-school levels;

(*b*) consideration of the content and methods in the post-graduate initial training of economics teachers: examination of actual and desirable practices;

(*c*) investigation of teacher attitudes to innovations in economics education, e.g. to new kits and other resources entailing specific methods of approach;

(*d*) consideration of the content and form of in-service courses for economics teachers: to what extent should these be geared to refresher courses in economics, to the examination of new developments in the subject, to new approaches and materials for teaching the subject?

Index